EXPLORING SPIRITUALITY

GOING DEEP

in LIFE *and* LEADERSHIP

IAN PERCY

••••

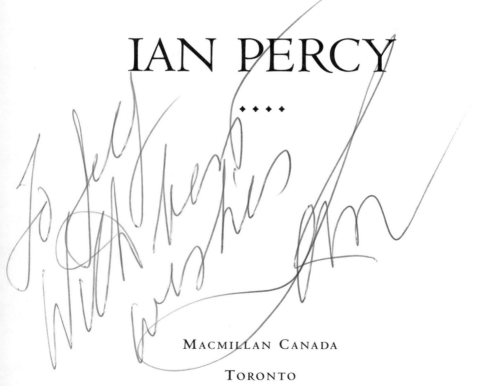

MACMILLAN CANADA

TORONTO

Copyright © Ian Percy 1997

Canadian Cataloguing in Publication Data

Percy, Ian D.
  Going deep : exploring spirituality in life and leadership

ISBN 0–7715–7552–1

1. Business – Religious aspects. 2. Spirituality.
I. Title.

HF5388.P47 1998   291.4'4'08622   C97–931393–7

1 2 3 4 5 TRI 01 00 99 98 97

This book is available at special discounts for bulk purchases by your group or organization for sales promotions, premiums, fundraising and seminars. For details, contact: Macmillan Canada, Special Sales Department, 29 Birch Avenue, Toronto, ON M4V 1E2. Tel: 416-963-8830.

Macmillan Canada
A Division of Canada Publishing Corporation
Toronto, Ontario, Canada

Printed in Canada

Georgia

"For my forever love,
I look up at the sky
sprinkled with silver stars
and blow a kiss to them,
for making you come true."

Acknowledgments

To my children, Karen and Nathan – my deepest love and thanks for your love and patience. You will never truly know how much you mean to me.

To my stepchildren, Erin and Ryan Kelly – thanks for being in my life and for welcoming me to yours.

To my parents, Harry and Joy Percy, from whom I learned so much in spite of myself – my deepest thanks.

To my in-laws, Bud and Babe Gardner – for the joy of being part of your family.

To Mary Anne Garnett who holds my life and office together – I am in your debt and am unlikely to get out of it.

To Peggy Roffey, my thought coach – heartfelt thanks for your provocations and language and lessons in syntax.

To the entire team at Macmillan Canada – thank you for taking the work of publishing to a deep and joyful place.

To a world of friends and coaches too numerous to mention – thank you for being on the journey with me.

Table of Contents

Welcome

Ian and Georgia Percy

On many more than one occasion I have shared good red
wine with business friends and
talked about the factors that most
cause us to grow personally and
professionally. Books, obviously,
are a major source of learning. One of my discoveries,
however, is that there is quite a difference between books
bought and books actually read. I was amazed at how many
books in the "best-seller" category, while proudly displayed
on mahogany credenzas, were never read through.
Whatever the reason for that, I figured it was probably parallel to the reason we don't use all the options on our
mobile phones, the programmable features on our VCRs or
the incredible capability of our laptop computers. Books
just aren't very friendly sometimes.

Everything about this book reflects our effort to be
friendly: the layout and design folks at Macmillan Canada
have done their best to ensure that this book is easy to read

because I've noticed that many of my friends are getting old and need reading glasses. I hope you find the content and flow of this book reader-friendly as well. I think that it is friendlier to talk *with* people through print, and not *to* them. One simply cannot connect on a deep, soul level by writing like an academic. When quoting other sources, for example, I will introduce them to you. I always feel ignorant when an author throws around names as if I'm supposed to know the people. I don't find that very friendly. You will also discover that I like to use metaphor as a teaching tool. Maybe it's just me, but I think this is the quickest and easiest way to get a point across. I may have overdone it a little, but to me it's like having a box of chocolates . . .

Finally, a friendly book has pictures. Real pictures. Not those emotionless corporate head-and-shoulders shots. My intention was to do everything I could to cause you to have a personal connection with the people who contributed to this book, particularly the men and women you will meet in the last chapter. We are all real people going through real challenges and enjoying real celebrations. It helps, I think, to have a face to put with the words.

Ian's son Nathan, our horse Bow and stepdaughter Erin

So, overall I have tried to share my heart in real conversation with you, anticipating what you might be thinking or wanting to ask. I hope it comes across that way. There are mail and electronic addresses at the bottom of the next page if you want to join the dialogue. I would enjoy hearing from you.

I believe in the interconnectedness of all things. As far as I am concerned, this

Ian's daughter Karen and stepson Ryan

means that you and I have a relationship. We always have had, but it is a stronger connection now that I've written this book and you've picked it up. My prayer is that our relationship will be synergistic – that it will get better and better the more it is experienced. Though this might be a strange way to put it, from my side I *need* to share this expression of my journey and the discoveries I've made along the way. That is the only way for me to make real the meaningful connections I yearn for. From the bottom of my heart, I cannot thank you enough for being here when I needed you. As far as you are concerned, I sincerely hope you get back whatever you need for your life, labor and leadership right now.

Go deep.

To reach Ian Percy or for information on his services and products, call or write :
   The Ian Percy Corporation
   20 Summerfeldt Cres.
   Unionville, ON   L3R 2B2
   Phone: 905-513-1950   Fax: 905-513-7873
   E-mail: percycor@inforamp.net   Web site: IanPercy.com

ONE

Your Invitation to the Deep

◆ ◆ ◆ ◆

Something in the universe has awakened us to the urgency of finding our souls. But where do we look? The 15th-century Hindu Master Kaber said, "Go wherever you like, to Calcutta or Tibet; if you can't find where your soul is hidden, for you the world will never be real." And we want – desperately want – a new reality. We want to find our soul, the true meaning of our existence. We long to be soul-full.

Marketing shamans have quickly recognized the consumer power of this deepest of all urgencies. If a product can be linked to the soul, they've discovered, you can pretty well consider it "souled." Take the Mazda truck commercial I saw the other day. Picture a trucklike scene. Desert, tumbling tumbleweeds. Arizona maybe. A kiln-dried cowboy leans back against his Mazda truck and drawls, "For me a truck is kind of a spiritual thing." Wow, I thought, must be some truck. A spiritual relationship with a horse I can understand. A horse can recognize you. Follow you around. Lovingly nuzzle you. But a truck? Depends on the options, I guess.

Actually, I've come to the conclusion that car and truck manufacturers must be very deep people. Infiniti's new Q45 model is being introduced with the tag line "Everything changes but the soul." An ad for the Lincoln Continental reads, "It gets into your soul, not your pocketbook." And at the 1997 Swiss Auto Show in Geneva, the Rover company unveiled the 21st-century version of the (Austin) Mini – they're calling it the "Spiritual." The four-door version is called "Spiritual Too." Apparently, we can now drive to our new and soulful reality, which will make it a much easier pilgrimage.

It is not just in products and consumables that we find trace evidence of the spiritual; we find it in our routine experiences as well. Let me tell you about 250 senior bankers at a four-day conference on strategic planning I led in Niagara-on-the-Lake, a quaint, pretty town on the Ontario – New York border. White picket fences with flower baskets hanging from the streetlights. The participants were ordinary, eat-too-much, work-too-hard, don't-get-enough-exercise kind of folks. I figured that the last thing on their minds was a spiritual pilgrimage. One just doesn't expect a conference made up of 250 mostly male banking types to send one's heart to aerobic levels of emotion. Running up three flights to your hotel room might do it, but not a group like this.

I couldn't have been more wrong. Or more baffled at what happened. From the opening welcome, everyone seemed to know something magical was taking place. There was anticipation, that wonderful sense of eager restlessness you feel when your team is about to make a comeback, or when you're about to hit the climax of a suspenseful movie. Maybe it was more than magical – perhaps the word to describe this experience is *mystical*. The organization and venue of the conference were excellent, but I expected that from this client. This "spontaneous combustion of the spirit" was far removed from any physical or logistical factor in the conference room. Could have been the negative ions misted into the air by the thundering falls nearby. Or had Jupiter lined up with Mars?

Every participant lucky enough to make a presentation to the group returned to his seat amid a standing ovation and high fives. People talked openly about the fears and hopes aroused in them by the prospect of re-engineering and restructuring within the corporation. There was an amazing combination of honesty and joy. Their expression of commitment to the group's fiscal goals brought tears to the eyes of their leader. We'd play music to signal the end of a break and to bring them back into the conference room. These guys actually danced to the music. Bankers. Male bankers! I didn't know bankers had a rhythmic bone in their bodies. This wasn't an Amway convention. None of it was staged, planned or expected. What on earth happened?

We're still not sure. Over the last 25 years, I've spoken at, facilitated and/or designed hundreds of conferences and I'm left with no choice but to declare this one a truly spiritual event. Explaining why I say that isn't easy. It's like asking why people go quiet when they enter a cathedral. You just know that if you yell or talk out loud, God will kill you. It was the participants' openness, lack of fear, spontaneity, a real feeling of love in the room. It went way past being merely a motivational experience. Somehow they had broken through all the usual corporate barriers and had made deeply felt connections with each other, their leader and their purpose together. There was *unity* – that's it – a transcendent unity.

Perhaps even more amazing is that, pushed by these bank managers, we found a way to infuse their 12,000 employees with this same spirit. A group of us went on what became known as the Quality Tour, traveling from city to city inviting the employees to take their bank to an unsurpassed level of service to its customers. The "Tour" climaxed in an unforgettable event held near Toronto that was experienced by more than 3,000 wonderfully and passionately possessed employees. To this day, those who were there tell the story to newcomers with the same reverence that aging hippies show when they talk about Woodstock. It has become part of the folklore of the bank. Occasionally I have shown video clips from the Quality Tour at other conferences to demonstrate what can happen when people's spirits are set free. We've heard more than one story of people moving their accounts to this bank just because of the passion they saw in the video. The spirit set free is irresistible.

This anecdote raises very valid skepticism in every managerial mind. I wondered about it too, though the skepticism may come from a darker side. We're suspicious of such supposedly "spiritual" events, I suspect. No, it's more than suspicion; we are just downright afraid of the spiritual. We can't always measure it so what are we to do with it? The lesson, drilled into every manager, is "If you can't measure it, you can't manage it." So naturally the skepticism leads, at least for bottom-line and control-oriented types, to thoughts like, "I'm glad everybody had warm fuzzy feelings, but did this spirit translate into any meaningful statistics?" and "Can this energy be made profitable?" Others might demand, "Show me the money." All I know, in this case at least, is that profitability, productivity and customer satisfaction measurements became increasingly favorable. The relationship between such spiritual breakthroughs and the corporate bottom line is a very interesting and important issue. It brings us face-to-face with the fact that, almost regardless of what business you're in, the workplace is also a human place. A place where human beings seek connection, fulfillment, meaning. It is a place, like almost anyplace where people are, in which the rich potential of spirituality lies dormant, waiting for expression on both a material and a mystical level. "Material" because spiritually connected teams fulfilling spiritually centered customer service experience greater success. You can see it, measure it, document it. "Mystical" because we feel that hard-to-define link with our internal Self and with the rest of creation. We can *sense* all of this, but we need to ask ourselves, what *is* "spirituality" and is it really any earthly good?

Around the 5th or 6th century B.C., the words of a man named Agur were included in the Old Testament Book of

Proverbs. He wrote that there were four things just too wonderful for him to understand:

> *The way of an eagle in the air;*
> *The way of a serpent upon a rock;*
> *The way of a ship in the midst of the sea;*
> *And the way of a man with a maid.*

If you read these beautiful lines the way they were intended to be read, they are rich with meaning. Read them another
way and you'd say he's talking about a bird, a snake, a ship
and sex. Birds make a mess. The snake you probably want to
beat with a stick. The navigation of a ship is an application of
mathematics and physics. Hardly spiritual stuff. And sex?
How many people do you know talk about sex as a spiritual
experience?

Actually, I know of one who did. He was a clergyman who
had given many, many years of his life to serving his God. A
devoted and committed man who saw no other purpose to life
than his religious calling. As happens in so many similar cases,
though, not only did he give up his own life, he gave up the
lives of his wife and children as well. So intent on celestial service, he had little meaningful relationship with his wife –
specifically, no sexual relationship. They were celibate for
more than 25 years. As an elderly man he went through some
kind of awakening about how narrow and shallow his supposedly spiritual life had been. Part of his spiritual awakening
was to establish true and full reconciliation with his wife, rela-
tionally and sexually.

At this point the story becomes both tender and funny. He
described to a mutual friend how his first sexual experience
with his wife, after all those years of abstinence, was not primarily a physical experience, but a spiritual one. They both
found that sexual intimacy, in the context of a renewed and
unconditional love, led to a spiritual unity, the power of which
caused them to understand even the nature of God differently.

Not for a moment do I doubt a wonderful and significant spiritual breakthrough for this couple. That's the tender and purposeful dimension to the story. On the other hand, it's impossible to read this story without musing on the fact that sex after a 25-year period of abstinence would be a spiritual experience for just about anybody!

Human sexual connection is, at least potentially, the ultimate metaphor for divine spiritual connection. Sex is naturally holy. In *Soulful Sex,* a book I wish I'd read years ago, Dr. Victoria Lee writes that "spiritual consciousness intensifies sexual exchange in wonderful ways. Lovemaking can become an experience of spirit manifesting through the body, transcending time and space, temporarily blurring the boundaries between self and others. It can put us in touch with a dimension in which there is no sadness, only joy." In another inspiring book, *Getting the Love You Want,* Dr. Harville Hendrix writes about "the humble path of marriage" and describes conjugal love as one of the surest routes to an awareness not only of our own inner unity, but our unity with the whole of the universe. "When we gather the courage to search for the truth of our being and the truth of our partner's being," he concludes, "we begin a journey of psychological and spiritual healing."

We are, we mortals, on that journey. Right through all the mundane and wonderful stuff of life, from a truck commercial, a bankers' conference, to a 500 B.C. mystic who waxes poetic at the thought of birds, snakes, ships and sex. That journey starts on one level and takes us to another.

There are two main levels on which to see, experience and create life. On one level, you and a million others can drive virtually identical trucks with a V-6 engine, 4-WD and a bed that'll carry a sheet of drywall flat. On another level, you can experience something beyond the mechanics, calling *your* truck by name, feeling *your* truck's unique heart, character and faithfulness. Patting the dashboard after it has successfully climbed a particularly steep hill. Finding in the performance of a mundane *object* a metaphor for meaning and excellence and, in the same moment, experience something come alive with your own intense sense of *being*.

You can attend yet another kickoff conference, the highlight of which is getting yet another sweatshirt with "Quality: Our Competitive Edge" written across the chest, singing along with Tina Turner's *"Simply the best, better than all the rest . . ."* or, you can watch in wonder and delight as people's lives and hearts change right in front of your eyes, and have your own changed just by watching.

You can happen to see an eagle flying around, or you can let your own soul take flight with it. A soaring, gliding soul.

You can recoil in revulsion at the sight of a snake, or you can marvel at how anything so feared can be so beautifully fluid in its own self-assurance.

You can go on a boat ride, or you can be deeply grateful that something as immense, majestic and powerful as the ocean actually allows you, in all your frailty, to sail across it. A voyage of awe and humility.

You can have sex or you can make love, becoming one flesh in a physical metaphor of spiritual unity.

What do you suggest we call these two levels? Is one lower and the other higher? Or how about labeling one "physical" and the other "spiritual?" That may be the simplest way to do it, and yet it seems almost too obvious. Does natural and supernatural do? Earthly and heavenly? Finite and infinite? Philosopher Immanuel Kant calls these levels "phenomenon" and "noumenon." Or how about psychologist Ron Browning's suggestion of "asleep" and "awake?" Then we have the choice of New Age physician Larry Dossey's "local" and "nonlocal." There are just too many choices for me. Spirituality is best kept simple.

So, for myself, I've begun by simply numbering these worlds. I decided that if I can't find the right words I might as well resort to numbers. The First World, then, is the obvious world. Drive that truck. Go to the conference. Look at that eagle. Watch out for that snake. Take a boat ride. Practice safe sex. See. Touch. Taste. Science. Measurement. A consciousness consumed with the question "How?"

The Second World is this spiritual world we are hearing so much about lately. Life seen in terms of meaning, worth. What is right, true and good. Answers to "Why?" Art rather than science. Those aspects of life that can't fully be researched or measured. On a First World level, for example, I work as a consultant and professional speaker. But a few will also know, on the higher secondary level, who and how I really am. Beyond "what I do" to "who I am." In the Second World, we see God everywhere and in everybody. We experience the confidence of faith and trust. We are energized by hope and love. Our lives become peaceful and whole.

You may feel that trying to demonstrate the difference between the First and Second Worlds by discussing a great truck, a great conference and great sex is irreverent and irrelevant. Not at all. The spiritual pervades even the mundane and it is in the mundane that we must first learn to recognize the spiritual. In the simplest, most incidental, most ordinary aspects of life there is the potential to see and experience differently. In telling people not to be so worried about things like food, drink and clothes, Christ suggested that they look at the simple and common field lily because even King Solomon, reputed to be the richest man who has ever lived, and whose stables were lined with gold, was never clothed as beautifully. Apparently there are two ways to look at lilies too. On one level, it's just another plant. On the other, a living metaphor for faith. With much the same insight, the Talmud says, "Every blade of grass has its Angel that bends over it and whispers 'Grow, grow.' " The world is alive with spirit and holiness.

That spirit, that "wholiness," is here, in us, around us. Another world to live in. But what is it and can we really come to understand and talk about it? This book is an attempt to bring at least a partial answer to these questions. Furthermore, I am trying to be relevant to your personal life *and* to your work life. From time to time it may be hard to know exactly which I am focusing on. Frankly I am glad for the occasional ambiguity because I think we draw far too heavy a line between what we call "personal" and what we call "professional" or "work." This distinction is particularly prevalent in our society because so many people, miserable at work, are trying to isolate the pain. The tight distinction allows them to quarantine their unhappiness to a period between nine and five. That's why Happy Hour starts *after* work.

Something is desperately wrong with this picture. No one aspect is more sacred or holy than any other. It is all one thing called LIFE. In part of life you sleep. In another part you make love. In another part you eat. And in another part you work. You wash the car, you worship, you ground your teenager, you watch the Super Bowl, you light the barbecue and you do all the stuff of life. I do not believe it is possible to claim spiritual awareness in your home life and then switch that off to go to work with such a shallow perspective that you don't even know the sun is shining. God doesn't do 9:00 – 5:00; he loves you 24 hours a day. Anyone who has truly connected with Spirit knows that it seeps into every pore and into every second. It seeps under your office door as easily as it seeps under your bedroom door.

Having said all that, and at the risk of contradicting myself, I do try to focus on the corporate context, as you will find. This is because many people in bottom line-driven–organizations have not, traditionally, been open to looking at their corporate soul. For the most part, they don't even know there is such a thing, so there is a lot of educating and exploring to do. This corporate resistance to the spiritual, I am thrilled to tell you, is weakening by the minute all over the business world as you'll see continually throughout this book. As I have learned, painfully, to explore my own spirituality, I am inviting you to explore yours. As I have slowly come to understand that my work is spiritual, I hope you will find that yours is too.

I debated within myself for some time as to whether this "exploration of the spirit" was a journey, a search or an uncovering. If it's a journey, I reasoned, we cannot stay where we are and must trek insightfully to a better place. If it's a search, then we are able to stay where we are but need to know that place much more intimately. The concept of "uncovering" says to me that all we are searching for is already within us and we don't have to "go" anywhere. Our task, in that case, is to peel back the disguises that keep us from seeing our worth as God's ultimate creation. Being the decisive decision-maker that I am, I've decided that the answer is "yes" to all three. Yes we can choose to go to a better place where we will not be as we are at this moment. Yes we need to look more carefully around us because we trample the holy and don't even know it. And yes we need to be scoured clean, unwrapped, unmasked. Liberated to sing the song of the soul set free.

Harry Houdini is remembered as one of the world's greatest escape artists. To achieve that notoriety, he had to become a great contortionist. Obtaining freedom from the shackles required him to twist around and see his situation from every conceivable angle. First, he'd be on his side, then suddenly on his back. Feet-over-head and then head-over-feet. Our struggle to set our souls free may not be that physically convulsive, but it will test and strain every part of our political, intellectual, emotional and spiritual selves. All of our twists and turns have the same intention of helping us see the rich spiritual power and freedom with which our lives have been gifted.

Throughout this book we will "journey" together, moving from the "First World" to the "Second World," while recognizing that we live in both. We will find that the real meaning of our lives is not an issue of our jobs and busyness, but is a matter of discovering the truth and purpose of our inner, sacred "Self." On our inner journey we will visit six places, "Stations" as they are called, each meant to move us to a deeper and more unifying experience of Life.

"Searching" will be part of our contortions as well. Every experience we have becomes a "lens" that gives us the opportunity to see what is truly good and holy in our life, labor and leadership. This wonderful opportunity, however, is negated by our persistent tendency to look *at* the experience rather than *through* it. Somewhat like the 3-D computer-generated art you see everywhere. When you look *at* the piece, it's a bunch of chaotic squiggly lines. Literally look *through* it and you see a clear, amazing, three-dimensional picture that was not visible before. There is so much we have yet to see in this life.

Finally, to round out the experience, we will also do some "uncovering." Sadly, too many aspects of our upbringing, education, religious teaching and work experience have clouded or disguised the reality that we are, first and foremost, spiritual beings. We are not just human resources and head count, meant only to be re-engineered and deconstructed. We are the sacred handiwork of God. We are meant for purposeful connection – to our Selves, each other and to our Creator.

This is an invitation to join hands, heads, hearts and souls in courageous community. It is not an invitation from me; I am privileged only to be one of the invitees. The invitation comes from the deep yearning of our own souls. It is one we can't refuse.

In *The Celebration of Life,* Norman Cousins writes that "one of the interesting characteristics of the English language is that the words that mean the most to us often lack precise meaning." Like love, peace, happiness and joy. That is part of our challenge here – to find word symbols we can paste on something not everyone sees, and that those who do see, see in kaleidoscopic variety. "I want to know," continues Cousins, "whether my life is an end in itself or whether there is something beyond my life that has meaning, even though I may not be able to define it." Is there a dimension of existence or experience that is "too wonderful" for us too? And if so, what language can we use to talk about it?

I had to smile to myself while on a flight the other day. Behind me was a young boy, maybe nine or ten years old, on his first flight ever – a point he made many times before we even pushed back from the gate. The excitement of first-time flyers is always fun to experience because they want to share it with everybody. There was the usual exhilaration about the takeoff, things looking so small, and he swore he saw his dad's car on the highway below. As we climbed through the clouds, bursting into the brilliant blue of the sky, he just kept saying, "Ho-ly! Ho-ly! Ho-ly!" Must have said it a hundred times, over and over. I know he meant it as in "holy cow," but I thought what more appropriate expression could there be? It *is* a holy moment when you leave one world and experience another one you've never seen before. It is this other, Second World, that we want to understand more fully, so let me elaborate on it.

Abraham Maslow, a name many of us remember from Psychology 101, wrote: "The unhappiness, unease and unrest in the world today are caused by people living far below their capacity." My first reaction on reading this was to discard Maslow's insight because I couldn't see its relevance to my life. I am a very busy guy so it is not me causing the unhappiness, unease and unrest out there. Reading the sentence again brought the realization that Maslow wasn't writing about being busy. Erroneously, I thought this was a First World statement when it really was about the Second World. Maslow is saying that people who haven't found any meaning in their lives, who have not found their way to the Second World, create unhappiness and unrest in the First World. Busy has nothing to do with it.

When he talks about "capacity," he is not talking about workaholism. That is quite another matter. Realizing your true capacity is about getting a grip. It's about getting your life back. Not easy to do because most of us don't remember giving it away in the first place. You probably have children and friends who repeatedly urge you to "get a life." Their point is for you to get your *own* life back, not the one your boss or someone else has designed for you. Apart from the extra money, the company car, the golf club membership and the corner office, do you really want a life that comes down to just that?

Like Adam of old, we are cursed with and through our work. Work has become our punishment for violating or ignoring that which is spiritual. On too many nights, you finally head for home around 7:30 or 8:00. Some of you reading this will think that's early. In the kitchen you find your supper on a plastic-wrapped plate with a Post-it note telling you to microwave it for a couple of minutes. That'll probably be the warmest thing you'll hold all night. About every other Saturday you've got to go into work just to get caught up. Great life, eh? Exactly what is it that you're so busy doing? Or let me ask you an even bigger question, "Why?" *Working Harder Isn't Working* is the title of a good book by Bruce O'Hara and I am convinced that he's absolutely right.

So how do we free ourselves from some of the demands of the First World so we can explore the Second? Let's use airplane behavior, which I've made the focus of considerable advanced research, to help us understand the difference between the two. After the safety instructions about seat belts and tray tables, a two-part airplane dance begins between the two strangers sitting next to each other. The first movement contains the question, "Hi, how are ya?" The correct answer, of course, is "Fine." You could be leaving the love of your life never to see him or her again, your heart shattered irreparably into a million pieces, tears streaming down your face, and the answer is still "Fine." Say, "Hi, how are ya?" to someone from another culture and you may get the response, "Thank you for asking because I am really wrestling with several issues in my life right now and . . . ." We think of interjecting, "Tell someone who cares. I'm North American and the right answer is 'Fine!' " "Hi, how are ya?" is a First World query. "How are you *really*?" is of the Second World.

The second dance movement in our airplane scenario proceeds in this fashion: "And what do you do?" We, of course, respond with the appropriate vocational term. The answer dictates whether or not there will be any further conversation. If you say that you're an actuary or a computer programmer, that will pretty well be it for the flight. I used to say that I was a psychologist, but I learned quickly not to say that anymore. I'd end up doing four hours of therapy when all I wanted to do was watch the movie. Instead of asking us what we do, what if this new seat mate asks, "And what is it that you are *accomplishing* with your life?" A horrified look comes over our face. What kind of a question is that? Can we find an answer or do we mumble something about not knowing and offer instead to tell them what we do? We all know what we do, and we know that we are incredibly busy doing it.

I can't speak for you, but I have to admit that telling some-one what I do is a lot easier than telling them what I am actu-ally accomplishing with my life. I have a suspicion that this would be true for a lot of people. I'll also bet that it's true for many businesses. In my case I *do* professional speaking, while what I want to *accomplish* is helping people and organizations find meaning and purposeful passion. What we *do* is a matter of First World existence, while what we *accomplish* is a prop-erty of the Second.

It has been suggested that hell might be discovering what you *could have* accomplished with your life. What an awful thought. Can you imagine? At the gateway to the damnation of eternal disappointment and unfulfillment, you are com-pletely informed of all the possibilities that had been yours. If only you had had the eyes to see. If only you had had a little more "accomplishing" and a little less of that frenetic "doing."

This is what our friend Maslow was telling us. Accomplishment, not busy doing, is the measure of capacity. I believe there is a mysterious and spiritual vessel in the universe in my shape and with my name on it. There is also one in your shape and with your name on it. My life's responsibility, with my unique gifts, strengths, knowledge, relationships and opportunities, is to fill this vessel to capacity. Yours too. Some people fill the promise of their lives to overflowing and everyone they touch is transformed in a wonderful way. Theirs is the abundant life. They know "why." We are hard put to explain how some people have come to be so possessed, so aligned, so irresistible. The good and faithful servant. We know that it is a wondrous thing and we are grateful to be one of the touched.

Sadly, there are those who return their vessels to the black hole unused. They put nothing in it. They have no idea of their potential. They touch no one and accomplish little. This may bring into your mind a vision of someone caught in the web of alcohol, glue sniffing and drugs. The wreck of their life is real and stark, but emptiness is not theirs alone. Emptiness is the curse of all who remain rooted in the First World, the empty Eden. Emptiness is not a respecter of persons. Indeed, as the Bible tells us, it is easier for a camel to go through the eye of a needle than for a rich man to gain access to Heaven.

Life in the Second World is a gift available to those with faith, not fortune. It is the wealth of the Second, not the First, that we seek when we try to fulfill our potential.

In addition to the First and Second, there is a Third World (not to be confused with underdeveloped nations) to which we have access, I believe, after the death of the First. It's the world in which the soul spends eternity. Everything is crystal clear and all the connections made. Some of those connections add up to eternal happiness and some to eternal unhappiness. We get a glimpse of both alternatives of this Third World from the vantage point of the Second, but only as through a glass darkly. In other words, we can, in every moment, obtain a cloudy glimpse of both heaven and hell. What the heavenly version of this Third or eternal World may be is the permanent existence of the Second World without the limitations of the First. Others suggest that the Third eternal World is the First World made perfect, a unification of the First and Second. Both provide an interesting vision of the afterlife or what some call eternal life. The hellish version of the Third World may be the permanent existence of the First World without the spiritual cushioning of the Second. Humankind left unhampered to its own eternal fate.

We are also obliged, before we go on, to recognize that many people feel there is only the First World. What you see is what you get. There is nothing more.

In 1623, the great English preacher and metaphysical poet, John Donne, was battling a serious illness which led him to meditations that he recorded as *Devotions Upon Emergent Occasions*. In his third meditation, Donne wrote that Man had but one privilege:

> *That he is not as others, groveling, but of an erect,*
> *of an upright form, naturally built, and disposed to the*
> *contemplation of Heaven . . . Other creatures look to the*
> *earth; and even that is no unfit object, no unfit*
> *contemplation for Man . . . but because Man is not to stay*
> *there, as other creatures are. Man in his natural*
> *form is carried to the contemplation of that place,*
> *which is his home, Heaven.*

We of the earth are meant to see things beyond the First World. Eventually we will find ourselves more at home in this otherworldly contemplation, the Second World, however elusive it seems right now. It is our natural form. This may mean that we are currently acting unnaturally, which would help to explain why we have such stress in our lives.

Let's be clear that the earth is filled with real things that are deserving of real contemplation. That's the heart of the trap. The First World we meet is sophisticated and complicated enough that people can and do spend their whole lives trying to understand it. We develop theoretical models to explain it. We rework it to make it more controllable and efficient. We measure and record its movements in more ways than a baseball statistician. We get Ph.D.'s in it. We set up corporations so we can sell parts of it to reap the profit that establishes much of our pecking order. The First World invites us to be very busy indeed. Unfortunately, it's like being so busy waxing your Ferrari that you never get around to driving it. "Existence involves two different kinds of reality," writes Copthorne Macdonald in *Toward Wisdom*. "One is a transient, fragmented surface reality which most of us mistake as THE reality. The other is an eternal, enabling oneness which . . . is our deepest, truest Self."

G. K. Chesterton, a 20th-century English author and poet, wrote:

We all feel the riddle of the earth
without anyone to point it out.
The mystery of life is
the plainest part of it.
The clouds and curtains of darkness,
the confounding vapours,
these are the daily weather
of this world.
Whatever else we have grown accustomed to,
we have grown accustomed
to the unaccountable.
Every stone or flower is a hieroglyphic
of which we have lost the key;
With every step of our lives we enter into
the middle of some story
which we are certain
to misunderstand . . .

Some will misunderstand the story I am trying to write too. In the writing and rewriting there have been constant reminders of my own misunderstanding. And maybe that's a good thing. To misunderstand keeps that searching part of ourselves alive. To think we fully understand would cause us to rest. Life itself is a hieroglyphic. May we all find our key.

There is another place. There is another way to live. There is an untapped mystery out there. My contention is that literally everything we have done since birth has been an attempt to find it. From dependently seeking the warm comfort of our mother's breast to the fantasy games of our childhood; from the studies, searchings and rebellions of our adolescence to the adult sophistication of our corporate-leadership strategies. How you dress is part of your search. So is the major you choose in college. The friends you have. The career through which you make a living is part of your search too. Likewise your religion. So are drugs and alcohol, although they are not very good guides to the key. Everything is part of the quest for meaning. The books you read and the movies you see. Our entire life is one long search. It's just that many of us do not recognize that we are searching.

It is very hard to even admit that there is another reality beyond the First World. Additional courage is required to go looking for it. And to talk about the search as a work in progress is to hold out your life for all to see and judge. In all likelihood you'll be judged a failure, or a hypocrite, because you will have found and declared things that your life has not caught up to. For most of us, there is a time lag between seeing truth and actually living it. The ultimate challenge of living the truth has generally been written off as impractical if not impossible. Nevertheless, as humans we don't have a choice about being searchers for truth. Nor do we have a choice about making choices. We have already eaten of Eden's tree of Knowledge of Good and Evil. We are cursed to a life of choices. Or is it *blessed* to a life of choices?

Imagine a living board game on which all the squares form life's spiritual journey. The goal of the game is to see how far around the board you can get before you die. The Power has put you and me on the square marked START. From there on it's up to you. Up to me. You don't have to move if you don't want to. But the further you go, the deeper your understanding of the spiritual life. The clearer you see what there really is to see; the more you see who God is and the depth of relationship God wants to have with you, and the more even the most incidental of experiences point to the Second World, to the richness that lies beyond the obvious.

This is a lot easier to write about than it is to experience. Sometimes I feel my life is a cyclical two steps forward, one step back on this spiritual game board. On more than one occasion it's been three steps back. No, I'm not being completely honest. There are also sideways steps that seem to produce little. Other times I spin around as if on figure skates, never sure what direction I'll be facing when I stop. I can be on my feet and a day later be standing on my head. In your quiet and honest moments, you too might confess that your dance has been full of these steps and missteps, and at the same time express a deep yearning for something more. That said, how do we learn to see the world differently?

TWO

Through the Glass Darkly

◆ ◆ ◆ ◆

If we are willing to recognize the existence of the First World of "how" and the Second World of "why," we also accept the challenge of learning to live on both levels simultaneously. The complication is that, while we need to keep the entire panorama in focus, we see and experience each level of it quite differently. We may need to wear a set of spiritual corrective lenses.

Those of you who wear corrective lenses will, of necessity, require an occasional visit to the optometrist's. At some point in your consultation you will put your face against a machine called an auto-refractor. The doctor will flip various lenses in front of each eye, asking constantly, "Does this make it clearer or worse?"

Let's make the eye chart a Life Chart and our experiences the lenses. Does your job make your ability to see what is really there, what is really important, clearer or worse? **Flip.** Did (or do) your parents make your vision of the world clearer or worse? **Flip.** How about your education? How much of your education do you think blurred your vision? **Flip.** What contribution has your marriage made to your vision? **Flip.** Did going through a divorce bring anything into focus for you? **Flip.** How about the death of someone you loved dearly? **Flip.** Your own heart attack? **Flip.** If you have the privilege of being a leader of people, do you see "head count" and "human resources," or are you able to see through their employee numbers to the real potential of their lives? **Flip.**

Experiences are positive factors in our lives only if we can see through them to something beyond the experience itself. If lenses are smudged and dirty, we start to focus on them rather than on what they were meant to reveal to us. We start to look *AT* the lens rather than *THROUGH* the lens. In the same way, most of us look *at* our experiences rather than *through* them. For example, let's start with the concept that your job isn't a job anymore, it's an experience *through* which you see a new level of meaning. Why be there if all you long for is to get to the end of the day, to get the report in or get the meeting over with? Why not learn how to live *through* your work and never have to be *at* anything ever again? This may be overly blunt, but none of us was born to do the job we are doing. On the other hand, it would be wonderful if we were confident that we were indeed born to accomplish whatever it is we are accomplishing *through* our job.

In the First World, there are millions of lenses available to you: accounting and medicine; art and homemaking; psychology and law enforcement; marriage and divorce; death and birth; poverty and wealth; imprisonment and freedom. Your experiences will differ depending on your gender. You have innumerable lenses to help you see your life and not one of them is an end in itself, although that is how many people regard them. Each is simply a viewpoint *through* which to get a glimpse of the landscape beyond.

Reality, for most of us, probably means that some of the experiences of our lives make things clearer in the spiritual sense, while others fog and cloud both our out-sight and in-sight. What I want to learn to do for myself, and what I invite you to do, is to affect the ratio of the two positively. It's a spiritual version of what the *Endeavor* astronauts had to do for the ailing Hubble Space Telescope. In addition to installing a couple of gyroscopes to keep things in balance, they replaced the Wide Field Planetary Camera so the telescope could see and record things more clearly. That's what we need – a Wide Field Planetary Camera for our personal and corporate souls. Come to think of it, we need a gyroscope too.

Let's switch to the workplace for a while. Organizations worldwide have long been searching for an "It," a Holy Grail. The secret lens of success. That one magical, mystical element that will unlock the secret of life, not as they know it, but as they hope it can be. The energy, time and money that have been spent in this search defy quantification. Life, as corporations have classically defined it, is a commercial life. The bottom-line life. At once so vital to human community and yet so narrow and superficial in its meaning. Their elusive "It" will, they hope, keep customers happy and loyal, employees energized and committed, and, at the same time, allow the corporation to make pots full of money. Generally, however, we have not been particularly wise or insightful searchers. We have been looking *at* things like strategies, systems and structures rather than *through* them to meaning. Meaning that will provide the happiness and peace we seek so fervently.

In his book *Searching for the Spirit of Enterprise*, international consultant Larry Farrell writes that "The bottom line on all this looking in the wrong places is not good. We've been left with an ever-growing stockpile of management fads, revolving people theories, and financial black magic – all of which has virtually nothing to do with growing a business . . . And while the experts fiddle, Rome keeps right on burning." He is right. Corporations have fiddled with automation, robotics and other technologies. They've even fiddled with self-actualization and meditation, explorations that come as close to other-worldliness as anything can. During the Canadian federal elections of 1993 and 1997, the Natural Law Party, based on the teachings of Maharishi Mahesh Yogi, fielded a candidate in virtually every riding across the nation. Their most unique plank was the promise that the stresses of the country would be borne by 7,000 people practicing yogic flying. Well, why not? We've tried everything else.

Other "fiddlers" tried management by objectives and managerial grids on which we could all plot our styles of management and thereby gain insight into our otherwise unidentified lives. On to mission and vision statements. (Are we having fun yet?) What did we do before mission statements? Maybe we need a lot more mission and fewer statements. It is interesting that words like *mission, vision* and *values* have spiritual roots and yet business has claimed them as its own creation. Teamwork (yawn) has been around forever. Fiddlers have deflated, decentralized, deconstructed and re-engineered. Almost anything that would go well with the prefix "de" or "re" became an annual conference theme or a Book Of The Month selection. Every "de" and "re" word simply means that what we have now isn't right. We are yearning people working in yearning organizations. We've looked at our values and principles, we've declared them in print, corporate videos, executive speeches and advertising. Spent a fortune trying to convince employees that they are now empowered when they weren't yesterday or the day before or the day before that. *At. At. At.* It's been one *at* after another. There is no *at* last. No wonder we never feel that we're *through*. This is why so many have made change an enemy. When you look *at* change, it becomes an obstacle. When you look *through* change to a better world that you can help create, it becomes a source of energy.

I don't know another book in which "The Search" was so thorough and so global as in Larry Farrell's *Searching for the Spirit of Enterprise*. It's an incredibly informative volume. The author went looking worldwide for the "spirit" of enterprise and describes his quest as a search for common sense. But is common sense really the missing "It?" I thought we wanted to sense something beyond the common.

"America is at a crossroads," Farrell concludes. "Our share of the world economic pie is shrinking. Our standard of living is at great risk . . . the challenge of our time is to get busy creating America's future prosperity." On the First World level such an admonition excites me. Makes me want to shout "Yes! Let's get busy!" But to do what really? Just get more pie? This isn't quite It for me, I'm looking for something else.

Getting busy, throwing energy into organizational and educational initiatives has some merit. I, and many others, have spent many years helping corporate clients search for ways to revitalize their organizations. In particular, the exercise of helping them declare their values and then pulling back the curtains to reveal their corporate vision, has been most satisfying. On occasion, awesome. But we want to be honest about many of these corporate initiatives. Dr. James Medoff, an economics professor at Harvard University, was quoted in the *Wall Street Journal* as saying he knows of "no empirical evidence that any of these things increase productivity." And so even the First World continues to roll along, immune to our clever initiatives. The management consulting firm Sibson and Co. reports that, after questioning 4,000 focus groups over a period of three years, they peg "the effectiveness of these management fads at between just 10–20 percent." It's no wonder that the phrase "flavor of the month" has become indigenous to most corporate cultures. Says Professor Dan Mitchell of UCLA, "Somebody's writing a book right now that will come up with a more popular phrase, and we'll all be doing that."

"The problem with these corporate efforts," my friend and novelist Sue Reynolds says, "stems from the fact that they are all tools and not ends in themselves. Without a basic spiritual perspective, basic spiritual values to operate from, they are pointless exercises. But they are not necessarily the wrong tool, given the right ends." Our challenge is to change these activities from *at* to *through* experiences. We have to learn to see *through* them all – literally and spiritually.

In that spirit then, a passing comment on one recent and particularly powerful corporate movement – Total Quality Management (TQM). In this area, I do not have a client for whom I have more admiration, respect and, frankly, love, than the folks at St. Joseph's Health Centre in London, Ontario. A major teaching hospital, "St. Joe's" is led by one of the country's most innovative management teams. Under the guidance of President Philip Hassen and Director of Quality Jane Parkinson, St. Joe's has literally written the book on TQM in health care.

I remember sitting in the boardroom with members of the senior executive team, having reviewed and celebrated the truly incredible accomplishments they achieved through TQM. In the midst of that very positive conversation, I turned to Phil and asked, "Well, Phil, do you think we've finally found it?" With every right to feel content, if not downright victorious, he said, "No, this isn't it." Was it wonderful stuff? Without question. Had hundreds of staff thrown themselves fully into the exercise? Yes, like few other groups have done. Had we found the "It" all corporations seek? Nope. Disappointing in one way. Exhilarating in another. It meant we had the opportunity to keep on searching. For Phil, TQM couldn't rest as an *at*; St. Joe's had to keep trying to see it, and other initiatives, as ways to work *through* to meaning in the life of the organization.

Maybe the corporate world's eternal search for "excellence" should be called off. There's talk about it. If the excellence we search for is limited to the First World, then we are rapidly tiring of it. We've searched everywhere and are not happy because we have found nothing of lasting substance. We thought in 1982 that management consultants Tom Peters and Robert Waterman had led us to the ten secrets of excellence, at least as defined by profitability and market share, measures used by the First World. Even on that level, we learned, within months, of the failure of several of the companies cited by *In Search of Excellence* as the best models of those secrets. Obviously something was missing. Something had eluded the research process. Something mysterious. It has taken us a long time to realize that excellence is not an *at,* it's a *through.* But we want to thank all of you great organizations for playing our game, and Bob, what do we have for these fine folks? We have some wonderful parting gifts including the new home version of "Guess the Meaning of Work." Tune in tomorrow when once again we try to give away our grand prize – Eternal Happiness.

It can be extremely difficult to find meaning in our corporate initiatives, just as it is in our own lives. In a brilliant *Time* magazine essay titled "Who's Afraid of the Big Bad Bang?," Dennis Overbye raises powerful questions about our scientific and pseudoscientific attempts to make sense of the world. "We have in life," he writes, "quantum uncertainty. There is no reason to think we even know the right questions yet, let alone ultimate answers." This is why so many are discouraged with The Search as they have known it so far. Continues Overbye:

> The currency of science is not truth but doubt. And, paradoxically, faith. Science is nothing if not a spiritual undertaking. The idea that nature forms some sort of coherent whole, a universe, ruled by laws accessible to us, is a faith. The creation and end of the universe are theological notions, not astronomical ones.
>
> We can only wonder whether some law of laws will stand revealed someday at the end of the grudging trial-and-error process of science. The theory of everything, even if it existed, however, could not pretend to tell us what we most want to know. It could not tell us why the universe exists – why there is something rather than nothing at all. And it could not tell us if our lives have meaning, if God loves us.
>
> Written on a piece of paper or on a T-shirt, the theory of everything would just lie there waiting for something else to breathe fire into it . . .

On God's love, science is also silent, and that silence is the wind of liberation. Physicists can neither prove nor disprove that Jesus turned water into wine, only that such a transformation is improbable under the present admittedly provisional physical laws . . . The fact that science cannot find any purpose to the universe does not mean there is not one. We are free to construct parables for our moral edification out of the law of the jungle, or out of the evolution and interdependence of species. But the parables we choose will only reflect the values we have already decided to enshrine.

That piece from Overbye is beautiful writing. I'm almost hesitant to pick up on it for fear of spoiling the moment. It invites; it tantalizes; and his comment about parables makes us wonder about the values we have chosen. Just what values have we enshrined?

In a report titled "Values of American Managers," researchers Barry Posner and Warren Schmidt update their ten-year-old study on the "personal values" of American managers. First- and second-place winners in the *personal* values in the "Organizational Goals" category were "quality" and "customer service," respectively. Brings tears to your eyes, doesn't it? In 1981 it was "organizational effectiveness" and "productivity." This was described as a "striking difference" but, frankly, it doesn't seem to be a quantum leap in values to me. Isn't it also interesting that much of the flattening, downsizing and re-engineering activity so prevalent right now is actually more relevant to the effectiveness and productivity values held by managers in 1981? Maybe this implies that many managers were dancing to the music long before the band started to play. Sometimes we can be very untimely fiddlers.

One-third of the respondents in both studies felt that their bosses engaged in unethical behavior. Fewer of the more recent group, however, would have the courage and conviction to resign over an ethical conflict. If our values aren't for sale, they sure seem to be for rent. On the other hand, two-thirds in 1991 said family brought more satisfaction than career. That compares to half the group ten years earlier. Does all this add up to you? Apparently we now love our families more than our careers, but we're much more likely to compromise our values. There are many, many studies like this. To tell you the truth, I'm starting to wonder if very many of us really do know what we stand for, what we truly believe in.

The relevant question here is whether or not people generally, and corporate leaders particularly, are actually getting somewhere in The Search for whatever it is that will satisfy the yearning of their hearts. We are wandering in a spiritual wilderness following best-seller after best-seller. Filling in values questionnaires for researchers who are trying to make statistical sense out of a spiritual world. Like the original, our modern-day Moses heroes do not seem able actually to take us to the promised land. Some aren't even able to show it to us. We drop them one after another as they disappoint us. Next!

Just how much more can we endure? How much longer do we have to be *at* this?

In a thorough and fascinating exploration of the role of courage in organizational regeneration, Harvey Hornstein recapped the history of The Search in a book titled *Managerial Courage*. Some of that history is also my history. I received most of my university training during the late sixties and early seventies, caught up in the human-potential movement, running around in work boots and worn-out sweaters experiencing "The Now." We didn't take coffee breaks in those days, we became One with the coffee. This was an important time for me. I found myself. Surely, I remember thinking as I looked disdainfully on the capitalistic bourgeois pigs of the corporate world, I have found the "It," while they have not. But coming very close to sacrilege, Hornstein writes of this period:

The human relations movement was properly concerned with dysfunctional, competitive and autocratic behavior in social life in general, and in organizations in particular, but evangelistic zeal, combined with a natural process, whereby individuals and groups try to become pure, perhaps purer than others in their commitment to the new norms and values, fatally transformed what began as a legitimate criticism of relationships and leadership into a new tyranny. Autocratic leadership was harshly stereotyped as ineffective, ruthless, unconstrained self-interest. Harmony and cooperation became indisputably good, without any undesirable costs, and disrupters of that atmosphere were treated as if they were indisputably flawed, lacking the essential and redeeming insight.

Fatal? A new tyranny? Say it ain't so, Harvey. You mean that wasn't the "It?" You mean that was just another *at*? He goes on to say that our searching can be as much stifled by the excessive zeal for social harmony as by an autocratic tyrant. Does that mean no more group hugs? No more bonding? For old time's sake, everybody link arms. That's it. OK, together now – "*Kum by yah, m'lawd, kum by yah . . .*"

Entertainment, the industry designed to flavor the First World and make it more palatable, has, apparently, been searching too. Every new season brings out a new area of searching as viewers gradually decide what is to be "popular." "Families have returned to the big screen" observes an article in a 1996 *Maclean's* magazine. "It's getting safe to go to the movies again," it begins, noting the increasing number of movies in which character is valued over action. Where will this shift take us? Can the entertainment media, a primary tool of the First World, eventually bring us Second World awareness? Can a medium whose primary goal is to communicate bring us both human and divine meaning, a sense of intrinsic worth, a purpose beyond mere consumption and self-seeking?

Television, claimed *USA Today,* is showing renewed reverence for religion. "In a medium often criticized for depicting the devout as extreme fanatics or fools, this [1996] TV season is showing refreshing respect for religion," the article says. It goes on to say that renowned producer Norman Lear is on record as being against "a terrible drift in our culture away from all recognition and discussion of that part of us that makes up our inner lives." An entertaining search for our spirituality is a rather interesting proposition. Maybe we'll be inclined to move a few more spaces on the game board of life if we can be entertained at the same time.

Television is not, however, the answer. Indeed, Canadian media guru and philosopher Marshall McLuhan once said that the Gospel cannot be preached over a microphone because the medium and the message are contradictory. Technology requires intermediate channels between sender and receiver while the Gospel requires direct connection. In a 1993 study commissioned by a Canadian multifaith channel, the Environics Research Group found that 47 percent say they never get spiritual inspiration from TV and only 6 percent reported that their viewing of religious programming reflected any effort to explore their spirituality. Overall, it is hard to expect television to help us in the search for meaning when 85 percent of the population feel television generally broadcasts the wrong moral and ethical values.

Let's look briefly at religion itself. Is it helping us in our search for spirituality? Is it making capital "L" Life more visible to you? You'd think that of all human organizations religion would make things clearer. Not necessarily so, unfortunately. We can be *at* church, *at* synagogue or *at* worship and never experience the *through* of faith.

It's not that most religions aren't trying. In an article in the *Toronto Star,* religion editor Michael McAteer looks at the changes in the Unitarian Church, a denomination generally known for its "none-of-the-above" approach to theology. Indeed, most Unitarians describe themselves as humanists, rational humanists and/or existentialists. It's the uncola of religion. Unitarian leaders readily agree that their church had – and has – a strong appeal to those who want to escape religion or perhaps have been hurt by it. To belong to this 500-year-old denomination, you need not pledge yourself to any doctrine, belief or theology. For this group at least, the article said, there has been a "stunning shift in direction." The headline caused me to shake my head and at the same time see rays of hope for the spiritual value of religion. It read: "Congregations grow as ritual and spirituality return to church." The alarming word, of course, is "return." When we have to talk about spirituality *returning* to a church, you know something has gone terribly wrong. "Spirituality is making a comeback," McAteer writes, "in a denomination where at one time the mention of God or spirituality was unthinkable and a complacent orthodoxy of dissent held sway."

I happen to have used Unitarianism as the focus of our first cut at reconciling religion and spirituality. Frankly, it would be my hope that the media could use the same headline for virtually every denomination and religious organization. At this point, however, it is sad but true that religion and spirituality are not synonymous. At times they are downright antithetical – a conflict between *at* behavior and *through* yearning.

"For too many sensitive minds," writes Theodore Roszak, "religion means the censorship of experience, not its liberation. The very word groans with mind-binding orthodoxies." Writing in the 1960s in *Unfinished Animal,* he states, "we find in this rising curiosity for the marvelous, the popular unfolding of an authentically spiritual quest, which has been driven into a variety of unorthodox channels by the rigidity of conventional religion in the Western world." As American comedian and secular critic Lenny Bruce once quipped, "Every day people are straying away from the church and going back to God." While there are many channels *through* which to find parts of our spiritual selves, it is unfortunate that religion isn't always one of them.

Organized religion itself is searching. During a March 16, 1995, ABC television special, journalist/broadcaster Peter Jennings explored the New Age, user-friendly modes of Christian worship. Showing examples of well-staged pop music and even stand-up comedy, Jennings wonders whether such programming simultaneously draws sellout crowds and sells out God. "Jesus lite," suggests TV critic Matt Roush. "We found it hard to analyze people's spirituality," concludes Jennings. It is hard to analyze because it is hard to find.

"A religious man," someone once said, "goes to church and thinks about going fishing. A spiritual man goes fishing and thinks about God." I wonder which God would see as the most genuine act of worship: "*at* church" or "*through* fishing?" While this book is not an exploration of religion, it is impossible not to discuss religion here. We want to explore spirituality and the temporal and eternal implications of a spiritual life view. But, as University of California professor Dr. Rachel Naomi Remen writes in *Vision* magazine, "Religion is a bridge to the spiritual – but the spiritual lies beyond religion. Unfortunately, in seeking the spiritual we may become attached to the bridge rather than crossing over it." We want to cross over.

THREE

Has Our Search for Excellence Been Called Off?

❖ ❖ ❖ ❖

King Solomon became the third King of Israel around 971 B.C. While worshiping at the temple in Gibeon, Solomon was asked by God in a dream to name anything he wanted God to give him. Solomon said, "I feel like a little child and do not know how to carry out my duties. Some days I don't even know how to go in and out. Your servant is here among the people you have chosen, a great people, too numerous to count or number. So give your servant a discerning heart to govern your people and to distinguish between right and wrong." As the story goes, God was pleased that Solomon had asked for wisdom and replied, "Since you have asked for this and not for long life or wealth for yourself, nor have you asked for the death of your enemies . . . I will do what you have asked. I will give you a wise and discerning heart, so that there will never have been anyone like you, nor will there ever be."

Like Solomon, you and I feel inadequate, inexperienced and overwhelmed at times. There is just too much going on in our lives. We don't know how we are going to deal with it all –

33

the kids, the mortgage, the Bre-X shares, the arthritis, the lay-offs at work, the boss with a fetish for reports, the transmission, the water in the basement. What would we have asked God for? Would we look internally or externally for the ingredients of an excellent life? If we were to pattern our personal lives after the typical corporate model, we'd look externally. Most corporations would have asked God for capital, market share, record-setting return on equity and the death of their enemies. They have defined excellence in these ways for a very long time. The search for external excellence has never fully satisfied corporate yearnings, and it won't satisfy our personal yearnings either. We've got to search new territory.

The story of Solomon goes on. God adds, "Moreover, I will give you what you have not asked for – both riches and honor – so that in your lifetime you will have no equal among kings." Just maybe, if we truly seek *inner* excellence, we will not have to worry about the outer symbols.

I rather like building projects around the house. It's a wonderful physical release providing a very real sense of accomplishment. All of this is an enjoyable part of my spiritual journey, though I sure don't think about these projects in that context while I'm doing them. Unfortunately, when something goes wrong, my impatience often provides evidence of spiritual regression. Anyway, somewhere along the way, the kids get involved in these projects and I become an instant shop teacher. The joke, of course, is that my projects involve only major motor skills and big-muscle utilization. Mitering a corner is the ultimate in fine carpentry as far as I am concerned. The one lesson in construction that I am clear about is "Use the right tool for the right job." It drives me nuts when I find the kids using my good wrench for a hammer or my screwdriver as a crowbar. Such substitutions never work very well, but that is not the fault of the tool. Clearly then, it would be foolish, having experienced futility in using the wrench as a hammer, to pick up the pliers for the same purpose.

A lot of us are making this metaphoric mistake in our own lives. Someone works hard to become a physician, sacrifices his or her marriage for the sake of the practice, burns out, gets into financial difficulty and maybe develops a drug dependency. In short, makes a mess out of life. Sad, but not uncommon. As a matter of fact, in June 1996, Britain's *Evening Standard* reported on a British Medical Association study that found that 10 percent of physicians in the United Kingdom were addicted to alcohol and/or drugs. Well, the demands of modern medicine will do that to a person, right? One solution for a troubled doctor might be to abandon the stress of medicine and pick up, oh, say real estate. Ah, real estate – freedom, independence, reward for performance. Now the doctor can live from commission to commission. Hand out a hundred business cards a day. Be out every evening driving fickle clients to see homes they won't even get out of the car to inspect. Spend Saturdays and Sundays hosting open houses. The pliers don't work very well as a hammer either, do they?

Anything wrong with being a physician? Isn't real estate a perfectly good profession to be in? No to the first, yes to the second. The problem is in how one sees *through* each vocational lens in the first place. You can be a physician and stay in the First World, evaluating biological bodies, writing prescriptions, making money, developing your ego. Or you can use being a physician as a tool for spiritual intervention and understanding of how the Second World can benefit the First. Let's play this one out a little.

Medical schools in Canada are realizing in very dramatic fashion that the physician lens needs to be reground if it is to help practitioners see *through* it to what is really important. To look at human life with the help of a Wide Field Planetary Camera. Let me start with the wonderful news that half the medical students in Canada are women. God is in her heaven so there is hope for our world. There is another good sign: high marks in science are no longer the secret to a successful application. Marks for life are paramount. Students who hrough references, job history and community-service experience that they have a "humanitarian soul" are given priority. A typical class of medical students today will include clergy, social workers, schoolteachers, civil servants and homemakers, all of whom see medicine as a calling to care. The first time a University of Toronto medical student sees a patient it's a house call! In the United States, 117 out of 126 accredited medical schools require the study of physician-patient relationships. This is wonderful and long overdue; we have recognized for centuries that this relationship is critical to the healing process. On March 15, 1995, *USA Today* reported that the number of medical students choosing to go into family practice was at a historic high. Rather odd, given that specialists make significantly more money. Going into family practice is a choice that comes from the heart rather than the wallet, explained the article. "We are not just going to look at a hand and let them go," stated one doctor. "We intend to be with the family for the rest of their lives." There is a big difference between a physician treating a patient's ailments and one who enters a person's life. Now don't go off and accuse your specialist of being a nonspiritual person. Remember, it's not the lens, it's one's ability to see *through* it.

We could play this scenario out for the real-estate example and for every other profession and job. It's not the job, it's what you use it for. For example, even in that most revered journal, *People* magazine, there was the story of 83-year-old Tom Dorrance, the Zen master of horse trainers, whose gentle and spiritual approach to this macho-American profession is described in a book entitled *True Unity: Willing Communication between Horse and Human.* It's enough to make John Wayne turn over in his grave, but here is a man who sees something different from other horse trainers. Dorrance doesn't see a horse as an animal that needs to be "broken." He looks *through* horse training and sees what others do not – unity in creation.

It's hard to accept this, but our jobs are not really very important. They are not ends in themselves. It's what you see and understand *through* them. The concept, or better, obsession with finding job security is odd when you look at it from the perspective we've been discussing. Just what is job security anyway? It's just an *at*. If you do secure a job, that in no way means you have also secured Life. And it is Life we want, isn't it? I want to say to the security-obsessed, "Ever think that 'securing' a job may prevent you from finding Life?" It's like tying your boat *securely* to a dock and then setting out for a cruise.

I've used the metaphor of lenses as a way to gain a clear and focused perspective on life. Let me suggest another metaphor, that of searching through a field, to take our exploration further.

You've watched news coverage of searchers walking in a line across a field or woods looking for a body, weapon or some other crime clue. The unit of field is central to any systematic search process. Interesting, isn't it, that the word *field* is also used to denote what we are doing with our lives, as in, "What field are you in?" As mentioned in chapter 2, what if we were to ask a different question: "Where are you searching?" We might then answer in Second World language, "I'm searching *through* law right now." Or, "I'm searching *through* raising my children." Even, "I'm searching *through* retirement" or "I'm searching *through* unemployment."

So how is your search going? In your heart of hearts. How are you *really*? Have you and I been so manic, so busy, running around in our fields – work, family, community, sports, school, religion – that we long ago forgot what we're searching for? Maybe we've tricked ourselves into thinking that simply being in a field is enough. But it's not, is it? Not even a secure one. No matter how far we've gone. President. Chairman. Gold medalist. Tenured professor. Governor. Judge. Your Holiness. Millionaire. MVP.

What I am finally learning, though slowly, is that unless we look *through* what we do instead of *at* what we do, happiness, wholeness and peace will not be ours. They sure haven't been consistently mine so far. I remember a guy walking around during a conference with a huge button on his lapel that read, "I don't know about you, but I'm faking it." Can't count how many times I've thought I should get one of those. My own search has been a real roller-coaster ride and I've been to both heaven and hell several times. You too?

Recognizing that my personal story is important only to me and those who know and love me, let me, nevertheless, open up at least some of it for you. My hope is that we'll connect with each other. I can only speak from where I've been; if you've been there too, you may find yourself in my story. The story is not important, the lessons are.

Growing up for me happened in a fundamentalist and evangelical Christian context. I look back at my childhood and I realize that I never learned how to search because all the "right" answers were unarguably spelled out for me by loving and well-meaning parents and a well-meaning church. However, somewhere inside of me I was arguing with what I had been taught, although I didn't know it. I wanted *through* and I was getting *at*. My first degree was in religious education. I now think that during those four years of study I was trying to deny my own arguing by finding academic and theological proof that the answers I had been given were in fact right. I was trying to minimize the responsibility and danger of searching.

Didn't work. My search in the field of Christian religion wasn't a true search at all. It disappointed and angered me and I didn't want to be there anymore. The anger turned out to be a blessing in disguise. The problem for me was not Christianity, but my not knowing how to look *through* Christianity, to use it as a focusing lens, as a field to be searched. The organized church had conditioned me to simply look *at* it as though it were an end in itself.

My next field of search was psychology on both the undergraduate and graduate levels. Now I was cooking! This study was truly wonderful because for the first time I began to do my own real searching. As I mentioned earlier, the human-potential movement consumed me, introducing me to a spirituality I had never known. Not only that, but I learned how to help others search too. What fulfillment that brought! The secret was that I saw *through* psychology to a meaning beyond it. But it turned out that this was not exactly pain-free either, because I didn't fit neatly into one of the predetermined graduate-school categories. There were forces in the university bureaucracy that wanted me to regress to looking *at* psychology. Fit in, Ian. Pick two from column A; two from column B; and one from column C. In those days, psychologists taught other psychologists, did clinical therapy or wrote learned papers based on experiments with white albino rats.

My search *through* the field of psychology turned up a gift for speaking and influencing organizations. I joyfully began to use that gift, and started my own company before I finished university. And it's here I began to lose it. I was so taken with being in the psychology field that I lost my wide-field perspective. Already I was forgetting that I had another field, my family – my wife and my very young daughter, Karen. Here was a field flowing with the potential for spiritual discovery and unity and all I did was look *at* it. I didn't search in it or *through* it. Yes, I loved them both and I was a good dad as dads go. Just writing this brings tremendous sadness because the truth is, I wasn't connected, and I'll regret for the rest of my life what I missed. And do you see that it's not just what I missed, it's what they missed? The sins of the father really are visited upon the children.

There was one powerful time of connection with my family when my wife and I were expecting our second child. Just prior to the expected delivery date, we discovered to our horror that the baby had severe hydrocephalus complicated by spina bifida. The baby died during the delivery. We named her Meredith Anne. I remember the two of us holding this beautiful and lifeless baby and for the first time in my life I felt my soul exposed in all its emptiness.

Sometimes in life you discover things in spite of yourself. And those kinds of discoveries are usually painful. This experience did change me at some level, for a time. I did walk more softly among the lives precious to me. But life goes on. Not long after this awakening, I was back in the work field bigger, better and more consumed than ever. Some of us are very slow learners. No. *I* am a very slow learner.

Once more the family field beckoned me with the birth of my son, Nathan. What a joy it was to witness the entrance of this baby! So alive and so healthy. I felt so much a part of my children's lives and yet there was still something missing. If you are a wife and mother, do you ever get the feeling that you don't really live with your husband, that he just visits between work assignments? Sort of like being *at* marriage and *at* family? Well, that was me. I happily went to most of the ball games and even to a couple of teacher interviews. Again, the sad truth was that most of my searching was still happening in my work, and I loved it. It was all so legitimate. Me, just looking after the financial needs of my family. I was away all the time attending to the needs of my clients. Most businesspeople I know are much more concerned with the quality of their customer service than they are with the quality of their parenting and spousing. What we lose, what I lost in this spiritual myopia! We should steal a page from U.S. President Bill Clinton's book and have a sign in front of our desks, **"It's Your Family, Stupid!"**

Our divorce was inevitable and painful. Those of you who have been through it don't need any more explanation from me. I now live two thousand miles away from my children. Unless you've done it, you have no idea how wrenching it is to take your kids to the airport and watch them walk alone through security to their gate and the plane that will take them "home." Look around the next time you are at an airport and see how many dads and moms you can count saying goodbye to their kids. A lot of us need to wake up. We tend to open our eyes two weeks too late. To the blind, all things are sudden.

With the same blindness, I went immediately into another relationship. The passion, the energy, the shared goals and interests – all convinced me that finally I had found my way. Never mind that part of the price tag was the disruption of yet another family. Never mind that I virtually abandoned the family and friends of my world to join hers. And with my positive attitude, of course I was up to the challenge of looking after two families financially. Surely I could get used to living in her house with her furniture and her pictures on the wall. After all, I tried to convince myself, the need for personal space belongs to the emotionally immature. There was no factor that could not be overcome. Love and lust would see us through!

The success rate of relationships born out of adultery is not good and my experience can be added to the negative column. Though it lasted almost six years, the battles for control and the constant competitiveness meant that the relationship died in anger. I realize now that it was also born in anger. I've learned a lot about anger, and it's devastating. Devastating to ourselves and to those around us who are wounded by the shrapnel of our lives.

I was visiting my children in Vancouver when I got the early-morning call that the locks on our house in Toronto had been changed and that I would find all my clothes in my car when I returned. Stunned, I looked across the hotel room at my sleeping son and couldn't help but relive the first devastation all over again. Somehow it seemed even worse in the light of this new implosion. My life didn't flash before my eyes, it came crashing down on me. It felt as if every failure I had ever experienced, every foolish decision I had ever made, every fall and scrape, every missed opportunity of the 47 years I had used up so far, decided to have a reunion in my soul. I thought I had known emptiness before, but I hadn't even been close to what I was feeling in that moment.

Keeping up happy appearances for the sake of my kids that weekend took everything I had and more. Where would I go? Where could I stay? What should I do? Who could I call for help? Only two friends came to mind – Linda and Jane back in Toronto. We'd been colleagues and close friends for years and had already helped each other through our various devastations. I called. They weren't home. All weekend I'd sneak frantic and fruitless calls to their answering machine. In despair I walked friendless into the airport lounge to await the flight back to my packed car. I also walked right into Linda and Jane. Unknown to me, they had spent the weekend in Vancouver, were headed back to Toronto, were on the same flight, and of course I would be living in their house for as long as I needed. And in that serendipitous moment, I once again began to feel the gentle guiding hand of God in my life.

Life is sometimes kind, and we do get a chance to heal. With humility and great joy, I can tell you that all of this pain did help me redirect my search. It helped me work for and achieve a relationship with my children that nothing will take away. The experience of divorce and separation did bring many things into focus for me. I am finally learning how to listen to my own kids and to share honestly with them my thoughts, feelings, hopes and fears. We talk about us, about searching for life, about what happened. Much more so than when I lived with them. While we still have our rocky moments because the wounds are deep, I couldn't be more grateful. They are the pride of my life. But what a price to pay for something that was right in front of me all along. If only I had opened my eyes and searched years earlier.

Life has a way of carrying on regardless of our experiences. "You can't have a better past," wrote Dr. Wayne Dyer in his incredible book *Your Sacred Self*. That statement of the obvious pierced me like an arrow. You and I can rethink old choices until the day we die. We can toss and turn with guilt and regret. But you know what? Ain't nothin' back there going to change! As one favored-to-win Olympic athlete said when asked how he felt about finishing fourth, "Of course you feel bad, but there comes a point where you've just got to change channels."

Because some of you, like me, have been in a process of moving from your past toward your future, let me share with you a little more of Dyer's insight:

> You cannot have a better past, so abandon the idea right now. You did what you knew how to do, given the circumstances of your life. Those mistakes of the past were driven by your ego, which wanted to keep you in its grasp. You listened to your false self and recoiled in fear over the idea of anyone knowing your true self.
>
> You moved away from love, but now you are back and making the choice for love. You know deep within you that at your primal level you have been designed for love and happiness. You simply let that false self direct you away from the loving presence that is your essence.
>
> You can choose to return to the brilliant light of love that is always with you. Who you are is that unclouded love. Go there often and all of your fears will be replaced by the love that is always within you.
>
> Let your thoughts remain on love, and let your actions stem from this love. This is the realization of your higher self. It is the realization of your sacred quest. You can truly make the decision to be free from fear and doubt.
>
> There is no greater Freedom!

For me it can't be said any better than that. I want to live in the brilliant light of love. It is so much easier to find what you are looking for in life if your life is well lit. After a couple of years of being single, the lights finally came on for me. I am in a new and wonderfully happy relationship with my wife, Georgia. There are no battles for control, no competitiveness. Just unconditional love that grows with each day. She has taught me much about how to find peace while still maintaining excitement about life. Life provides so many opportunities through which we can search. For me the lessons continue to be both joyful and painful. And yet, at the same time, they are all rewarding. Sometimes I think I've learned, sometimes I know I haven't. Slow one day and fast the next. Gratefully, God is patient, and, most of the time, so are the people around me.

On one hand, I wonder how I dare to write this book since I can see so much more than I can live. On the other hand, if you will accept me simply as a fellow searcher for what is right, true and good, we may be able to help each other move to an understanding of life that taps into the spiritual power readily available within us if we could but see it.

What I hope for all of us is that our search for internal excellence has not been called off. Life is meant for meaning, wholeness and joy. It is not about jobs and work, as important as they are in the First World. So, regardless of discouragement or setbacks, it is important not to call off the search. We need to find a new way to search, a new and deeper meaning to the experiences of our lives. A new meaning for family, for work, for learning, for faith. Once we understand that the kind of searching we need to do is spiritual, the benefits will bring harvest in every field of our lives. When we learn the real meaning of fathering or mothering, we will learn the real meaning of corporate leadership. When we redefine what excellence and success really mean in business, we will have also redefined what it means at home. It is all one and the same if we look deeply enough.

FOUR

The Meaning of Spirituality

✦ ✦ ✦ ✦

"Can you send us a list of your talks?" the woman from the speakers' bureau asks. I've always found that an odd request because it sounds as if I should have four of them or maybe a David Letterman–style top-ten list. So I go into general descriptions of the topics that are of current interest to me. As you would expect, somewhere in the top three I mention "Spiritual Leadership," particularly as it applies to the workplace. "Sounds intriguing," she says with a hint of that anxiety you feel when someone sounds as though they want to mess with your soul. "What exactly is that about?" she asks. Good question. All of a sudden I realize that while I could talk for hours about spiritual leadership, I can't give this woman two sentences describing what "It" is.

Just what are we talking about anyway? Were we spiritual in the tie-dyed psychedelic sixties and early seventies? Did romping naked through the surf of Big Sur, California, help us find our souls? Should U.S. President Bill Clinton have inhaled? Was Johnson & Johnson being spiritual in 1982 when it pulled 31 million Tylenol capsules off the shelves, sending the entire corporate world off into a values kick? Is being an equal-opportunity employer a manifestation of spirituality? What if we recycle a lot? Which was the most spiritual event – the Republican or Democrat Convention of 1992? Anything change in 1996? Both Republicans and Democrats claimed to have God on their side. Is the Canadian federal government showing spiritual leadership when it slashes social services in order to reduce the deficit? Is there really such a thing as a holy war? Is Jack Welch demonstrating spiritual leadership in revolutionizing General Electric? For all his notoriety and brilliance, will Lee Iacocca be remembered as a truly spiritual leader? How about televangelist Jimmy Swaggart? How about you? How about me? For that matter, do we even want to be spiritual?

Let's start this exploration with a basic principle of effective group dynamics: your process (how you go about doing things) and your content (the subject matter or agenda) must be synergistic; they need to be mutually supportive. If, for example, I were to give a lecture on why the lecture format is not an effective educational process for adults, the crowd should ask for their money back. Then there was the conference I went to in Atlanta, Georgia, on the integration of psychology and theology, only to discover that no real theologians had been invited – we were all psychologists. Or the time an organization put on a course for self-directed work teams and began by pre-assigning the seating for the participants. In many corporations this contradiction is expressed by the rank and file who say, pointing up to the corner offices in mahogany row, "They don't walk the talk." People are divining rods for truth. When your process and content are not consistent with each other, you lose credibility and integrity.

We clearly run that risk in trying to define spiritual leadership. It is pointless to define a Second World concept using First World terminology. We will lose integrity if we try to do so. You can't create new paradigms by using old paradigms. Putting new wine in old skins will cause those skins to leak and spoil the wine. Am I positioning the dilemma clearly? If your 12-year-old, poised on the brink of puberty, asks you to tell her what love is, would you send her to the dictionary? Webster won't help us here, either, and I am going to resist the urge to look up the words *spiritual* and *leadership*. We'll try to find a Second World answer to a Second World question without this aid.

One member of the team coaching me through this book suggests that first we need to understand what "spiritual" means and not worry about "spiritual leadership." Spiritual leadership is a red herring, the coach says. If we understand what being spiritual means, she insists, we will automatically evidence spiritual leadership. That sounds deep enough to be worth a try.

However, right away we run into one of those circular conundrums like: "If God can do anything, can he make a rock so heavy he can't lift it?" In our case it's: "Can one understand spirituality if one is not already spiritual?" If the answer is no and only those who are spiritual can understand spirituality, then there is no need to explain it. Those who are spiritual will already understand while those who are not will never understand regardless of our best effort. St. Matthew quotes Christ's teaching that insight into spiritual things is a gift not possessed by everybody. Fortunately, the text goes on to say, "Whenever someone has a ready heart for this, the insights and understandings flow freely. But if there is no readiness, any trace of receptivity soon disappears." What is vital to understanding is not spirituality, but a *readiness* to be spiritual. Assuming that we are at least ready to understand, and given that people are fundamentally spiritual beings, we have to conclude that spirituality can be explained and understood. The caveat is that we will understand spirituality only to the degree we have opened ourselves to its meaning.

A black belt's concept of karate is a full spectrum away from a white belt's concept. The latter does not really understand karate and won't for some time. At a white-belt level, it seems to me, students spend a good deal of time pretending they're a black belt. While no one is likely to issue colored belts for each level of spirituality, there are some rich similarities to explore. Apart from having Karate Kid videos in the family library, and taking kids to karate lessons, I am not a karate person. How can I, from this elementary starting point, come to understand this complex and mystical martial art? "Sign up for some lessons," will be the first reaction. Fair enough. That fits with our desire to understand spirituality too. We've got to take some lessons.

Our exploration of First- and Second-World differences, the encouragement to look *through* the experiences of our lives to find the holy, and my personal story of how hard it is to do that are all intended as introductory lessons. Getting our white and yellow belts in spirituality requires us to see the spiritual in the simple and mundane. Once we learn to do that, we graduate to the higher belts. Some people don't have the patience for this process and end up deciding that the spiritual world does not exist, that it is not worth reaching if it does exist, or they become angry and cynical about others who persist with the journey. It is like the little kid at his very first karate class who asks the Sensei, "When do we get to break boards?" Somehow you just know that this kid is going to last two or three classes at the most. Ask him why he quit and you'll get something like, "It was boring, we never did anything. All we did were these stupid exercises." Something happens inside the hearts of those who persist and reach the ethereal world of degreed black belt. Something mysterious clicks into place. The time, pain and discipline of those "stupid exercises" are reasonable payment for a journey to another world. But they had to get through the quitting point.

Likewise, it seems to me that in the process of understanding anything meaningful in life – love, leadership, anger, forgiveness, self, parenting, spirituality – there is a veil one must pass through. Everything on this side of the veil is learned through labor – lessons, if you will. We look for answers without knowing the questions, and the answers we do find seem to change with the wind. We eat but remain hungry. Our searching is cyclical and we visit points of truth over and over, never really confident that it's actually truth we're visiting. We get hurt a lot and wonder why learning has to be so painful. Like nervous children waiting for the school play to begin, energy heightened every time someone brushes past the curtains, parting them briefly enough to show that there really is an audience out there, we too brush the veil and are rewarded with flashes of insight into another kind of existence. It is out there and it's inside of us. We know. We've seen it.

But the veil. How do we get through the veil? We have already learned that there must be a readiness to understand. That is the prerequisite. It is readiness that begins to rend the veil. How then do you and I get ourselves into a posture of readiness? Perhaps readiness is created by what psychologist Dr. Morris Massey once labeled a Significant Emotional Event. An experience so full of impact, so powerful, that it causes us to S.E.E. the world differently. There is no question that significant emotional events can disrupt our lives and put us on another course. There may be a question, however, about whether or not an emotional event can propel us to the other side of the veil. It seems to me that we need a significant *spiritual* event to propel us to a spiritual world. Emotional events just don't have enough thrust on their own. Remember, for our search to have integrity, our process has to be consistent with our content. A spiritual voyage eventually requires spiritual fuel. Emotional fuel alone will give us only an emotional voyage. Emotional fuel is needed to start, but it is not enough in and of itself.

This is the most important and difficult journey we will ever take. In preparation, we must first explore this readiness aspect a little more.

So what precedes readiness? Awareness does. Learning to truly see and recognize what is around and within us. When you learn to see, you cannot help but be led to the spiritual.

Now here we go almost getting stuck with language again because awareness is much more than just actually "seeing" things. There are three ways through which we are aware or "see." One is through our **senses**: we are "aware" of what we observe with our eyes, what we taste, feel, hear and so on. This vehicle of awareness is so routine that many of us no longer marvel at what the senses can bring us. Watch a baby and you will observe that she innately knows that all of the senses are necessary to fully experience something. It won't be long before someone comes along to tell her not to touch and not to put things in her mouth, just to name two of the most popular parental commands. When was the last time you felt your food the way a toddler does, or even looked at it, for that matter? Some cultures do eat with their hands, though in our society we stay away from our food by using long instruments with sharp points or edges. Maybe I'll start a new culinary program called "Feel Your Food." Getting a little ridiculous? Stay with me and think about it for a while. Is there anything more beautiful in the world than a mother breast-feeding her baby? All of the senses becoming a single experience, a single spiritual experience, I would guess. The warmth, the taste, the feel, the sound of a familiar heartbeat. And have you ever seen a breast-feeding baby look up at her mother and her mother look down at her? If that's not spiritual, I don't know what is.

The second way in which we can have awareness is through our own **internal** knowing: what we know within ourselves. It is possible, for example, to feel fear and not let that fear be observed by anyone else. Only we know within ourselves that we are afraid. There is an exception in that others very closely connected to us, and particularly those who deeply love us, sometimes have access to our internal awareness. That is, they are able to sense something going on inside of us. Generally, however, this awareness belongs fully only to us.

I suggest that we do not use this internal knowing very well either. How often are we quiet enough in our lives to really experience what is going on inside of us? How much denial clouds what could be a very helpful picture? Some time ago I spoke at a conference in London, England. At lunch that day I had the privilege of hearing another speaker who talked about stillness. I've never forgotten it. He referred to the overused metaphor of dropping a pebble into the middle of a pond and how the impact of something so small ripples out across the entire pond. Usually the metaphor is used to illustrate the impact all of us can have in our world no matter how insignificant we feel. Most people who use this illustration, the speaker said, forget to mention one thing: for the rippling effect to be truly observable, the pond must be still. Sometimes in our stillness we can find our greatest strength and understanding. Our greatest awareness. This, in turn, leads to a great readiness.

Imagination is the third way in which we have awareness. We can also use related words like *intuition* or *fantasy,* although these words are superficial and inadequate in some way. Imagination is the most mysterious vehicle of them all. It leads us to what we believe about our existence, about the meaning of our lives. Here we get into the realm of faith and hope. Imagination brings our inner and outer worlds together. Our faith and our beliefs actually contribute to the creation of our total world, the seen and the unseen. It is at this point that the leap comes. As philosopher Sam Keen notes, "Anything that transcends eating, drinking, and making money must begin with a leap of faith."

This vehicle of imagination and intuition takes both our sensory awareness and our internal awareness and uses them to take us to a whole new level of understanding and experience. When I ask you to tell me about your children, about someone you love or about your relationship with God, it is likely that you will go from a visual picture in your mind, to an internal response to that picture, to describing to me a relationship that is not subject to proof or disproof. It is simply there and is very real to you in all of its unseen majesty and mystery. You have deeply imagined it, richly imagined it; that is, you have known it in your heart. This is what imagination does. This is what brings us to the brink of the spiritual.

Imagination has a dark side too. Awareness through imagination can expand or contract your world, depending on what you *do* with your imagination. Most of the conclusions we have come to in our lives are more the product of our imagination than anything else. Parents and teachers sometimes have imaginary and limiting conclusions about the academic potential of children and, unfortunately, often act as if that conclusion were the only reality possible. Employees imagine conclusions about the degree of freedom and choice they have in their work and then act accordingly with great courage and creativity or with timid dependency. We can imagine ourselves giving a reasonable, if not enthralling, presentation to the board or we can imagine ourselves bumbling, drooling, with our zipper down and our new tie dotted with gravy.

What we call reality is recognized through what we imagine the world to be. This makes imagination, and its amazing cousin, intuition, very powerful tools indeed. All of creation began out of God's imagination. Everything around us, including ourselves in some cases, came out of somebody's imagination. Surely, then, there must be some way in which we can become more fully aware of the spiritual level of reality we've been talking about. If faith is the substance of things hoped for and the evidence of things not seen, then faith and imagination must come together at some point. What a grand thought that is! Grand because it means that we are quite capable of a spiritually centered life. All that will be, is already. Around us. Within us. All of nature is full of wonders! Even more mind-boggling is the realization that all that God is, is just waiting to be seen and trusted. For some, God is known, and for others, unknown. There is an inviting mystery in both the knowing and the unknowing. And just to round out this awesome picture, we, and all our wonder-fullness, become available to ourselves as well. For some, the Self is known, and for others, unknown. In both cases, the journey has only begun.

In July 1995, I took a shamanic journey into the rain forest of Peru. If you want to be guaranteed an experience in which all of these awareness-forces merge to take you into the Second World, take a trip like that. My conclusion is that it would be impossible to walk through that threatened environment without being affected deeply, spiritually. The trees made me touch them. I was overwhelmed by the healing power of the plants in the hands of one who knew what to do with them. The place felt holy. It is a place of energy and spirit. I believe it was created by God. For me, it pointed to God. The devastation of this forest, which I knew was happening not far from me, cried out even more loudly: "God is, and the goodness of his creation calls you and draws you; you refuse it, or, worse, destroy it at your peril." Both the beauty and the devastation opened my eyes and brought me home, longing for goodness, for the world of meaning. Landing late at night on God's creation smothered with concrete by civilization, feeling with new sensitivity the anger of the crowds impatient with the process of arriving, and seeing a thousand cars all warning each other with their brake lights that progress had come to an abrupt end, I felt sad and yearned for meaning even more.

Our moments of awareness will come both painfully and joyfully in myriad ways. When we become fully aware, we also become fully ready. Once we become ready, the spiritual will happen all by itself. Believe it and it will come.

Let me back up and show you a model that has been very helpful to my understanding of the "spiritual." This is certainly not original and I wish I could tell you who first put this simple framework together. Though I can't, my deepest thanks goes out to her or him.

There are four approaches we can take to virtually everything. We'll also call them levels of commitment. They are:

POLITICAL

INTELLECTUAL

EMOTIONAL

SPIRITUAL

Everything we do in our lives is done at one of these four levels.

POLITICAL

Even this most shallow of levels has value. Take environmental protection, for example. Green is politically correct. If you are not recycling waste, or at least look as if you are recycling – get with it. No one is asking you to believe in it, just to do it. Put the recycle bins out where people can see them, put up posters about the Amazon rain forest just outside the cafeteria, and for Pete's sake, use recycled paper for at least some of your letterhead and definitely for the annual report. You can hardly print, "This paper was made from freshly cut trees" on the back cover, now, can you? In short, you don't have to like it, just do it!

Many of us spend the majority of our time on a political level. We go along with the system because the benefits of changing it are not worth the fight. We've all had to go to a reception when doing so was the last thing in the world we wanted to do. But politically we couldn't safely get out of it and we participated only as long as we felt necessary to minimize any risk to our careers. Or we've gone to a retirement tea for someone we didn't even like. He was your department head – you had to go. Furthermore, having put in your ten bucks for the present, you were determined to at least get your money's worth in food.

INTELLECTUAL

Obviously, all of these political activities are superficially motivated, so it is not hard to go a little deeper than that. Not only is recycling a politically correct activity, it just may make business sense. It is an intelligent thing to do. Check it out. Get some numbers together. Put forward a business case. That's how most businesses make their decisions, isn't it? Then at the end of the second quarter and the fourth quarter you can get a printout on how much money you are saving by recycling. Whether or not it is good for the planet is not nearly so important as whether it's a good deal for you.

EMOTIONAL

There is deeper water still. Beyond the political and intellectual levels lies the emotional. Now you are actually going out of your way to recycle. You rinse out your empty tin cans and carry your disposable cup past the more handy garbage can to the recycle bin that happens to be next to the suggestion box where you dropped in a strongly worded suggestion that we shouldn't be using disposables in the first place. You've taken your kids to see *Free Willy I* and *II,* to say nothing of that rainy Saturday morning when you took them to Tree Day in the park, where they lovingly planted tiny saplings with roots wrapped in little burlap bags. Your heart is in this recycling thing. You inconvenience yourself to protect our planet. Thank you!

SPIRITUAL

As wonderful and powerful as emotional commitment is, we can go deeper still. There remains the spiritual level. You and the object of your commitment are one and the same. Let's run through our recycling chain quickly. Politically – just do it. Intellectually – have a business case for doing it. Emotionally – joyfully go out of your way to recycle. Spiritually – you go to the west coast of North America and chain yourself to one of the giant redwoods of California or a majestic cedar in British Columbia, defying the lumber barons to cut through your body with their chain saws. The tree and you will live or die together.

While the example may seem extreme, it is not meant to trivialize the point. Spiritual commitment *is* extreme. On this level, we knit up the whole. We take true political action that is grounded in intellectual conviction and emotional commitment. We put our whole Self on the line because something matters deeply. It is in putting our Self on the line that we discover a depth of meaning that brings us home to Life itself.

The key point to understanding this spiritual level is the recognition that *there is no separation between you and the object of your commitment.* Keep in mind that this object can be a person, a belief, a thing, a philosophy, a dream and so on. Deeply religious people, to illustrate, want to feel unity with their God. Christians, for instance, aspire to oneness in God through Jesus Christ. Christ prayed that his followers would all be one. St. John recorded the prayer as follows: "Just as you, Father, live in me and I in you, I am asking that they may live in us, that the world may believe that you did send me. I have given them the honor that you gave me, that they may be one, as we are one – I in them and you in me, that they may grow complete into one, so that the world may realize that you sent me and have loved them as you have loved me."

Adherents of Baha'i have a spiritual commitment to the inevitability of world peace through the oneness of all people, or what has been called "the planetization of mankind." This is not a hope for these believers, it is a surety. In a 1995 declaration to the National Spiritual Assemblies worldwide, the Baha'i Universal House of Justice stated, "With the physical unification of the planet in this century and acknowledgment of the interdependence of all who live on it, the history of humanity as one people is now beginning." The peace and security of mankind, wrote Baha'u'llah, founder of the Baha'i faith, "are unattainable unless and until its unity is firmly established."

You can see that the idea of unity quickly becomes central to any discussion of spirituality. When you behave politically, merely out of calculated self-interest, there is a huge gap between what you believe and what you say or do. That's why political correctness and hypocrisy are the same thing. The intellectual level narrows that gap considerably because you have engaged facts, logic and reasoning. Movement to the emotional level goes even further because your heart and feelings are now reflected in your actions. When you hit spiritual, there is no gap and no separation between belief and action. The gap has been filled by the very essence of who you are. You and the object of your commitment have become one.

If I were to examine the reality of the modern-day Christian Church, I would begin at precisely this point because the truth is that one can, functionally, be politically, intellectually, emotionally or spiritually "Christian." It is often said that North America is a Christian society. On what level is that said? Every American president that I can remember, regardless of what was really in his heart, has sponsored a prayer breakfast with Reverend Billy Graham. Obviously, this has long been at least a political custom, providing "official" evidence that America is a Christian society. For some, of course, it may have been a truly spiritual experience.

For us more common folk, the matter of charitable donations presents a better example. Some of us will give to charities providing there is a tax receipt. This is something like presenting a business case to God. However, it seems from Christ's prayer quoted earlier, that the evidence of God's love is directly contingent on a *spiritual* oneness, *not* on political, intellectual or emotional unity.

On the corporate level, one can help organizations evaluate themselves based on what, if anything, they are spiritually committed to; what central issue or vision makes them "one." Unity on the first three levels has some real benefits, but it is insufficient without the spiritual. Corporate statements of vision, mission and values, for example, must point and lead to unity. If they do not, it is difficult for me to see how they could constitute a spiritual core to corporate life. Most such statements focus on market position or profit rather than on a quest for unity. More about corporate purpose later.

Let's get back to something a little more mundane. Remember, these four levels of commitment apply to everything. You have a family reunion coming up next week. That event will be, primarily, either political, intellectual, emotional or spiritual. Let's say that your family isn't very close, never has been and never will be. You do not want to go, the conversation is mindless and all people do is sit and watch TV. Someone points out to you that your great-aunt is 103 and this might be her last family gathering and you really should go. So you make a political decision to attend because there will be more aggravation in not going than in going. Clearly, you do not have your mind, heart or soul in it, do you? At least you'll eat well.

Happily, you learn that your cousin, Norm "Mr. Internet" Thompson, is going to be there. As a surfer, you can hardly wait to talk computers and techie things with this guy. May not be such a bad way to spend a day, after all. Now your head is engaged and you are making an intellectual commitment to attend the reunion. Just remember to take your new laptop to show him.

Can you believe your luck? This is going to be a great family reunion! Your sister just called to see if you could pick her up on your way. Turns out that she is bringing a friend of hers who doesn't have any family here, a bright, warm, beautiful woman you met at one of your sister's parties last summer, someone with whom you would very much like to develop a relationship. Not only will you pick them up, you'll wash and wax the car. Think she'll remember you? No question, your emotions are fully engaged in this reunion now.

The reunion is well under way. You've kissed your great-aunt dutifully, wondering if maybe she has already passed away but no one knows it yet. "Mr. Internet" has thrilled you and bored everyone else by talking about the power of technology, pointing out that your laptop is more powerful than two stories full of computers were 25 years ago and that if automobiles had experienced the same advancements, you'd be able to keep your car in your pocket. "Amazing," everyone had gasped at once. And you might as well have been handcuffed to your sister's friend, for all the room you gave her. She seemed to like the attention though.

It's midafternoon and the five still-single adults are sitting together in the backyard under the old maple tree. You get to talking about what you are each doing with your lives and what is meaningful and not so meaningful about work, relationships and so on. This is all stuff you have been thinking about but have never talked about openly like this. It was when your sister's friend asked you what you really wanted out of life that the conversation went a little deeper. Plumbing these depths was a little scary; you truly yearned for this level of connection and yet you fought against letting the others know what was really in your soul. Your sister's friend wouldn't let you off the hook; gently and persistently she kept searching for the real you. Her own openness and honesty left you stunned and encouraged at the same time. Though the others had joined in with almost equal intimacy, there seemed to be an unspoken agreement that this was your time. Where did the two hours go? You didn't know whether to feel exhausted or refreshed. There was a sense of communion about the experience that you can't explain to this day. You do remember your sister's hug and her whispered words, "I'm proud of you."

So what level was your last family reunion on?

Let's try this **PIES** model out on your last executive-team meeting. Was it primarily a **political, intellectual, emotional** or **spiritual** experience? A political meeting would be one during which the president heard what she or he wanted to hear; people playing the game, nodding at just the right moment and being careful to rehearse what they wanted to say to ensure that it was politically correct. You could see a couple of your colleagues holding off just long enough on their vote until they could see which would be the winning side. They were consumed with self-protection, power games and turf wars. An unbelievable waste of energy, time and spirit, to say nothing of the foolish decisions that are made by people stuck at this level.

If the meeting wasn't totally political, I'll bet it was largely intellectual. Each head of a Strategic Business Unit carefully presenting "the numbers." The challenge here is to use all your creativity to manipulate the numbers so that you come as close as possible to "plan," or at least, to look closer to plan than the next presenter. Want a capital-budget decision to go in your favor? Don't argue for it emotionally or spiritually. Put your business case forward using your best political and intellectual skills accompanied by endless graphs and charts. Your motto is "Give me data or give me death!"

Most executive teams that I have observed over the years spend 95 percent of their time operating on political and/or intellectual levels. This is exactly why, after a relatively short time, an emptiness begins to grow inside. Just as your body can be protein-starved, your soul can become meaning-starved. While this is mostly where the game of business is played, it is simply not satisfying in the long run.

Let me hasten to clarify that I am not denying a value in being politically astute. The virtue of "prudence" is as old as humankind; we wouldn't have survived without it in a less than perfect world. Nor am I suggesting that one shouldn't use one's head in interpreting any accurate data that might be available. The point is that, if this is all you have – self-protective prudence and argument-stopping data – you are living on very barren ground.

Some executive teams incorporate the emotional level of connection. Gradually it is becoming more acceptable to express one's feelings, whether you have data to back them up or not. Some suggest that this is largely due to the increasing influence of women on senior-executive levels. As good as this news is, have you observed that the expression of feelings, by male or female, is invariably accompanied by an apology? Where did we learn that we have to apologize for our feelings? During one of my executive-team coaching sessions, a gifted female executive tearfully expressed her absolute exasperation over the group's unwillingness to make a key decision. If I had been given a dollar for every time she apologized for those tears I could have bought the entire group lunch. What was interesting, though, was how her heartfelt expression gave everyone else permission to talk about their own feelings, many for the first time. One man talked about how he felt that he was losing his family because of the demands of the work-place. If he had to choose one or the other, he admitted, he was choosing his family. These were powerful moments, to say the least. For most of us, this is not the usual boardroom fare.

Before I move the discussion off the emotional level, let me expose a trap I don't want us to fall into. The expression of emotion is often equated with tears, sadness, discouragement and so on. This accounts for only half of the emotional possibilities. We have much the same trouble expressing joy, delight and celebration. When is the last time your team did the wave around the boardroom table, whooped and hollered in delight or gave each other hugs of celebration? Have you ever seen tears of joy in the eyes of your colleagues or felt them on your own cheeks?

Remember my story in chapter 1 of the bankers' conference that was so magical? The senior executive who enabled that unforgettable event to happen was Mike Baptista of the Royal Bank of Canada. What all of us remember most was the time Mike, with tears in his eyes, told his troops how much he loved them. Mike died suddenly on July 10, 1995, at 51 years of age. He was a brilliant banker and during his career achieved some amazing and unequaled accomplishments. But at his funeral there was no talk about that by those of us who worked with him. All we could do was throw our arms around each other and talk about the time Mike told us he loved us. The tears flowed without apology that day and they do again as I write this. I want to honor Mike by telling you about him as the best example of someone who had unique political and intellectual skills, but who led his people from his heart and his spirit. My last point of connection with him was the bank's premier recognition event, the Royal Performer's Cruise. He had invited me to speak: "I want them to have a spiritual experience." That was the last bit of instruction I received from Mike Baptista.

When was the last time your executive team felt a spiritual connection with each other and with the leadership decisions you had to make? If it's happened to you, you will remember an almost alarming sense of freedom and openness as people talked out of their deepest selves. It didn't matter who was president, who was in charge of marketing, who was young or who was old, who was female or who was male. The whole was greater than the sum of its parts. The right thing to do became self-evident as though directed from somewhere else. Each individual recognized at once how powerless and how powerful he or she was. Yes, political and intellectual factors were there but somehow the group transcended those. It even went beyond emotion. You've agreed on things as a team before but this experience went beyond agreeing; it touched true unity of spirit. No policy or directive can cause this to happen.

If you've never been to this place, my attempt at description will sound incredibly naive, foolish and far-fetched. If you have had this kind of experience, you long to have it again. Unfortunately, we are given these moments only occasionally. My hope is that we can learn to change that.

For another look at where unifying corporate spirit can wither or flower, how about a quick run at two favorite corporate pastimes, re-engineering and corporate mergers. Go get a snack and a cold one because this will be brief but brutal.

There is a slight chance I'd lose my money, but I'd still bet that every corporation that has gone through a re-engineering process or a corporate merger has hanging somewhere in its executive corridor a declaration of values that includes the phrase "People are our greatest resource." Talk about a political statement. Everyone knows people are our most expendable resource, especially the expendable people themselves. In my presence one president said to his staff, "Look to the left and look to the right. A year from now one of you won't be here. Now let's work as a team." Enough, enough. Let's look at these two events – re-engineering and mergers – in an objective and unbiased way.

Do you think re-engineering is primarily a political, intellectual, emotional or spiritual experience? You know from my tone that I think it is clearly political (the in thing to do to keep boards and shareholders thinking that the executive is actually in control of the situation) and, because of the reliance on

THE MEANING OF SPIRITUALITY 63

technology and systems analysis, also somewhat intellectual. Now remember that many experts are saying that the effectiveness of these re-engineering efforts is at best 20 percent. Though that's clearly not great, let's be kind and give a passing grade on political and intellectual. What about emotional and spiritual? In all of my exposure to re-engineering, I have yet to see an example that didn't include dead bodies being buried by emaciated and frightened survivors. There are actually consultants running around giving workshops on how to care for the *survivors* of re-engineering. And the pruned people are given over to relocation counselors. Makes you wonder which group is the lucky one. At least re-engineering has helped launch two new business opportunities.

One of the highlights of my career has been to be double-billed with Peter Drucker at a conference in Geneva. This man is an icon. The Father of Modern Management. More important, he is humble, gracious and totally without pretension. It was an honor to be there, to watch him on stage leaning on the edge of a table, as is his habit, and to hear him talk for almost three hours about his life. He warned us that all was not what it seemed to be on the world stage. We may admire the production capabilities of the Asian countries, he said by way of example, but some of what they are producing is of such poor quality, it is being stored in warehouses rather than being sold. What appears to be successful industrialization may be a facade, Drucker warned the audience of international businesspeople. Then it was my turn to talk about my assigned topic, "The Post-Re-engineering Era." Has re-engineering been a facade too?

I talked about what I thought re-engineering had left in its wake. "It's like we have learned to build the world's best, most efficient fireplace," I said. "We have taken thermal science to an all-time high. The firebox is lined with eternal space age poly-something. A masterpiece of efficiency and design science." The only problem, I suggested, is that "there is no fire." We have no fire in the fireplace. What, then, is the point of the fireplace?

Frankly, I don't know a better way to put it. In so many re-engineered corporations there is no fire left in the fireplace. No wind in the sails. No fire in the belly. No sparkle in the eyes. Just watch: those who have written the best-selling re-engineering books will soon be writing best-selling sequels in which they will apologize for disregarding the majesty and holiness of the human spirit. If they don't, they should be made to as part of their penance. How we long to have passion again!

Ever been in someone's house where there is a "front room?" You know, the good room that no one is allowed to use? The one with the cover on the couch and the plastic runners on the carpet. There is always a fireplace in that room and the firebrick is as clean and yellow as the day it was laid. There hasn't been a fire in that fireplace in fifteen years. If that's your house, light a fire! A house filled with spirit turns into a home. Bring warmth, passion and memories into the room. You and it will never be the same again.

How about a quick shot at mergers? There really is no such thing as a merger, you know; but I digress. Two financial institutions with which I was familiar decided to come together. I was not at all involved but I did have occasion to suggest that they look after the emotional and spiritual dimensions before dealing with the intellectual and political. Guess how far that advice went? Two or three years were spent on "merging" assets, unifying computer systems, working out those precious numbers, designing a unified front for the marketplace and rather coldly discarding those people made redundant by the whole venture. Can you imagine actually being declared redundant? "Oh, it's not *you* that's redundant," the self-righteous rush to say, "it's your *job* that's redundant." Well, don't we feel precious now! That is like saying, "Let's leave personalities out of it." Can't be done.

After all this political and intellectual merging, they start to get a little alarmed. Seems that among the so-called survivors, there was an unusually high number of deaths, particularly among managers. When the "Manager of the Year" died unexpectedly, it was finally decided that something should be done. This is not a metaphor. We're talking about dead people. Not poor morale – dead people. Real funerals being held for real people who had actually survived the downsizing. As I wrote earlier, it's hard to tell which group was the lucky one.

Let me give you one final illustration of how the four levels of commitment apply to very common experiences. Many organizations have some form of annual conference, retreat, sales-kickoff meeting, management workshop or what have you. Here is how it usually goes as the group tries to work its way through the levels I've been describing. Lest anyone get defensive and think that I am being unfair, I joyfully acknowledge many exceptions to the example below. I am just trying to make my point unequivocally clear.

We start with the president's annual address, often written by somebody in public relations. On the whole, this is usually a political experience. We laugh heartily at the opening joke though we've heard it a hundred times. We take note of key phrases that we can use strategically during the reception to follow that evening. The obligation to applaud enthusiastically at the end goes without saying. If the group is particularly enthusiastic they could try out the politically motivated standing ovation. There are documented occasions where a standing ovation for the president has turned the reception from a cash bar into an open one. For all the effort it takes, it's worth it. Some groups are even more politically overt by inviting a high-ranking government official to kick off the conference. This is particularly wise if you are going after a government contract of some sort. We all know that nothing of any substance will be said, but then we aren't intellectually motivated at this point in the conference anyway.

The intellectual head stuff comes with the industry specialist who tells us with considerable authority about the challenges facing the industry in the global marketplace. You are given a binder bulging with the data backing him or her up.

This usually scares us half to death but it sure gets us thinking. Time for the coffee break.

Regional reports follow. Not much to be said here. The guys from Central always take more time than they are supposed to. Lunch.

We're still in intellectual mode and so are invited to sign up for various breakout groups focused on certain key issues such as improving customer service, increasing cross-functional teamwork, cost reduction and so on. If your corporation is highly controlling, you are preassigned to your group because they know you won't mix with other departments on your own. Once there, you fill up several pages of newsprint with brainstormed solutions for your particular problem and spend the remaining time trying to talk someone into giving the report to the whole group. Whoever gets the job is obliged to begin his or her report with the reminder that they are only the messenger, absolving themselves of any responsibility for what they are about to say. See how we're slipping back into political here?

The president acknowledges the plethora of great ideas and reassures the audience that each one will be given the attention it deserves. We all know what that means in terms of real change. The closing motivational speaker is now introduced. This at least should be fun and upbeat. This is the emotional part. The anatomy of a good closing motivational speech is Laugh, Laugh, Cry, Laugh, Poem. If the speaker is responsible, he's been there for most of the conference and knows what you are all about. If he isn't, he's arrived ten minutes ago and is giving exactly the same speech he gave in Dallas yesterday. All of this is wrapped up by the sweatshirt ceremony in large or X-large. The conference will get much better evaluations if the sweatshirts are any color but white.

Does this not sound all too familiar? Where in all of this well-intentioned effort do we get real? Where do we, without fear, make the kind of connections with each other that enable us to truly transform our work and our world? We easily accommodate the political and intellectual levels and nibble on the emotional. The true foundation of our personal and corporate life, however, is spiritual and we don't even come close to touching it. That is where the real power and permanence is. The real force for change lies in our spirit, not in our strategies or our systems.

I've used the environment, family reunions, executive-team meetings, re-engineering, mergers and corporate conferences as illustrations. Parenting, sales calls, tourism, strategic planning and marketing strategies could as easily have been used. What I want to make clear is that everything has a spiritual core, a spiritual center. Every experience has spiritual potential. Once we learn to connect to that core, the world changes color. As the old hymn says, the greens become a greener green and the blues a bluer blue. Were the sky of parchment made, with ink the oceans filled and every blade of grass a quill we could not adequately describe how great and wonderful this "It" is. We never quite can, but the trying is filled with the energizing magic of creativity, the evidence of Life – and our Love of Life. There is such abundance. Everything that is possible to know about God's love has been made available to us, hidden in the heart of things tangible and intangible. In every tree, flower and mountaintop. In every experience and every relationship. And so, with the poets, we will spend our Life trying to paint word pictures of Love and never come close to reaching the limits of its breadth and depth. There are too many ways of Love to count and yet we delight in beginning. Then we will know our way around the Second World. We will be living *through* our work, not *at* our work, *through* our relationships, not *at* them. Lives inspired by Love.

FIVE

The Great Shuddering

◆ ◆ ◆ ◆

Most of us want to live out of our center. We want to be in that deeper place. Somewhere inside us we also know where we have to go to find this richer, fuller life. The political and intellectual perspectives on life and work can be found in the shallow end of the pool. The emotional and spiritual perspectives are found in the deep end. But is it just a matter of floating from one to the other? That sounds so enticingly simple. And yet it's not, it truly is not.

We have a modest in-ground pool in our backyard, which means that the shallow half dips away rather steeply to become the deep half. The faded vinyl lining has become slippery with age and so, if people are not careful as they approach the invisible line between shallow and deep, what they thought was a secure footing, isn't. There is that brief moment between realizing that their footing is gone and that they now have to swim. One can almost witness the switching device working in their brains during that split second: Stand! No, swim! No, you can stand! No, swim! That's it, swim! For that moment the person is neither here nor there. In the pool, of course, reorientation is easy and part of the fun of being in the water. Were it so simple in life's rough seas.

In the shallow end of life, we have the political and the intellectual levels described in the last chapter. Do not equate the metaphor of "shallow" with useless or unnecessary. You can have a lot of fun in the shallow end. Shallow denotes that you can be very adept politically and intellectually and yet give up or expose very little of your true self. Living in the deep end on the emotional and spiritual levels requires you to expose all of your Self. It is between the two approaches to life where the dance of uncertainty – to stand? to swim? – plays out.

I truly want to be in touch with my spiritual, sacred Self. I want to learn to see and interpret my experience of this world from a spiritual perspective. But I would be less than honest if I were not to tell you that I don't want to have this depth of connection everywhere I go. Sometimes I want to go to a cocktail party only to schmooze with interesting people, to have a few laughs with funny folks, maybe pick up a few ideas about this or that. Other times I truly enjoy the stimulation of an intellectual discussion and do so without putting my whole inner soulful-self into it. Sometimes I just want to stand in the shallow end.

Doing so means putting the political and intellectual together into a general approach to life that we might call "economic." The word *economy* was given to us by the Greeks – the *oikos nomos*, which means the house laws or rules, those aspects of life that are measured, predictable, managed, dictated and ruled. If you are the gambling sort and go into a casino you don't know, you immediately ask about the house rules, their *nomos*. Is there a five-dollar or a ten-dollar minimum? Are the drinks free? What are the rules around here? Are there credit facilities? The idea is that you simply want to fit into the casino's system and feel no need to bring about radical change in how things are done there. Given the size of the bouncer at the door, this is a politically intelligent move on your part. Large parts of our personal and professional lives are lived on an economic plane; that is, politically and intellectually.

At the same time, however, we know that if spirituality is to be real, it must pervade our lives. Spirituality is not something that is "on call," to be summoned on a still summer night as we watch an orange sun back-light the pine-covered hills around the lake. For me there are increasingly frequent times in my life when I *do* want in-depth connection, I *do* want to let people in on my inner self and want to be let in on theirs. I want to experience the freedom of emotional and spiritual engagement.

We can put the emotional and spiritual levels together and attach the single heading "ecological" to them. This word is also a gift from the Greeks – the *oikos logos*. You may already have a sense of what the familiar and powerful word *logos* means – a *meaningful* utterance. It was used in ancient writings to signify the divine power by which the universe is given unity, coherence and meaning. So what we are getting at here is the *deep* meaning or structure of the house. To keep with the casino imagery, after you've asked the *nomos* questions, you might ask a couple of *logos* questions like: Are people friendly here? Is there a supportive relationship among the patrons? Will there be an intimate discussion group later in the evening about why we gamble?

If I were to ask you to tell me about your company, you might describe your product or service, tell me how many employees there are in what capacity and location, and perhaps, even tell me your market share or gross revenue. "Oh, I'm sorry," I might interject, "you thought I was asking an economic question, I meant it ecologically." Ecologically, I'd want to know about your corporate spiritual purpose and about whether there is evidence of unity among the people who work in the company. I'd want to know if there is love and passion in their hearts for what they are accomplishing *through* their work. These are dramatically different interpretations of the question.

We are continually moving between the political/intellectual/ economic (or First World) interpretation of life and the emotional/spiritual/ecological (or Second World) interpretation. Which one we choose depends on a great number of circumstances ranging from our upbringing to our view of destiny. Were mealtimes as a child an economic or ecological experience for you? If you ate supper at 5:30 sharp because that's when your dad came home from work, spoke only when spoken to, had to finish your peas because there were starving people in Africa and usually had the dishes done and put away by 6:00, then I suggest dinner was an economic experience. Some families might have taken quite a different approach. Dinner happened whenever everybody was ready for it. It often took over an hour and a half to complete because people would keep talking about everything that was happening to them. You ate only until you were full and the dishes weren't done until much later in the evening. An ecological experience.

A newlywed couple used up their fifteen minutes of fame on television recently by showing the world their incredibly long prenuptial agreement. It covered everything in minute detail: how grocery shopping was to be done, who did what household chores and when, what each was to do to correct bad driving habits, how each was to keep track of money and how often they were to have sex. If that isn't the shallow end of the pool, I don't know what is. No guesswork and no spontaneity. Just follow the marriage manual, the nuptial notes. It is not for me, but some people don't want to live any other way than economically. Since I am going to spend the rest of my life with Georgia, I need our relationship to be ecological because economic ties just aren't strong enough.

So back to the issue of how we move from the First World of economy to the Second World of ecology in our lives. My insight here has come both painfully and joyfully, mostly the former. Between these two levels hangs that thick and heavy veil we talked about earlier, the one that our readiness and awareness only begin to push aside. To fully move aside that veil, which is really a veil inside us, to make it tremble and part so that the First World is illuminated by the Second World, so that the economic is infused by the ecological, we must ourselves be shaken by a Great Shuddering. No way around it, under it or over it. As the old spiritual says, we've got to walk that valley ourselves because there ain't no one who can walk it for us. And, as we'll soon see, it can get awfully lonely.

My sense of this rending of the inner veil as *shuddering* can be illustrated by reference to two image-sources: a movie and a book. The movie *Apollo XIII* took a lot of us back to the days when we would get up in the middle of the night to watch a blastoff with Walter Cronkite. It was exciting and tense television, disaster looming with each unexpected circumstance. The whole world was an audience. Today, of course, only a few people care enough to stay up-to-date with the shuttle program. Fifty-three-year-old American Shannon Lucid returned from a record-setting 188 days in space. I didn't even know she had gone. Nobody told me.

Back during those late nights with Walter, we all knew what was going on. Up the rocket would go and disappear like a flickering flame into the darkness of space. Walter would excitedly tell us what was happening until the space capsule hit the LOS zone. His voice would become hushed and concerned. For every launch and every return, this "Loss of Signal" zone posed incredible and mysterious danger. If the craft didn't enter it exactly at the right angle, it was all over for the crew. We watched the capsule go through: it shook violently at its point of greatest stress. Suddenly all was quiet, the astronauts had broken through to effortless and unlimited speed.

Coming back was a different story. You've likely seen the *Apollo XIII* movie so you'll recall that the real drama was on reentry: a major power failure in the space capsule! As the crew and ground control scrambled to meet a very small window of opportunity, they also had to confront their relationships and their circumstances. They had to confront their own destiny and mortality. Every aspect of their physical, intellectual, emotional and spiritual selves seemed to be on the line. During the reentry, the whole theater again shook with the shuddering of the craft: the heat shields were white-hot with uncertainty. Would it hold together through this enormous stress? We held our breath for that three or four minutes. There was no communication. The crew was very much alone. Everyone else was helpless. It was a lonesome valley. Suddenly we could see a speck in the sky and there it was, safe in the gentle web of its parachutes. They were home. Relationships were reconciled, all was forgiven. Each man landed at a different spiritual place than he was at the beginning of the adventure. Each had seen himself and his world from a whole new perspective. There was a new appreciation for life and love. Together, they had made it *through* the shuddering.

Author Marilyn Ferguson also pointed me to the concept of shuddering as the passageway between here and there, between the First and Second Worlds. Her insightful book *The Aquarian Conspiracy* was published in 1980, years ahead of its time. There is a conspiracy of renewal happening throughout the world, she told us prophetically. And if we want to be part of this renewal, we need "a great shuddering, an irrevocable shift, a new mind – a turnabout in consciousness in critical numbers of individuals, a network powerful enough to bring about radical change in our culture."

Do you too feel the power of those words? How can we not want to be part of this transformative network? Where do we sign up for such service? Well, we may indeed be eager to enlist, but we would also be wise to note what she says about the membership fees. First, we've got to go through a shuddering that will test the heat shields of our very souls. Second, once we are through, we can't go back. There is no buyback or escape clause. Third, we have to give up our current way of thinking, the way that got us everything we have so far, in favor of a new way that we will never fully understand. Fourth, the deepest part of ourselves, our awareness, our values and our perspectives, are going to be turned 180 degrees.

We were facing west to see what was ending; we will now face east to see the rising sun of a new dawn. If we have the wisdom and courage to see where it leads, we will powerfully transform our life, our love, our labor and our leadership.

I was, and continue to be, amazed at Ferguson's insight. How was she able to see such things in the universe when all the rest of us were busy looking at ourselves? Amazing as that may be, the truth is, there have been people since the beginning of time who have seen the power and the mystery. Did they too go through the shudderings, the shifts, the turnabouts? Is this the only course through which we can bring ultimate wholeness to our lives? Must our corporations also go through some kind of collective shuddering if we are ever to find meaning *through* our work?

Let's deal with this last question first because in many ways it is the easiest to answer. Yes, corporations must go through a shuddering if they are to discover and fulfill their spiritual purpose. They must go through a shuddering if they want to release the awesome creative power of their people. They must go through the irrevocable shift if they intend to redefine leadership within the organization. It is my firm belief that *every* organization today stands at the threshold of a shuddering. As with *Apollo XIII,* the window of opportunity is small and organizations will have to go through their own LOS zone at just the right angle or they will perish.

I do not know what the shuddering is for your organization. My guess is that you and your team could list many issues that need exploration or a clear and final decision. Likely, you've been going over and over the same issues for years now. Maybe it's time to get on with it. There is always one problem or another to deal with in our firefighting approach, isn't there?

I want to be gentle in saying this, but experience has taught me that most of the issues you'd raise in, say, a half-hour brainstorming session, would be red herrings, a diversion from the real shuddering you need to face. This does not mean they aren't real or important. It just means that while they may be shudderings, they are not THE shuddering. I believe there is one key shuddering awaiting the soul of most corporations. There is one veil, one barrier that we know beyond a shadow of a doubt, if we were ever able to call it for what it is and get through it, we'd experience effortless and unlimited momentum. At least that would be true until you hit the next stratosphere where you are likely to face an even more difficult shuddering. Fortunately, the more experience you have with shudderings the more insight you have to deal with them. We don't hear much mention of the LOS zone anymore, do we? The space program has gone on to other shudderings. For us right now, however, let's get through one shuddering at a time.

I will give you a hint as to where to look for your window of opportunity that will lead you smack into your corporate shuddering. Some will not believe this at first, but your corporate shuddering probably has to do with the ego-centered issue of power. Who has it and who doesn't. Most organizational transformation is prevented by people who have power and don't want to give it up. Detractors of this notion will instead point to re-engineering and the quest for efficiency as the shuddering. Some may point to your recent merger as the source of shuddering. Or perhaps to a sudden downturn in the market that has dropped your profit margin to 2 percent. Maybe it's the attempt to ratify a union in your traditionally nonunionized company that you think is the shuddering. Maybe it's hundreds of dispirited people who somehow survived three rounds of downsizing. These are all big, big issues and will be shudderings for you, but do not be deceived or distracted. They are mere vibrations compared to THE shuddering waiting for you. Courageously look within them and I think you'll find that you most have to confront the issue of power. This is why this book concludes with a chapter on the beloved corporate spiritual leader, one who has finally worked through the control factor and has claimed the real secret of power.

Get your team together and ask the simple question, What is it? What is it that is at the bottom of all of our issues? What is it that we never really talk about in front of each other? If you do this in quietness, humility and openness, you will find it. Every time someone suggests an answer to the great shuddering question, have the team take a short time of quiet reflection during which each person asks his or her heart, "Is that it?" If the answer is no, then keep looking until the whole team arrives at a unanimous "Yes, that's it!"

Once you are there, don't stop. Keep working and talking until you achieve the breakthrough you need. This breakthrough must not be limited to the development of strategic action plans, assigned responsibilities and time lines. You've been there and done that. We are looking for a change of heart, a spiritual turnaround, a transformation. That "click" inside your soul. You "get it."

Nothing will be more hurtful than quitting halfway through the LOS zone. You will all be left stranded in space because of a power failure. Many organizations come face-to-face with their shuddering and it threatens and scares them. Through deft political and intellectual maneuvering, they manage to escape, not toward freedom but *away* from it. Like long-term convicts, sometimes we can live under corporate control for so long that the prospect of being free is actually frightening. We'll complain about it, of course, but there is something safe about captivity.

Of course, no one has to go through all of this. You know well the thousand ways organizations have of avoiding the shuddering. You've been frustrated by some of them yourself. Sending the issue off to be studied by a task force is one intellectually justifiable approach we learned from our friends in government. Or you can select a lesser shuddering and inflate it to the point where absolutely everybody has to get involved, leaving no time for the real thing. If you are desperate, you can cause a diversion by reorganizing the company, moving the plant to the suburbs or even redesigning the corporate logo.

Heck, even getting a smoking policy is good for at least 18 months of avoidance.

The sad thing is that we employ similar avoidance strategies in our personal lives as well. Couples often avoid dealing with a shuddering in their relationship by doing one or both of two disastrous things: they have another baby or buy a bigger house. Obviously there is nothing wrong with having a baby or getting a bigger house if the couple's relationship is strong and loving. If that is the case, these decisions can indeed enrich and strengthen their relationship. However, if you are in a relationship that is struggling and you need a diversion for some reason, get a dog. It's a *lot* cheaper, less harmful emotionally and hardly anyone ends up making dog-support payments. Most of us learned a long time ago that what you avoid now, you will still need to deal with later. Perhaps unfortunately, the world is round and the faster you run away from something, the faster you run back to it.

Going through your great corporate shuddering can be a tense experience, to say the least. Chapter 9 contains stories of shudderings from a variety of organizations. It is a very subjective, soul-searching process. How do you know if you have found your shuddering? How do you know if your shuddering has brought you closer to your spiritual core? Well, as foolish as it sounds, you just know. There is a melody created when spirit, meaning and purpose come together. It is the ring of truth. The human heart is made to resonate to the timbre of truth. Truth is connected to freedom. We are created for freedom and because going through our shudderings takes us to the edge of freedom, we are like a divining rod. We know when freedom is nearby. Freedom awakens our creativity, intelligence and energy. Freedom calls on our strengths to unite us through our weaknesses, and together we are able to overcome the rigors of the First World.

Let's move carefully to our personal shudderings. Imagine that the five or six people with whom you work most closely are seated around a conference-room table with you. As you think of each one, ask yourself how well you *really* know that person. If our experiences have been at all similar, we have to admit that we really do not know our colleagues very well at all. Some of them have been in your life for many years and you still don't know each other. Not really. You may know if they are married or divorced, what part of town they live in, how many children they have and whether they golf or not. But you don't know them. Until you know their shudderings, you don't know them.

Now imagine that behind each person is a four-drawer file cabinet filled with the records of their life. Their visits to heaven and their visits to hell are all in there. What is home like for them: do you have any idea? What addiction are they fighting? What critical choice are they facing in terror? Which child keeps them awake at night in worry and helplessness? Do you know who has fallen completely and utterly in love and is ecstatically happy for the first time in years? What tragedy has your colleague endured and what scars do you think remain under that business suit? What lab-test results are they waiting for? Which teammate is overwhelmed with gratitude because her tests came back negative? Who has an elderly parent who makes excessive emotional and physical demands? Which one has decided that bankruptcy is the only way out of his financial dilemma? Which one is dreading Friday night because that's the night she and her husband are going to tell their children that their parents are splitting up? Who is trying to weigh an incredible overseas job offer against the disruption of his children's education? These are the shudderings of their lives.

As you go around the imaginary table wondering what is in the imaginary file cabinets, you eventually come to yourself. No guesswork needed here because you have the key to your file cabinet. You know the shudderings of your life, just as I know mine. Some of you reading this have just come out on the far side of your shuddering. You've broken *through!* Your life is becoming your own. Stabilized. Moving toward integration and wholeness. Are you all right? You weren't sure there for a while, were you? The old heat shields took quite a beating. That period of feeling isolated with no wise or even supportive communication coming from anywhere was awful, wasn't it? It's like no one else in the world had the foggiest idea what you were going through. And guess what, they didn't. This is exactly the problem. We have been taught to be alone and have rarely experienced what it is like to be in community. Consequently, in our businesses, our churches, temples and synagogues, our schools, our social network and even in our own families, we do not often have the degree of unity necessary to have shuddering partners. But you stayed with it and you are beginning to experience the freedom of the other side.

When I look back on my own shudderings, I not only wonder how I got through them, I wonder how I got into them in the first place. There has to be an easier way to learn and grow. As the son of missionary parents, moving from Nigeria to Canada was a cultural shuddering for me as a child. Failing two consecutive grades in high school was a tremendous shuddering for me as a teenager. And as you have already read, the death of a baby and two failed relationships were terrible shudderings for me as an adult. Even a few financial shudderings seem to have been thrown into the mix. Underneath these was the greatest shuddering of them all. I had to get through my anger. That journey and the insights that I gained from it are shared in chapter 6. I'll tell you, it was sure lonely sometimes. Friends disappeared, family disappeared and even God seemed to be busy elsewhere. I don't really need to tell you, you've been there.

My heart really goes out to those of you who are in the middle of a shuddering right now. Part of me wishes that somehow I could know what it is, and in the knowing share it with you. Is it your health? If you've been told you have cancer, MS or AIDS, you know better than all of us what a shuddering is. I received an E-mail message circulated among a number of us who stay connected as professional speakers. It asked for prayer for our colleague Diana Golden who won an

Olympic Gold Medal for downhill skiing in 1988 with only one leg. She lost her leg to cancer as a child. A few years ago her breasts were lost to cancer, and now, for the third time, she must go to war again, this time against cancer of the spine. Frankly, if prayer weren't an option, I wouldn't know what to do in a situation like this. Even in prayer, I find it difficult to know how to direct my thoughts. Overwhelmed, I just want to hand the message right over to God. I guess that's what prayer is.

There are times my shudderings seem so inconsequential, yet I know we need to be cautious about comparing them. My shuddering is mine; it is the most vital thing in my life right now. And so it is with yours. Knowing that a once-loving, promising relationship is turning bitter is also a shuddering. We know we've got to move on but that doesn't make it any easier. Not when we're in the middle of it. For some, that shuddering is complicated by worry over where they are going to live, or by the disapproval and judgment of the self-righteous around them. People who find themselves unemployed for the first time in their lives are shuddering too, as are their families. It just seems to go on and on. Sometimes I think musician and healer Kelly Walker is right when he says, "We are gracious and blessed messes!"

I am, at times, overwhelmed by the knowledge that the entire creation is shuddering in one way or another. Everything is being painstakingly re-created. Individuals. Corporations. Religions. Families. Why is it this way? I don't know. I don't know why the great majority of our shudderings are so painful. I do know that some never exit the shuddering, that some are devastated by it. Some stay in a half-life, perhaps learning a little here and there but never fully passing *through*. I do know too that the shudderings can, at best, take us to a deeper place. I do know there is freedom on the other side. I do know, especially, that we cannot lead our organizations to a place we ourselves have not gone. I do know that all of our shudderings are different and that is why we can help each other go through the irrevocable shift and come to a new depth of meaning, to a renewed sense of Life.

I cannot conclude this chapter without at least a partial balance to our painful shudderings. The greatest and most powerful shuddering of all is love. Human love. God's love. It is love that will pick you up in its arms and safely see you *through*. To know that you are truly and unconditionally loved is all the heat shield you will ever need. Love is what is needed in our governments. Love is what will keep our families together. Love will bring passion back into the workplace. It is love that will energize corporate leaders all over the world to lead their people to a place where the soul is set free to create the life where the "why" behind the "how" is clear.

One of the highlights and honors of my career was to be asked to deliver the closing address at the 1995 annual convention of the National Speakers Association. I don't know if you can appreciate this, but speaking before 1,800 of the world's best professional speakers is quite a shuddering in itself. And what a treasured shuddering it was for me. The speech was titled "Baffled Angels and the Grand Why." I talked about the Inner Journey, about getting from "how" to "why." About getting through our shudderings and on to wholeness. When I finished, a blind musician by the name of Ken Medema was led to his piano and he began to sing a song that had come to him while I was talking. Without question, this amazing man is possessed by an equally amazing spiritual gift. I still get shivers when I listen to the tape of his performance. Here are his words. They were a tremendous gift to me and I want to pass the gift along.

Well I think I feel a shuddering
in my heart
Well I think I feel a shuddering
in my heart
Will it break me?
Will it shake me?
Will it tear me apart?
Well I think I feel a shuddering
in my heart.

I am longing now to move from
how to why
I am longing now to move from
how to why
Sometimes it makes me laugh
and sometimes it makes me cry
But I'm longing now to move from
how to why.

I can almost feel the freedom
on the other side
I can almost feel the freedom
on the other side
And I face a new tomorrow
like a baffled, blushing bride
I can almost feel the freedom
on the other side.

SIX

Six Stations of the Inner Journey

◆ ◆ ◆

T he view alone would have been worth the trip. The hotel looked down from the mountaintop over Lac Lucerne in Switzerland. Day and night you could hear the cowbells, each herd sounding different from the others. It was one of those environments that almost made you rise above all the details and mechanics of life. However, details and mechanics were what the conference was all about. One hundred and twenty senior, and mostly male, financial types from more than a dozen European and African countries had gathered for several days of professional development. They spent the first two days working on a complex and real-life business case. Their desks were covered with binders filled with information about the global marketplace. Detailed charts showing projections for everything imaginable lay strewn about. They loved this heady stuff and were very good at it. I, the token touchy-feely guy, was to have the closing day of the conference. Gosh, were they excited about that!

I had sat through their case study and watched them analyze and problem-solve. Just observing had pretty well exhausted my ability to understand what they were talking about. And then it was my turn. How could my message about the human spirit, about love and relationships, about spiritual leadership in both familial and corporate contexts compete with these financial issues that could mean tens of millions in revenue to them? There was little option but to share my heart and soul in the best and most human way I knew how. That is what I did. Although much of my time is spent speaking to groups filled with brilliant, intellectual people, I knew that the intellect can be used by the skillful owner to block anyone or anything from reaching the heart. Nevertheless, the heart was my goal and I went after it, never quite sure how close I was coming.

At the end of the day, I proposed to the group that it was their responsibility to integrate my message about spirit with their earlier focus on systems and statistics. "I am not sure how you are going to do that," I admitted. "I know how I am going to do it," said a man at the back of the room. Now, before I finish the story, let me point out that when you are working with a primarily European audience, you just don't expect much in the way of personal disclosure, at least not in front of a roomful of professional colleagues. I swear some of these guys weren't even using their real names. "Please tell us," I said with an inviting gesture toward the man who had spoken, thrilled at such an immediate response. "My daughter," he continued, "has been wanting to teach me piano for years and I've never been home to do it. I phoned her during the break this morning and told her that I was going to give one night a week for a year to learn how to play the piano." You could see in the faces of others that they were wondering if his medication was wearing off. And to tell you the truth, even I found a query forming in my mind. What do piano lessons have to do with international finance? "Do you think piano lessons will help him become a better financial manager?" I asked the group. "Of course," they said, as though I had just asked the stupidest question of all time.

"I've learned something today," volunteered one of the German participants from the middle of the room. He didn't even stand to speak, and I came to the conclusion that he didn't have the strength to do so at that moment. "I've learned that I don't have any real friends," he confessed. The room went suddenly and reverently quiet as he continued to share his heart. "I've spent my whole adult life building my career and this business and I've just realized that I don't have any friends." His comment hung over the room and you couldn't help but know that he was confessing on behalf of us all. There was hardly a dry eye in the place as he told us of his plans to go back and reestablish long-ignored relationships and to find his life again.

It was pretty clear that whatever was happening in the room at that moment had nothing to do with the beautifully colored overheads I had been showing them all day. Nothing to do with my insightful models explaining the human condition. Something spiritual was taking place and it felt right and it felt good. Some readers may groan and roll their eyes at this point, but I'm telling you, when there is a true and healthy expression of spirit in a room, you just know it.

"I've got something to say," volunteered a third man from near the front. This was not my meeting anymore so he needed no permission from me to carry on. "I was planning to stay here in Europe for another few days to visit other offices. But I phoned home this afternoon to tell my wife and kids that I was coming home tonight. They couldn't believe it," he said. Frankly, I don't think he could believe it either.

So, why this story? There is an awakening happening all over the corporate world. In every culture. In every profession and corporate context. People are yearning for meaning. The First World does not satisfy. Life on the level of economy leaves one hungry – hungry for the Second World, for ecology. Never mind the learning organization, these people make up *yearning* organizations, hungry and thirsty for what they know is out there somewhere. Many are desert-dry, spiritually speaking, and even a little water brings out a flowering soul. Bouquets of beautiful, beautiful souls. Lately I've seen people who appeared so tough and unreachable release their spiritual selves to such a degree that even their appearance changed. This is not street-gang tough. We're talking white-collar tough. Politically and intellectually tough. Powerful, brilliant and incredibly successful people who have had enough. Not all, obviously, but the numbers are growing exponentially. They have come to realize that what they have been doing just isn't worth the cost anymore. They are not living life naturally. There must be something else. They are tired. They don't want to play the corporate game any longer, even if they are winning. Success means nothing if there is no significance. The luxury of money is momentary if there is no meaning.

I quote again from one of my favorite books, *Hymns to an Unknown God* by Sam Keen: "You and I are destined to live out our lives in the middle of the Great Paradigm War, a worldwide conflict between three mythic systems – the technological-economic myth of progress, authoritarian religion, and the emerging spiritual worldview." One of these three influences is winning the war for your corporate soul. Some corporations honestly believe that once they have their systems upgrade integrated into their business they will reach new levels of quality, service, teamwork and profitability. Wall Street is on a never-ending search for THE economic model that will make the American dream a reality for all. Both quests are futile. Yet others count on finding the right bureaucratic structure and control processes to assure their success in a market that seems out of control. We did, after all, learn about authoritarianism, bureaucracy, structure and control from organized religion. If it works for God, we reason, surely it will work for us.

Then we have the third warring paradigm – the "emerging spiritual worldview." What the heck is an emerging spiritual worldview? Well, I just gave you an example of it in my story about the financial conference. The group actually employed all three of Keen's influential paradigms. They discussed at length the technological and economic complexity of the business case. They were adamant that a total change in structure was needed and that someone needed to take control. But it was not these intellectual insights that made the difference to the conference participants. Sometimes we exhaust ourselves in our political and intellectual exercises and, in our exhaustion, we are left little choice but to reach for the emotional and spiritual. What made the event a life-changing event for many was that a few dared to get in touch with their souls.

It's not that any of us has actually *lost* what psychologist Wayne Dyer calls our sacred selves. That mystical part that makes us sacred creations and creators has been imprisoned, or even exiled, by our education and our employment. By our religions, our roles and our reward systems. By the expectations of our parents and our partners. And mostly by the choices we ourselves have made. But it's not lost, we know exactly where it is. We are wanting to recover, uncover, discover the sacred within. Its mystery makes us nervous, but somehow we know that if we can learn to live and relate out of our spirit, our life, labor and leadership will be dramatically and forever changed.

What pathway is bringing so many of us to this point? Our inner journeys are so different and yet I have long wondered if there isn't some underlying framework common to us all. It is the discovery of what I think that framework is that I want to explore with you now.

In some of my relationships there has been, to varying degrees, an unhealthy intimacy-resistant element that I was contributing. Depending on with whom, where and in what context, this characteristic has been expressed in attitudes and behaviors that demonstrated competitiveness, jealousy, possessiveness, confrontation or judgment. I've recently learned that this is a problem of ego; we'll get to that matter shortly.

For much of my life I have been restless for peace; I have longed for an end to my longing. Longed for peace and a generous measure of joy. Just like my European friends in the story above, I know, and have known for a long time, that the things we usually use to give ourselves value are hollow. They do not give us peace. Status, income, possessions and celebrity are not satisfying end points in and of themselves; they do not bring joy. They are not worth the cost. We've known this truth since before Christ walked the earth, so what's really holding us back? Why don't we act?

Two factors have finally broken me open to see what is really going on in my life. Relational frustrations and financial frustrations, mostly the former. Motivated largely by a broken heart, I went looking for the path that I felt God meant for me to be on. I knew I was stuck somewhere or had fallen off or something. A reasonable starting point, it seemed to me, was to come to a new understanding of what the path was all about. Pretty hard to tell if we've gone off the path when we don't know where the path is.

My insights into this path do not come from years of psychoanalyzing other people's journeys, nor from any formal academic or research exercise. They come from reading the insights of many authors, from reflections during long silent drives or while lying awake at night. From long talks with friends, colleagues and clients who are also trying to find their paths. What I have learned is true for me. My hope is that my truth will help you find your truth. I have found my way; I do not presume to have found yours.

I have also come to see a clear parallel between one's personal inner journey and the inner journey that many corporations are going through. Most corporations, of course, don't see themselves on a spiritual journey, but they are on one, nevertheless. The sooner organizations realize that their real problems are spiritual problems, the sooner they will experience true transformation and not have to muck around in what are largely destructive strategies of re-engineering, right-sizing, rationalizing and so on. But first let's walk this path in the personal world.

There seem to be six components of any journey along this path. I don't want to call them "steps" because that implies one moves in linear fashion from one to the other. Nor am I comfortable with "stages" because that suggests that once you've passed a stage you're done with it. "Stations" is the best solution that I can see. The Six Spiritual Stations of our Inner Journey. There is an implied developmental movement among these stations and one might visit them in that way. Frankly, I can't imagine that actually happening. The more likely scenario is that you will grow as you experience one station then another. Often you will go back and revisit them all over again. Furthermore, you can be at several different stations at once, depending on what circumstances or aspects of your life you are looking at.

I talked about these "Stations" at a conference last summer and in the audience was a speaker and poet named Sidney Madwed. He turned my presentation into a delightful poem and I pass along his gift as an introduction to this part of our exploration.

Everyone must go on an inner journey, the journey
of the "I's."
There are six stations which when completed
make one wise.
The first station is **INNOCENCE**, it is based on total trust
And a belief that everything in life is fair and just.
The second station is **INDEPENDENCE**, when you
want personal control
So you can be master of your fate and captain of your soul.
The third station is **INSTITUTION** which pressures you to
conform
And uses their expectations to make you meet their norm.
The fourth station is **IRRITATION** which makes you resist
external control
You want to be self-directed and self-determine
your life's role.
The fifth station is **INSIGHT** when the extraneous
you remove

And you become spirit-driven and focused to improve.
The sixth station is **INTEGRATION** when your life you own
And you've found your uniqueness and are not
anyone's clone.
If you complete your inner journey, the journey of the "I's,"
You will have great wisdom and become one of the wise.

STATION ONE: INNOCENCE

This is the station of absolute trust. The world is fair and
good. No one will hurt you. People stand behind their word.
The best metaphor is infancy, and keep in mind that it is only
a metaphor. Adults can be at the Innocence Station too. The
infant, on some level, assumes that "because Mom fed me yesterday and is feeding me now, chances are extremely good that
she'll feed me tomorrow." Babies at least start life thinking evil
of no one. This is why we just cannot fathom why anyone
would hurt one of the Innocents. Remember when your child
was three or four and would leap off one of the steps on the
stairway into your arms? "Of course Dad or Mom will catch
me," she'd think. "That's just the way the world works, isn't
it?" Sometimes she'd jump off the stair and you weren't even
looking. Scared you half to death. "Don't do that!" you'd
exclaim in your fright. "Why not?" the child would think.
"You're God, aren't you?" God wouldn't let her get hurt, why
would a parent?

For the Innocent, there is a natural oneness with the rest of
the universe. I am part of everything and everything is part of
me. Take a child to someone else's house and he automatically assumes that he can go into any of the rooms, play with
their stuff, ask for a cookie and so on. Your house is my house.
When you want a drink of soda pop, you just go ask for it.
Not like adults who sit around muttering about why no one
has offered them a drink. This natural oneness is an important
characteristic of this first Station. The memory of it will
become a major driving force two Stations from now.

Yes, the world is good and right and kind and filled with
unifying abundance. Don't we wish it could continue to be so

for us all? Unfortunately, we are not able to stay at this Station for very long.

Before we visit the other Stations, let me give an example of how the relatively worldly-wise can return to the Innocence Station. I have a project that is very important to me. It involves manufacturing and marketing a product designed to help strengthen family communication. While I hope it does well financially, the primary motivation behind this endeavor is pretty honorable, perhaps even spiritual. Have you noticed that banks are very hesitant to fund spiritual projects? So off I ventured into the venture-capital world for the first time. In round figures I needed to raise a million dollars – too big for anyone I know and too small to interest any of the investment houses I had worked for. I met a man who puts such deals together – recommended by trusted friends, came across well, was a faithful churchgoer . . . you get the picture. He was given a rather substantial retainer and sent off to find my million. A few weeks later I got a call from the police asking if this guy worked for me and informing me that he was being held for extradition on fraud charges.

I sat in my lawyer's office strategizing how to get my money back. She looked at me from across the room with the most pitying expression I have ever seen outside of a puppy farm. "You don't believe anyone would actually do this to you, do you?" she asked. I guess the lesson is, "Don't make deals while you are at the Innocence Station!" Lots of lessons learned here, but to tell you the truth, if I have to choose between trusting people and getting hurt every once in a while, and not trusting anyone, I'm going for trusting. There is a part of the Innocence Station that I don't ever want to leave.

In far too short a time we realize that there are people who want to hurt us, that the world is not always good. In reaction, we begin to feel the need to separate ourselves by defining and defending ourselves. This drive is what leads us to explore the second spiritual station.

STATION TWO: INDEPENDENCE

As we bounce from experience to experience, it does not take long to begin to wonder if, just maybe, not all of the influences in our lives have our good at heart. The universe does not always share its bounty at our whim. There seems to be some form of pain at almost very turn. This catches us by surprise and we wonder what on earth is going on here. What all of this is, is the arousal of our "Beingness." God's Spirit, that highest common denominator connecting all of existence, is enthroned within every one of us. It whispers, "Now become what is within you." In Innocence we simply "are," and in Independence we are "to be." Absolutely everything we need to become what we are to become has been within us from the beginning. Every molecule of our being is programmed with the instruction, "Go and find it! Uncover it! Let it out!" And so off we go into the chaos of life "to find ourselves," as we used to say in the sixties.

In the same way that the majestic cedar tree demonstrates God's Spirit differently than the willowy birch tree, and the lion demonstrates it differently than the lamb, so I must demonstrate it differently than you. Though all of existence is in what Martin Luther King, Jr. called "an inescapable net-work of mutuality," we are each to give our own unique testi-mony to that common spirit. This is the sacred quest that you and I are on – go out there and be a one-of-a-kind evidence of God's Spirit and Love. Our calling is not, "Go out there and work at the bank or be a schoolteacher." As I have been claim-ing, these activities are only tools or conduits for something far greater, something to live *through*, not *at*, conduits to meaning in the Second World, to what we want to accomplish.

Our visit to the Independence Station is filled with discov-ery. The child discovers that her hand is not part of the crib, it's part of her. She can manipulate, see and taste it at will. It belongs to her alone. A youngster refusing to be fed any longer declares, "I want to do it myself!" A creative six-year-old wears the most obnoxious color combination imaginable, often mixing winter and summer clothes. And Lord help the adolescent if he wants to wear a ring through his eyebrow. All of these are developmental demonstrations of the Independence Station. On a First World level you may think that it's only a matter of silly physical expressions of identity. Not so. It is really a deep Second World expression. It is a human Be-ing wanting to see the world for herself, through her *own* eyes. There is no substitute for that. You can be told about the Rocky Mountains, see pictures of the Rocky Mountains, but until you *see* them, you haven't seen them.

While trying to find our differences by separating ourselves from the rest of the universe, we cut the umbilical cord of Innocence. Consequently, independence happens on much more than a physical level – there is philosophical independence as well. The incessant question "Why?" is undoubtedly the best and most universal example. No matter when or about what the "Why?" question is asked, what is really being said is this: "I know *you* think that way or want things done that way, but I am separate from you and I would like to think and do things *my* way." Frank and Elvis sang that they had done it "My Way" too. At the final curtain there was one thing of which they were certain – that they had done it their way. Every once in a while you'll hear some poor struggling lounge singer singing that song. "A tribute to Frank, thank you, you're a beautiful audience." But the singer is not doing it his way; he is mimicking somebody else's way. Were he to find his *own* way, who knows how his life might change? Independence is a very critical station, but it isn't even close to where we're heading. When we face our final curtain, I hope we've moved a lot further along our inner journey.

Why? Because much of this original quest for independence is misplaced. In our immaturity we think that we have to give up unity with the universe in order to give identity to ourselves. We forget about the connectedness of all creation and existence and consequently become easy pickins' at the next Station.

STATION THREE: INSTITUTION

No sooner do we get into the swing of searching for Independence than something apparently beyond our control starts to happen. We end up in some form of organizational context in which some other power or source of authority wants to take over our choices and life. It's not that these new powers have evil intentions, necessarily; they simply aren't aware of the potentially damaging impact they can have. By institution I mean church, school, club, gang, business organization or even family – any situation in which someone else is able to dictate what you are to believe, think or do. Let's look at some of these.

Bureaucracy was taught to us by the church. In pre-Reformation days it was only the clergy who knew how to read and write and so the general population was ripe for control. That control came to be imposed through rules, regulations, dogma and (the ace card) the threat of hell and damnation. To a considerable extent, that need to control still exists in the organized church.

Those of us who were raised in churchgoing families do not have to go back very far to recall the tension between what we were told to believe and what we were actually wondering about in the secrecy of our own hearts. We could create a great deal of anxiety by starting to muse about whether or not the miracles of the Bible really happened or, may God have mercy on our souls, should we wonder if God exists at all. Frankly, I think God enjoys people who wrestle with such difficult concepts. I can't imagine God being easily threatened by this, though our parents, ministers, priests, prophets, shamans and rabbis often seem to be.

On a more mundane level, we have all fought against being forced to conform to various liturgies and rituals, standing when told to stand, sitting when told to sit and so on. As children, we were to sit still and be quiet during church. If you went to a Catholic school, you probably still pull your hand back every time you see a wooden ruler. The important thing to note in this, and in the other examples that follow, is that all of this external control is being imposed on us just as we are trying to define our independent selves. We have barely begun to "find ourselves" and an authority bigger than us is telling us who we are. What we want to say back to religious authority is, "Who are you to tell me who I am?"

Let's go on to school. Did you fit in or not? Generally, and sadly, very little of our schooling was designed to help us find out who we are and what the divine purpose of our life is. Your interests, how you learned best, your aptitudes, gifts and dreams were not likely taken into account. The capital "Y" You didn't really seem to matter and that's where the tension started because You mattered more to you than anything.

Some of us were lucky enough to have a teacher somewhere along the way who thought we were more important than the system. That person reached deep into our souls, grabbed hold, rescued us and pointed to the mountaintop. He or she saw who we really were and helped us to see it too. There will be a few exceptions, but most of us would be hard-pressed to name more than two or three teachers from our entire school experience who actually had that kind of impact on our lives.

Now, you would think that, of all institutions, the family would be the one place devoted to helping you find You. Not necessarily so, though I sincerely hope that actually was the case for you. In your family, were you encouraged to think things through for yourself, maybe even to the point of debating or exercising your beliefs against the beliefs of your siblings or parents? Or were the answers to life's questions dictated to you whether you asked them or not? Does this sound familiar? "As long as you are under my roof, you'll abide by my rules!"

I am a parent and I believe in putting limits on children. I am not questioning whether or not your kids should abide by your rules. What we need to realize, however, is that the being on which we impose our limitations, discipline, rules or whatever, is an independent human trying to figure out who she is and what divine purpose she is to fulfill. There is an inherent tension here that we often don't think about. When my children were young, I erred far too much on the side of rules and regulations. "Lighten up!" was the most frequent plea I heard. What they were saying was, "Dad, give me room to be myself!" Making too many rules and imposing too many restrictions says, "You've got to be like me. Think and act like I do." Implementing too few guidelines, on the other hand, says "I don't care what you become." Parenting is, fundamentally, a matter of having the wisdom to know how fast to let go. While it's a little late, I now realize that my need to control our family institution became a negative factor in my children's early journey to discover their divine purpose. I am relieved by the confidence that I am now a much better coach and guide, and that they will, in their turn, be much better at this spiritual dimension of parenting than I was.

Finally, let's take a look at the institution of business. I believe that most work situations actually block the employee's movement on the inner journey. For starters, look at something as simple as your average job description and tell me how liberating that document is. Some list dozens of *do's* and *don'ts*, the last one being "And any other duties as shall be assigned," which is another way of saying, "In case I forgot something, you stupid little twit." If the document describing your life's work makes your life look like a paint-by-number set requiring nothing of you but compliance, you can kiss your quest for Independence goodbye. The Institution has taken over. Big Brother rules!

There is no end to the corporate examples at which we could look. We've been taught management principles like, "If you can't measure it, you can't manage it." And we are very, very determined to manage. The issue, after all, is power and control; consequently, we set up measurable structures and systems through which we can manage both people and things. The thought that people "under our command" might have lives of their own, or that they might actually make their own choices, is frightening to many of us. "Somebody must be held accountable," executives are fond of reminding anyone within earshot. I'm a big fan of accountability; it's the "holding" part that bothers me. In virtually every sport, except professional wrestling, you are penalized for holding, even though you are holding an opponent who is trying to beat you. Maybe it's just that the word is too close to the imagery of holding somebody down or holding somebody back. Wouldn't accountability have the most value and meaning in the context of freedom?

Perhaps the most pervasive evidence of the Institutional need to control can be found in the overreliance on structure. Everyone's time and energy, our Corporate Keepers seem to feel, should be kept safely in a box. The notorious agenda is one scepter of structural control. We've all had to live within an agenda: "9:00 to 9:03 – Welcoming Remarks." Who really lives like that? Whatever happened to nine-ish? "9:04 to 9:24 – Business Arising out of the Minutes." Sounds like methane gas escaping from a swamp. We select "Chairpeople" to control our meetings who sit in the control seat at the narrow end of the table, often employing "Robert's Rules of Order" to ensure that every word is uttered in correct sequence and form. Rules of order – a rather redundant phrase, don't you think? Just begs you to be free and creative. In more formal settings, the Chairperson commences the meeting by whacking the table with a hammer as a warning to one and all that there are dire consequences for stepping out of line. How judicial.

I've had agenda organizers from the other side of the planet call me six months before the event to say that they are putting the agenda together and what time did I want to schedule lunch? I say, "How about noon?" They write it down, grateful for the direction. I had the privilege of speaking at a high-level industrial conference in St. Louis, Missouri, a while ago. Included in the preconference material sent to the senior executives who would be attending the meeting was an entire page entitled "Dress," beginning with "Travel to the Conference – wear loose, comfortable clothing." Someone actually felt the need to tell senior executives what to wear on an airplane? I felt like writing back to ask that, since all I had were skintight jeans, would it still be okay for me to attend? The funniest part was the final dress directive. You guessed it – "Travel *from* the Conference – wear loose, comfortable clothing!" The memo did not specify whether they should be the same loose, comfortable clothes or not. I wasn't sure what to do and almost missed my flight home.

Start looking around your organization from this perspective and you will be amazed, perhaps embarrassed, at how the corporation tries to control people. Of what, exactly, are we so afraid? That someone might actually rise to leadership? That without our control, the entire organization would disintegrate into unimaginable chaos? That there just might be a creative idea somewhere that would require us to change something? Regardless of where it comes from, the Institutional Station is all about control and power over your life. This is very annoying; it's also too true.

STATION FOUR: IRRITATION

Just so you'll know right from the outset of our visit to this Station, this is the big one. My discoveries here are what really turned my thinking around about my own inner journey. "Irritation" says more to me than even anger, frustration or resentment, which are all part of this station. Irritation is a wake-up call; irritation invites the creativity that turns sand into pearls – *if* we recognize it in its spiritual dimension.

Look back at what happens when you journey from Independence to Institution. Just when you are beginning to think that you are responsible for your own life and choices, just when you first begin to discover that life is a creative process and that, maybe, the purpose of life is to demonstrate your own unique witness to the spirit of God that gives Life to your life, you end up in an institution. We have noted above that in every institution – family, school, religion or business – somebody wants to have power over you. The purpose of that power is to encourage you to fit into an institutional template. That template has attitudinal, behavioral and aesthetic dimensions. Some people quietly and with resignation fit in, either because they feel they have no choice in the matter or because they trustingly believe that doing so will be beneficial to them.

We may not recognize it at the time, but the Institution Station is really forcing its brand of unity on us. Look alike. Act alike. Believe alike. Have the same goals. Follow the manual. Be consistent and predictable. Follow the party line. Avoid spontaneity and creativity. Make life easier for yourself – just fit in! Don't rock the boat. As an external organizational consultant, I see this pressure constantly. What if you can't fall into line? The fear of not fitting into the template is not necessarily rational, so where does it come from? Here is the key. When unity is not born out of free choice, it is not unity at all. It may look like unity, have the language and symbols of unity, but it is not unity. It's the same as recognizing that a group of people is not necessarily a team. Teams become teams only when a group of people make the free choice to become one. Remember, we have already experienced natural oneness back at the Innocence Station, and something deep inside tells us that this ain't it. Somebody took our choice away, and we want it back.

So do you want to know how most of us react to this spiritual whiplash, this spiritual deception? We're angry. We're madder than hell. Only we are not likely to throw open our windows to scream to the institutional world that we are not going to take it anymore. That only happens in the movies. Oh no. We've been taking it for years. And you know what? We're likely to keep on taking it until we are truly ready to see our own anger and to understand where it comes from.

We are angry in so many ways. Tragically, a few show their anger through actual physical and emotional violence. Others get angry at themselves – the result of the remarkable and almost universal institutional ability to make people feel that they are at fault, not the institution. Sometimes this self-anger is called depression.

Here is a good example of an institution making individuals think it's their fault. The other day a Member of Parliament for the government of Ontario asked my advice about how the government might instill a "service attitude" into its 60,000 civil-service employees. Their plan at that point was to begin by conducting a huge attitudinal survey so there would be conclusive proof that the employees had a lousy attitude. "Great idea," I said, not so gently trying to redirect their planning. "Tell all 60,000 that they are the sick ones and that it's all their fault. That will really boost morale and win them over!" At no point, of course, could we expect the government as an organization to admit that just maybe they have bureaucratized themselves into being a negative and debilitating environment within which it is almost impossible to work in a positive, empowered and service-oriented fashion.

Some of us exercise our anger by becoming workaholics. Others angrily take up what could be a very worthwhile cause because it initially gives them a legitimate reason to be militant. Anti-abortionists who murder doctors and nurses fall into this category. In their minds there really is such a thing as a holy war and they will stop at nothing to win it. Some people show anger by having extramarital affairs. They could be angry at their spouses or angry because they themselves are getting old. Some try to drown their anger with alcohol. Ever hear the comment, "He's a happy drunk?" Maybe, but where do you think the anger went? Anger is drown-proof. Others do it through accumulation: collecting properties, possessions and people. They don't often realize that they are expressing anger about their institutional experience by setting up another institution that *they* can run. Success can, strangely, be an expression of anger. Their favorite expression is "Those that have the gold make the rules." You can almost see them drooling in delight as they repeat this mantra. No sir! No one will ever have control over them again. The fact that they are controlling everybody else does not seem to matter or even register in their minds. In some way, we all want that liberation, don't we? The popular goal to become "financially independent" is a socially acceptable way of saying, "When it comes to money, I'll never be under anybody's control again!"

Racism is a blatant expression of anger. Many of us now look back on documentaries of Martin Luther King, Jr., and the marches in Alabama and elsewhere and we gasp at the struggle. I know that I didn't really understand what was going on while it was going on. Now when I hear King's voice proclaiming, "Free at last! Free at last!" it goes right to my soul. Every one of us desperately longs to be free. What I long for us all to discover, if you have not already discovered it, is that your anger can set you free too. My discovery of this truth has been the greatest "shuddering" in my own spiritual journey. It is out of gratitude for this realization, at long last, that I write this now. Also to keep reminding myself. It's a lesson to learn daily, a station to revisit often.

In discussing certain forms of anger – and there are dozens of others that won't even be mentioned – I can begin to sound like a reformed smoker who just can't understand why anyone would smoke. I am an almost reformed angry person. Anger has been so hurtful to so many. Millions of people will never come close to their potential because of anger. Some will never experience love because of anger. We can see anger forming in our own children and we know in our hearts that we helped put it there and we'd do anything to get it out. It is so sad to see anger.

I know that I have been angry in many ways over the years. Until recently, the result of my anger has been an inability to have a committed, loving, trusting, noncompetitive relationship. Frankly, I am not helped by the logic that "it takes two" both to form a relationship and to break one up. Or that there are always "two sides to every coin." What I finally had to do, given that I had resolved to continue my inner journey regardless of the pain, was determine to look only at *my* anger. Whether or not the other parties looked at their anger was their business – though I have several thoughts about that if they ever ask! Please don't think about other people's anger as you read this. You think about you and I'll think about me. At least for now.

So anger is evil, right? People who do angry things, which includes all of us, are sick people who need to get fixed, right? Well, that's what I thought and, indeed, that's what I was always told at the Institution Station. But anger is not necessarily to be "fixed," I discovered. And what a discovery it was! *Anger* (and please read this part slowly and reflectively) *is an essential component of spiritual growth.* Without anger the inner journey stalls. Anger is meant to be used. It has spiritual energy trapped inside. It is meant to take us to another place. It has a divine purpose in our lives. Yes, I am an angry person and will always potentially be so. "Hi, I'm Ian and I'm angry," is how I'll begin our Anger Anonymous meetings. The challenge is to see the anger and understand it. Let it be transformed into Irritation and then you can move to a deeper place on the journey.

Those who do not use, or go *through,* their anger, but simply express it, whether violently or nonviolently, are the ones to be feared because they end up not only living in, and *at,* their own anger, but dragging everybody else into it too. I also worry a lot about those who pretend that they don't have any anger since they may be the most dangerous of all. It's like the classic Edward de Bono exercise in lateral thinking: QUESTION: What do you do when you have a guard dog that can't bark? ANSWER: Put up a sign that reads: "Extreme danger – Silent guard dog!" I have trouble connecting with people who don't bark at least once in a while.

Of course you are angry about losing your job and being told two days before Christmas. Of course your divorce has left you angry, especially if your anger was all you got to keep. Of course you are angry because someone more financially astute cheated you. She was unfaithful to you, of course you are angry. I'd be angry at God too if I had cancer or MS. Those wasted years at school because no one cared that you learned things differently from other kids should make you angry. Why wouldn't they? Be angry that your parents never said an affirming word to you your entire life. Your husband doesn't either, does he? Be angry about that! You trusted your priest and he violated you. Who wouldn't be livid? You get paid 25 percent less than your male counterpart who does exactly the same job with poorer results. You bet you're angry. And no, they didn't consult you before dividing up your department. How else could you feel but angry?

Most of us are angry in one way or another. Often, as in the examples above, we have a clear object of irritation to focus our anger on. Many times, however, we are just generally off balance for reasons that are not clear to us. How can a person who *seems* to "have everything going for her" be so unhappy? Well, sometimes we don't know what is making us angry. In many of these situations, I suggest, ambiguous anger points to a contradiction between our inner calling and our outer direction.

There is a toy that began life as a test for fine motor skills, in which a player tries to move an electronic stylus along a narrow, twisting channel without letting it touch the sides. At a couple of points the player can choose to follow an easy path to the goal or take a narrower, more difficult one that enables him to earn extra points. A buzzer is triggered should the player fail to stay in the center of the channel and he has to start all over again. The winner is the one who can get closest to the finish without setting off the buzzer.

We are not rats in a maze, life is not an experiment, and so this toy metaphor is not totally applicable to life. God is much more creative and loving than to have put each of us in narrow, predestined channels, punishing us every time we move off center. Nevertheless, let's think of the buzzer in the above example as the irritations in our lives. Each of us just living our life, trying to find a way to pay our bills and be happy at the same time, and we touch, or even hit, the wall. *BUZZZZZZZ!* The first couple of times we laugh and adjust. *BUZZZZZZZ!* A few more times and our response changes. *BUZZZZZZZ!* Stupid game! *BUZZZZZZZ!* How is anybody supposed to make it to the end? *BUZZZZZZZ!* There's barely enough room for anybody to get *through*. *BUZZZZZZZ!* And we begin to turn angry.

Is anger really essential to the inner journey? Yes! And that is what is so freeing. Anger can take us from the political/intellectual/economic First World to the emotional/spiritual/ecological Second World. We are not sick just because we are angry and we don't have to be fixed. However, it is vital that we each recognize that anger must be allowed to move us to a better place. When it does not, it becomes an emotional virus and it will kill us. So where should it take us? Ah, this is where we need some real insight.

STATION FIVE: INSIGHT

Anger *can* be a form of divine energy *if* we are able to recognize it as a springboard to the spiritual potential in our lives. Our anger, however, is not innately divine; we are the ones who make it so. In the same way that hydrogen and oxygen combine to make water, we add insight to anger to make wholeness, integration. This is not a process of problem solving in the purely political and intellectual sense, though some irritations can be minimized that way. For example, traffic jams in the morning anger us and so we figure out a more efficient route to the office. We are talking about a much more significant level of irritation than the minor stresses and strains of daily living. We are talking about anger that has become entrenched in our beings to the extent that it has formed part of who we are at this moment. Our minds *are* required for insight into this kind of anger, but the real force of insight's power comes from connection to our hearts and souls. In other words, there is the role of grace to be played by the Divine here. First, however, let us look at our part in this transformation.

Anger will always move us somewhere, even if it's into more anger. We can, however, begin to recognize anger's potential to move us to a *better* and *deeper* place if we think of anger as a signal to make a choice. I believe that choice and power are synonyms – that we have power in our lives *only* if we are making real choices. A whole and integrated life is powered by choice. Choice in attitude. Choice in relationships. Choice in work. Choice in worship. Choice is the one common characteristic of both the First and Second Worlds – we have to make choices in both. Make a choice and you have power. When you have power, you have life. So our work here is to, first, recognize the signal, and, second, to be *ready* to make a choice. There is just one complication – anger seems to enhance our tendency to apply the responsibility of choice to the source of our irritation, rather than to ourselves.

Usually, if I am angry about the way my team is performing, I express my anger to the team and demand that *they* make a choice to be or do something different so I won't have to be angry anymore. Not often do I have the insight that my anger, even though it is focused on the team for good cause, is a signal that *I* need to make a choice. Likewise, if the team is being irritated by a team member who is always angry, the team places the pressure to choose a more positive attitude back on the angry member. Not many teams would say, "Our colleague has gifted us with his anger so that we can make a choice and thus become a better team. Let us thank him for his anger."

Anger is the signal to both giver *and* receiver that a choice is pending. Which party might be "in the wrong" does not need to enter our discussion. If I am angry at you, I need to look *through* the anger to determine what choice is being presented to me. If you are angry at me, I still need to determine my choices. The primary responsibility of choice-making is mine in both cases. Concerning myself about whether or not *you* are making the choices *I* think are appropriate not only does not take me to a deeper and better place, it draws me even more deeply into the anger. Many couples spend years trying to get each other to change, and get angrier by the minute because the *other* person is clearly lacking insight. We need to deal with the "beams" of choice in our own eyes before we can point out the "slivers" of choice in the eyes of others. Our role is to see that a choice is being presented to us *through* the anger, and then to be willing to make it. The choice is not about "to be or not to be" angry. We are already angry. The choice can be about something relatively minor and immediate, like our attitude while standing in a ticket line in the rain, or about something of great consequence that has been left suspended in our lives, like being abused as a child. In each case there is the potential of healing transformation.

Where, then, does the role of the Divine come into the transformational process? Strange as it may sound, anger, transformed through insight, is the core of spirituality. The irritations of the First World reveal a chasm of anger separating us from the Second World. Insight is a divine gift, a life-saving bridge from the Second World that helps you cross over. If there were no irritation and no anger, we would not see our need for the bridge to a better and deeper place. Let us be grateful for the *BUZZZZZZZZ!*

But the truly amazing contribution of the Divine comes in the choice-making process itself. Since God's spirit flows throughout all of creation, his direction and wisdom are available to us for our choice-making. No one has expressed this truth better than theologian and teacher Glenn Clark who wrote: "I believe with the great artists that all creative power comes from great stillness. If then, we just quiet and afterwards act, the action will go further for there is alignment. We should not have to do much to change the whole world. When one is in perfect alignment with God and man, all work becomes play and all creative effort becomes effortless. An aligned person is an irresistible person." The power of this alignment is a grand mystery. If we could somehow experience what it would be like to watch electricity make a lightbulb glow, having never seen it before, we might come close to the wonder of our divine connection.

In 1946, a colleague of Clark's, architect and sculptor Dr. Walter Russell, put the mystery of connection this way: "I believe that when the Self of man thus walks and talks with God one as gradually ascends to the great heights and desires of his ambitions as the tree ascends from its seed . . . there is but One Thinker in the universe; that my thinking is his thinking, and that every man's thinking is an extension, through God, of every other man's thinking. I therefore think that the greater the exhalation and ecstasy of my thinking, the greater the standards of all man's thinking will be. Each man is thus empowered to uplift all men as each drop of water uplifts the entire ocean."

Though I too believe this with all my heart, in no way do I want even more of these anger-generated, choice-making opportunities in the world, and I certainly don't want any more in my life. The fact is, there is enough anger there already. For you. For me. We know the roots of some of our anger and how we are to use it. Some of our anger we don't understand at all. But I do know this: our anger has the potential to give us back our lives. You know the ones I mean – the ones we both almost found in Independence but then lost in Institution. Here are a few examples of how it works.

So you are angry at your parents. Let's just say they were nonaffirming, overly controlling and judgmental. Where can that anger take you? One place is into more anger. Just keep on angrily telling everyone about how nonaffirming, overly controlling and judgmental your parents were. Blaming parents for what is now happening in one's life is both popular and convenient, particularly if they're dead. Choose this option and guess what? You'll end up a nonaffirming, overly controlling and judgmental lonely person because you need those characteristics in order to remain angry.

The second choice is to ask yourself what insights you have learned from this most difficult school. What have you learned about affirming those you love? My guess is that you,

more than almost anyone, have a greater and deeper understanding of what the human heart craves. When your little girl
brings home her first wrinkled, still-wet, learning-to-glue,
construction-paper masterpiece with "Kelly" scrawled in
green crayon across the top, spelled with a very large "KEL"
and a very small "ly" because there was no room, doesn't the
pain of your lifetime open your heart to envelop her? In a single torrential moment, you somehow reclaim out of timeless
galaxies all the childhood affirmation that should have been
yours, and you give it to her. And suddenly you gain the
insight that you have never been so affirmed. Out of your own
emptiness has come abundance.

You go on to wonder why your own parents were so overly controlling. It's not as if you had a long delinquency record.
"What were they so afraid of?" you wonder. Then you ask the
same question of yourself and you stand eye-to-eye with your
own fears. It's the prospect of personal powerlessness, you
realize. Most everything in your life, as it was in your parents'
lives, is being controlled by Institutions, not by you. That realization quickly evolves into another awareness that the most
treasured possession in your life, your children, will spend
every day of their childhood and adolescence gradually and
deliberately moving out of your control. Where will that ulti-
mately leave you? With not much to control except maybe the
cat. Then again, scratch the cat off the list too.

Suddenly it hits you – you were all your parents had. Maybe
they were angry about their lot in life and so they tried to keep
you from getting away like everything else had. They had
made mistakes with their own lives and they were not about
to make any with yours. If only they could have understood
that by making that choice they almost lost you forever. The
other shoe drops. You don't want to lose your kids either, and
for the first time you see that parenting is primarily a matter
of reveling in the wise and gradual transfer of power from parent to child. From that point on, you delight (at least on a
good day you do) in their pulling and straining against you,

knowing that just every once in a wonderful while they will, in their exhaustion, abandon themselves to your cradled arms, resting so they can resume the struggle in the morning. As you look down at their sleeping forms you know they have had one more day of life-school, and that you, their teacher, have taught them well. You are teaching them to be free. Insight has led you to understand the struggle. Once you understand it, it holds no fear.

And why are your parents so judgmental, even to this day? They seem to have so little tolerance of anyone who thinks, believes or behaves differently than they do. Like they have a monopoly on the truth? Just thinking about it, you feel the tension crawling across your shoulders, the result of years of adverse conditioning. You do not believe what your parents believe. You do not see the world's diversity as the negative they imagine it to be. You do not have to fit in to what they think is right and, furthermore, you won't! There, at least you've finally said it out loud. But be careful! If you stop at this point, you will end up as intolerant and judgmental about your parents as they are intolerant and judgmental about you. And you will have caught the virus and imprisoned your soul. Remember that the goal, thanks to Insight, is to be set free *through* anger. The word *freedom* means to "live without judgment," refusing to blame and refusing to be blamed unjustly.

It is at this moment that my point can best be made. Be angry. Go ahead and reject everything that you were force-fed by your parents if you want to. But if you are going to reject those beliefs, what will *you* believe instead? On what will you take *your* stand? On the basis of what principles will you go on to live *your* life? Let your anger and frustration push you to work out your own plan of salvation. How wonderful that you are finally thinking things through for your Self. Even if you do come back to some of the beliefs held by your parents, you will believe them because they are *yours,* not theirs. That is an incredibly important difference.

Can you imagine how bland and inane the world would be without rebellion? None of the world's religions would exist and neither would our mighty corporations. Come to think of it, the world would still be flat with the sun revolving around it. It is rebellion that has led all kinds of disquieted people to life-changing discoveries. I am convinced that the last thing God would ever think of doing is to throw all our lives into some kind of spiritual blender, pouring us out a de-spirited, indistinguishable and impotent mass. How awfully boring and inconsequential that would be. Let's not have any more luke-warm living. Apathy is the most terrible trap of all. Be hot. Be cold. But be You!

Two long-term employees are laid off from the same firm. Both are 50-something. Both feel the belittling unfairness of the experience. Both want to literally spit on the new boss who wishes them "all the best" as he hands them each a cardboard box, telling them to empty their desks and turn in their keys. Both shed tears with their families that night, unable to distinguish angry tears from tears of terror. In the morning, each makes a choice about what to do with his or her anger.

One begins a lifelong rehearsal of the experience, getting angrier and more bitter with each mental replay. He summarily dismisses all corporate executives as direct instruments of the devil and spends endless hours at the neighborhood pub detailing for the patrons' enlightenment what the company owes him after all those years. His anger leads him to no new insights at all and he'll spend the restless rest of his life imprisoned in Anger, unable to use the gift of Irritation, never breaking through to the joy and power of the Second World, the world of spirit.

Our other friend, feeling equally angry, frightened and betrayed, gives herself a long gift of silence in which she asks her heart the questions: "What is this about? What is this new reality telling me?" Proud of her years of work there, she knows she accomplished much for the company. In return, the company paid her a good wage and extended many benefits to her and her family. Nothing unfair about that. Her friends, wanting to rescue her from the irritation and anger of being "downsized," rush to reassure her that this is not about her. But it *is* about her. She is being signaled to make a choice. However, the whole ordeal is not a negative comment on her past, she further reflects, so why should she regard it as a negative comment on her future? It never really was a matter of the job being so important, but what she was able to accomplish *through* the job. Out of this reflection comes the insight that the most important question has nothing to do with a particular job. It is about choosing to move to a better and deeper place. "I most want to understand," she thinks, "what it is that I am trying to accomplish with my life, not with my job. Then I want to explore what other choices will serve as ideal vehicles for that accomplishment." She goes insightfully through her Great Shuddering to the rest of her life *for* the rest of her life. Free at last! Free at last!

What wonderful Power leads us all to such freedom? In each of us is that God-given, inborn yearning for meaning. A biological and spiritual need to love and be loved. In each of us is that special divine grace that enables us to transform anger into insight. We are meant to be tools of that grace, opening our insights to our children, our organizations, our places of worship, our schools and our soul mates. We must be careful not to share our insights in a way that invites a form of spiritual mimicking. Each must walk his own unique journey and work out his own salvation. There is no other way.

Somehow and somewhere within us we know that our lives are meant to be something significant. We may not be able to articulate it, but we also know what that significance is. It's the Grand Why of our life. The Divine Spirit to find and be that significance was gifted to us in our creation. The metaphor is a little weak, but my mind goes to a go-cart-track experience of a few years ago. All helmeted and strapped in, my son Nathan in his cart and I in mine, ready to run the course. We just had to wait for the track guy to come and pull the cord to start the engine. Without that we just looked the part. Well, to state the obvious, our cords have got to be pulled. Something has to "yank" us into action. It is the only way for us to be off and running on our inner journey. Life calls on us, our spirit calls on us and God calls on us to do more than simply look the part.

The very best race courses don't just have straightaways. They have hairpin turns, S-curves and other obstacles, not to mention other far less skilled drivers also on the track. Guess what these challenges can do for us if we are open to it. They make us better drivers! In the course of our inner journey, we run, almost daily, into obstacles and shudderings of various intensities. Without insight we rail against these obstacles and want them removed. They make us angry because we see them as blocking the way. With insight we learn to see them *as* the way. They're gifts.

It does not matter whether you are angry about something at work or in a relationship. It could be about the weather ruining your crops for the third year in a row or about how you were treated at boarding school. It could be about a disease or about a bankruptcy. Some of what happens to people is beyond comprehension. My friend Paul Kells's 19-year-old son was burned to death on the first day of his new job. It's impossible to have insight sometimes. Yet today Paul and his family have gone *through* their unimaginable shuddering (though I don't think parents can ever get fully *through* the loss of a child), and are a major driving force for occupational safety right across Canada. *Through* his new calling, Paul will save hundreds of lives. My friend W. Mitchell has survived several major accidents that left him in a wheelchair, hands burned off and his face very badly scarred. The only thing untouched was his voice. Today he is one of the world's most gifted inspirational speakers, known as the "man who would not be defeated."

While the severity of what we experience varies enormously, the underlying principles of the Insight Station are the same. First, let's again thank God for reminding us that we are on an important, one-of-a-kind inner journey and that our anger has a divine energizing and directional purpose. Second, let's diminish our anger by using it to get our *own* life back and to help us on our *own* inner journey. Rather than let our rage blind us, let it give us sight – *in*sight into the life we are meant to live. If we use it, we will lose it. This is the purpose of the Insight Station.

STATION SIX: INTEGRATION

I have never experienced a point where everything comes together. Over the last few years, however, I have experienced many points where *some* things come together. Those moments bring such joy that, frankly, I don't really care if there is one cataclysmic point of fusion in my life. As we can easily foresee, the Integration Station is about things in our lives making sense. About us seeing the relationships among time, people, places, things and events as we have experienced them. Integration marks our return to wholeness, the experience of unity that we had in Innocence but lost during our visit to Independence. In Innocence it was uninformed unity, and in Integration it is informed and insightful unity. This is a return by free choice to real unity, not the counterfeit version we were force-fed at the Institution Station. We see here that our yearning for unity has always been there, like gravity, always pulling us back, asking to be recognized.

Integration is the accumulation of our Insights. The more insights we have, the more we are able to see the wonderful mystery that is our lives. As I quoted earlier, "The mystery of life is the plainest part of it." Without insight, of course, there is nothing plain or obvious about anything. With insight we at least begin to see the pattern of our lives' path. I almost used the word *logic* instead of *pattern,* then came to the quick conclusion that most of our lives are anything but logical.

At this point I begin to be cautious about writing beyond my actual experience. I will try to clearly indicate when I have experienced in my own life what I am writing about. It will also be clear when I am describing what I believe to be true, without the confidence of direct experience.

Can we get to a place where we are able to avoid anger entirely, when something most would call negative happens to us? In other words, can we go right from the Institution Station (where the stuff usually happens) to the Insight Station (where we learn why it happened) and then on to Integration (where we decide what to do with it)? At this last stop we assimilate our new learning into what we have already integrated. This process of Integration means that you and I gradually see Divine wisdom in literally everything. But even if we believe that this truly is possible, it can take a long time before we actually get to that depth of understanding and vision. Most of the time the "stuff" of our lives just happens. We don't give it a second's worth of thought. It does not click with us that routine, ordinary, everyday, no-big-deal occurrences are filled with Divine wisdom. It's like throwing out an old birthday card and then remembering that you also threw out the hundred-dollar check your aunt had enclosed. Our ordinary lives are holy and precious.

We will never access wisdom while we are living *at* anger. We only access it from integrated insights. We've heard beliefs like "There are no accidents" or "There are no coincidences" before and may even have made an attempt to see the wisdom of the mundane. However, until we take the Journey, use our anger to lead us to insights, then integrate these insights into an understanding of what our life is all about, we'll have to be content with little more than appetizers from the Second World. Just because we loved *The Celestine Prophesy*, read one of Deepak Chopra's wonderful books (or at least started it) and have just picked up a secondhand paperback about angels, we are not granted automatic access to understanding all things. There is no shortcut. We take the Journey, difficult as it may get, or we don't get to go. On the near side of the Shuddering we know that we are not where we are to be. We rejoice in the knowledge that there is more, and at the same time brace our souls because we know we will be deeply scoured and utterly shaken on the way. We've got to go through our Great Shudderings. Believe me, I have a thousand times wished it were not so. But, once we do experience those, we have access to the Second World of meaning. Goodness will prevail. There is freedom on the other side. There is Life.

In this Life, we can get to the point where we truly understand why certain people come into our lives. Why our old high-school friend calls us out of the blue 20 years after we last talked to her. Why we were put in seat 7C when the reservation agent said we had been assigned 4B for the 16-hour flight to Australia. Why our teenager decided to stay home for the weekend rather than go to his friend's cottage. Why we ended up taking a course in Early Childhood Education when the Psychology of Sex was already filled. Why our phone call to an overbooked holiday destination coincided with someone else's call to cancel their reservation. Pretty mundane stuff, huh? Look again! The obvious connection between every one of these examples is the question "Why?" The "Why" world is the spiritual world. Most people spend their whole lives trying to figure out the hows, which is the primary activity of the First World. In the integrated life, we actually know why and seek meaning and goodness in all that we do. This is not the revelation of an imposed, predestined plan. Life is not a paint-by-number set! Each "why" we understand is another color on our palette, and with these colors we finish the creation that God began. What incredible freedom this brings. I mean, can you imagine a state, even a partial state, where you know why?

Here is one of my favorite stories. If you are not a romantic, just skip the next few paragraphs. A short while ago, I was rearranging my banking situation. The bank was actually a client of mine and so one of the senior vice-presidents kindly took it upon himself to assign my account to one of the best account managers. That account manager decided he didn't have room for me, which was quite irritating given that I thought I had special status, and passed me off to a young woman relatively new to her account-manager position. The fact that Maureen Bradbury turned out to be the most valuable source of financial advice and management that I have ever had is a minor part of the why of this story.

While idly chatting about exercise one day, Maureen invited me to her country-line-dancing class. Klutz though I am, I went anyway, grateful for the chance to wear the cowboy boots I had bought in Tucson 10 years ago. After demonstrating to Maureen an almost total inability to remember the most simple of sequences and wondering why on earth I had agreed to come, I got passed off again. This time to a very beautiful woman who was clearly one of the best dancers in the room. Now, I was a single guy at the time, so while this was intimidating, it sure wasn't irritating. If anyone could teach me, apparently, Georgia could. The dancing outcome is also inconsequential to the why of this story, so I'll not comment further. At one rest point, Georgia and I talked about where we each grew up, our educational backgrounds and so on. Turns out her brother Ken and I were in the same remedial Grade 10 class. "Would I like to go to Ken's fiftieth birthday party as a surprise?" Georgia asks. That was our first date and, I am overjoyed to say, we are now married. I believe it was an event literally waiting to happen, even though the road to it was rough indeed.

After the fact, of course, the whys are easy to answer. Georgia and I can now see the wisdom of all the interconnected parts of our coming together although they were spread over many decades. But if you had come to me in Grade 10 and asked, "Why is Ken Gardner in your class?" I'd have answered, "How the heck do I know?" But if Ken hadn't been in that class, it is unlikely that I would have had my first date with Georgia. The *truly* romantic among us will be quick to point out that if Love had not found this way, it would have found another. Perhaps so.

As you'd expect, I love this story. And chances are, you've got an even better one that you love to tell. But here is an advanced aspect of the Integration Station. I believe that God has given us the spiritual power to see the wisdom and connectedness of every event in our lives *while* it is happening. We can actually grow to that depth of understanding. Kind of like the graduate school of spirituality. Not that I'm even close to that level of spiritual wisdom, except for a few rare and wonderful occasions. One grows to it gradually, I think. Probably at the same pace as one's anger gets mysteriously, painfully, beautifully transformed into insight.

You have been reading about options in responding to the stuff that happens in our lives. This can be a pretty comfortable discussion. The real challenge comes when shit happens. Thanks to Forrest Gump, we all know that it does. Quite simply, the principles behind stuff and shit are the same. It's just that one tests us a lot more. As we become more spiritually mature, we respond to either with the same confidence and expectation. Pull up the curtain and let us walk on stage, we are ready for all that life has to offer!

Until recently, I thought that this twilight zone kind of thinking applied, if at all, only to major, earth-shattering events. Certainly there could not be significance behind every mundane thing that happened. You'd end up in hours of meditation wondering why you got that taxi driver instead of the next one. Why you ordered a doughnut instead of a bagel. Maybe Freud was right, sometimes a cigar is just a cigar. I always thought the taxi example supported this argument until I heard Dr. Warren Bennis speak. I have known about and admired Bennis since graduate-school days. A prolific author, he is an insightful authority on leadership and service. The main thing I remember from this particular talk is his story of the enterprising taxi driver who offered him several newspapers to choose from, a cold drink if he wanted it and the use of his cellular phone if he needed to make a call. The lesson was that one can demonstrate leadership and service from any starting point. Bennis has probably told that story all over the world and for him the answer to "Why that taxi driver?" is abundantly clear. That man's ability to turn a job into art, service into graciousness, taught Bennis what he was trying to know, what he was ready to learn. The experience spoke to him because he was ready and had "ears to hear." Bennis told us that that anecdote would be the only thing we'd remember out of his lecture and he was right. Now I don't write off any experience as inconsequential. If it seems to be of no consequence, it is just because I don't have the insight to see its significance yet.

In the next chapter we are going to trace this same journey in the spiritual life of a corporation, and trust me, corporations do have spiritual lives. To help that transition happen smoothly, let me recap the Six Stations of the Inner Journey.

- The **Innocence Station** gives us our start and instills in our hearts the notion that life can be good. It gives us an experience of trust and a taste of the reality that the universe is filled with abundance. This is the birthplace of hope.

- The **Independence Station** gives us a chance to develop our spiritual, emotional, intellectual and physical muscles in the quest to find out who we really are. We begin to distinguish our own uniqueness from the other uniquenesses in the world. This is the birthplace of Self.

- The **Institution Station** brings our quest for independence to an abrupt halt and we learn that our lives are filled with institutions each of which would dearly love to have control over us and do everything they possibly can to fulfill that intention. Most of us find this belittling and disempowering, though often we don't even realize what is happening to us. This is the birthplace of struggle.

- The **Irritation Station** opens our eyes to the realization that we may have, on many fronts, compromised our lives in favor of these institutions. When we discover that this is indeed true, we get very angry, to say the least. Our anger gives us two choices: to remain imprisoned within it, or to actually use the anger to become what has been within us all along. Understanding that anger is an essential and divine component of the Inner Journey is tremendously freeing. This is the birthplace of liberation.

- The **Insight Station** takes us back to hope and trust. Visiting this station means that we have, at least to some extent, learned how to use anger to discover what we believe and what we stand for. We learn to accept the grace of Irritation that transforms anger into clarity and opens us to the "why" of our existence. In that openness to "why," to significance, we begin to touch the joy of Life. We begin to understand the mysterious and divine patterns of our existence. This is the birthplace of wisdom.

- The **Integration Station** brings it all together. As our insights begin to add up, we are able to more fully answer the whys of our life. The whys of the timing, choices, relationships, gains, losses, pains and delights of everyday living all begin to make sense and have divine purpose. We are no longer consumed with the hows of the First World and instead use that energy to find the wisdom of the Second. This is the birthplace of peace.

I can do no better in concluding this chapter than to remind us all that all of life is holy. All of life has a spiritual center. As we progress in our Inner Journey, the world will unfold like a flower and we will see what God saw when he said of his own creation, "It is good." From philosopher Sam Keen comes this inspired thought:

The holy may appear in the
flaming beauty of maple leaves falling,
or in the ecstatic meeting of flesh and flesh,
or in the haunted face of a Somalian mother
who holds her starving child,
or in the awesome patterns that
unite quirks and quasars.
Be Alert

SEVEN

The Corporate Journey

◆ ◆ ◆ ◆

"Be alert." If we ever had the inclination to turn the spiritual quest into a command, this would be as good as any. More and more over these last few years there has been a real awakening of the corporate soul. Those with eyes begin to see, those with ears begin to hear. Five or ten years ago the question of spirituality in the workplace would not be raised as a serious point of discussion in most boardrooms. Except, of course, if one of those prayer breakfasts I mentioned earlier was being held. In that case such a discussion would be expected and be over in about an hour anyway. It's different now. An almost universal corporate yearning is moving spirituality to the top of the agenda. I'd like briefly to trace that movement and then describe how the Six Stations apply to the corporate spiritual journey.

By corporate soul I mean that transcendent aura, feeling, sense, vibration, chemistry that occurs when two or more human beings try to achieve something worthwhile together, something that brings out the full potential for goodness and excellence in human nature. One soul plus one soul equals corporate soul. The more of these individual souls you get in the picture, the more difficult it becomes to discover the nature of the transcendent corporate soul. That soul is always greater than the sum of its parts.

Why has that whole soul been so hard to recognize and talk about? For years well-meaning speakers' bureaus and meeting planners have warned me about using the "S" word when I speak at business conferences and conventions. Yet we all know there is such a thing as being spiritual. Takes me back to the early struggles of those who tried to get sex education into the classrooms of the nation. They actually had to deal with people who didn't want the words *penis* and *vagina* used. Most of us have one or the other, including some of those who tried to block these programs. Some didn't even want the word *sex* said out loud. In case I too have been vague, let me shout it out: There is a Spirit that envelops everything. "Everything" includes you as you read this book. Me as I write it. Your children waiting for you to come and play like you promised. Your first date since your divorce. The purple mountain's majesty. The lilies of the field. The fourteenth annual convention of the international whatever. The closing ceremonies of the Olympics. Your board of directors and your Strategic Planning Task Force. And, yes, even your re-engineering project. Everything!

Furthermore, it is God's Spirit – not some happen-chance, divine-less harmonic manifestation. As I noted previously, it is because of God's Spirit that everything exists and exists in Martin Luther King, Jr.'s "inescapable network of mutuality." Back in 1947, French philosopher and theologian Pierre Teilhard de Chardin saw this mutuality and expressed it this way: "No one can deny that a world network of economic and psychic affiliations is being woven at ever increasing speed which envelops and constantly penetrates more deeply within each of us. With every day that passes it becomes a little more impossible for us to act or think otherwise than collectively." The universal task of the human being is to find unique and creative ways to give testimony to this mutuality. Unfortunately, we are not always up to this divine task. In acting "collectively," we have a choice of expressing spirit *exclusively* or *inclusively.*

When we fight and kill each other, we act *exclusively* and fail in our highest task. The fighting and killing can be literal, as when one race tries to eliminate another or when gangs fight for exclusive rights to an inner-city neighborhood. We also fail, however, when we demean women or minorities in the workplace and when we callously rid our companies of unwanted people for the sake of even greater profit. When we act in wisdom and love, we have succeeded because wisdom and love cannot be anything but *inclusive.* We succeed when we serve soup to the homeless. We succeed when we help an employee discover his or her giftedness or when we insist that a toy we manufacture be absolutely safe though it increases the cost and lowers our profit a little. God's spirit always unifies while cherishing the sacredness of the individual – that is the ultimate test of goodness in both our personal and corporate lives.

One – and it is only one – way of attempting to evidence God's unifying Spirit is called religion. Sometimes, I hope, God is proud and pleased with the effort. Sometimes, I suspect, he is not. Another form of attempt is called managing a business. Again, sometimes God must be proud and pleased with the effort and sometimes not. Other attempts are called being a lover, being a parent, teaching preschoolers, being unemployed, retiring, having a long talk with a hurting friend, giving a cup of water to someone who is thirsty and the million other things that give us lenses to see *through* and fields to search in. My belief is that all of our *inclusive* attempts to show wisdom and love are on a level playing field. There is no status given to one over another. I have heard some clergy express their passion by claiming that "there is no higher calling" than what they are doing to serve God. This is admirable in one sense but wrong and dangerous in another. The truth is, when you know that you are doing the good that *your* life was meant to do, *then* there is no higher calling. The job title is not important.

Right now we are going to explore the corporate world's natural yearning to wisely manifest the unifying spirit of God. While I believe this to be the ultimate purpose of all human endeavor, including commerce, I understand why this phrasing is not likely to be incorporated into your mission statement – at least not yet. We cling tenaciously to the notion of being a bottom-line-driven company. Any other purpose beyond improving the bottom line terrifies many of us. Let's explore the connection between profit-oriented work and the spirit within us.

We may not recognize it, but we have been moving toward corporate spiritual expression for some time, probably since time began. Not being an expert on that early period, let me begin from when I first got involved in the corporate world, back in the late sixties. My children think that *is* when time began, and so be it. The group movement of that period was, at its heart, a spiritual movement. We are talking here about Bob, Carol, Ted and Alice. T-groups. Hippies. Woodstock. Tell it like it is. Group gropes. Intimacy without responsibility. We had come out of the assembly-line era recognizing that we had lost our souls to the time-and-motion experts and we were desperate to find them again. Many did not think that was possible in the capitalistic world and for good reason. In my judgment and experience, the attempt to make real and honest connections with one another was a very spiritual intention.

Fortunately or unfortunately, many corporate executives had trouble walking around barefoot and blindfolded, trying to become one with their boardroom through the tactile exploration of its various textures. Achieving oneness with your environment is a spiritual thing, too. It was just that this way of getting it didn't have enough structure for some people. So off we went to more statistical approaches to finding out who we were, which, again, is all part of the spiritual quest. We learned about where we fit on various managerial grids. It was terrific! Just draw a line from the A axis and another from the B and where they intersect, there you is! This led to other attempts to define our identity such as job descriptions and managing by objectives. Identity. Purpose. All spiritual issues.

We started to get back the wonderful old feeling of actually being in control, but the truth was, something was still missing. Quality. That was it. Maybe if we learned to do our very best, there would be an inner peace. We were taught that quality is free, but still spent an incredible amount of time, energy and money measuring and documenting how close we were coming to what was called 100 percent compliance to standard. I still have old files of handout materials from when the gang in my company used to put on some of the best quality workshops in the world. The quality movement has stayed with us a long time in one form or another, most recently as Total Quality Management discussed earlier, and the newest quality standard called ISO 9000. The very latest offspring is the growing focus on Quality of Work-life, which is a rather interesting progression when you stop to think about it. In some companies, it's being called "work and family balance," a spiritual direction if I've ever seen one.

Still there was deep and painful yearning in the corporate heart. The next spiritual exploration was mentioned earlier, our obsession with vision, mission and values. The language can't get much more spiritual-sounding than that. Some voice inside our corporate mind told us that we had to move from the question of "How?" to the question of "Why?" Values, particularly, seemed to be the way. We didn't quite get it but the direction was right. Along with the mission and values movement came empowerment, overall a rather feeble admission that the institution had taken choice – and therefore power – away from employees and that maybe it should give them back. When you take away choice and power, you take away life itself. Again, right direction but very few organizations got to home plate on this one. They weren't really ready to give employees their lives back. To this day, most employees think empowerment is a clever management technique to reduce head count. How very sad.

This vision-and-values stuff was just too airy and we came back once more to processes like re-engineering and rationalization, where we reverted to the security of science and data for intellectual answers to the spiritual issues that troubled us.

Ironically, all the initiatives I've mentioned in this sketchy historical perspective have a spiritual center. You can see this if you look only at the basic intention of each initiative rather than at the overall process. Corporations generally didn't follow through with any of them because we, as leaders, have been afraid of moving too far from science and data. This is the crux of the issue right here. It's all about control and ego. And ego won't recognize anything it can't take credit for. First, we want it to be us who accomplishes great things: delivers 30 percent ROE, ranks number one or two in every selected market, wins the Baldridge prize for quality and so on. Second, we are incredibly frightened about being out of control. However, if we are intent on being connected to spiritual wisdom, we don't get to be in control, at least not in the way that we currently define it. Something bigger than you or I takes over. The fear of losing control is the major reason corporate leaders are unable to move from political/intellectual to emotional/spiritual.

Around all of this has been the timeless interest in "team." We love teams and will do almost anything to get them working in our companies. "Team" is another way of saying "community." To me, common unity is the ultimate demonstration of spirituality. True communities live as close to a state of perpetual spiritual wisdom as is possible. In the mid-eighties, I published a book in which I explored the Judeo-Christian heritage of community. To live in community and to show others how to do so was a direct assignment from God, I suggested. I now think that religion generally, and the Christian church specifically, has dropped the ball badly. There are wonderful exceptions, I know, but fundamentally I believe this to be true. God, working in mysterious ways, has revoked the assignment and given it instead to business. Which is why we are seeing the awakening of spirituality in the workplace. Should community fail to materialize in the work context, the assignment will be turned over yet again, next time to government. Given what goes on at some political conventions, this is a scary thought. How on earth will God pick which party to give it to? Anyway, this is a whole other issue. Perhaps we can come together around this topic some other time.

As we now approach the direct application of the Six Stations to the corporate context, keep in mind that organizations have been circling around their spiritual center for a very long time. They take a taste of it and then retreat. Taste and retreat. It is uncanny how close the corporate pattern parallels our individual journeys. Take a look.

INNOCENCE

At the **Innocence Station**, we see the world as fair and just. Hard work and determination have their own rewards. God bless our Dominion and God bless America. Land of the free. The American dream, symbolized by Liberty's torch, is a possibility for all. As long as you are honest, like apple pie and maple syrup, own a Chevrolet and know who the Beav was. Your word is your bond, why would you need a lawyer? Miracles do happen on Thirty-fourth Street. Jimmy Stewart will go to Washington and fight for you because it is government by the people for the people, and that means you, little buckaroo.

Innocence is what the Olympics are all about, isn't it? Athletes temporarily giving up their lives for the sake of pure victory and pride of country. Surely it is not about drug-enhanced performance, political interference, corporate money and terrorism. All right, so the Olympics aren't innocent anymore. Haven't been for a long time. But look how innocent the founding principles of the first Olympic games in 776 B.C. sound from our modern perspective:

- the value of the whole person in spirit, body and mind;
- the belief in individual freedom and merit;
- a consciousness of our individual and collective responsibilities to each other;

- an acceptance of our democratic right to participate in public affairs.

Innocence is also the starting assumption for most people who decide to launch out on their own. Their lives become their work, and their work becomes their life. It is all one grand unified experience. The absolute thrill of seeing your name for the first time on letterhead and business cards. Of being able to say, "I'm self-employed" with the same voice of freedom that a convict would use in declaring that he had "served his time." Fledgling entrepreneurs have a great new idea and of course the banks will provide start-up capital and of course the market will respond and nobody would ever want to steal or copy their product. After all, this is what being free to "enter-the-prize" is all about. Small entrepreneurial partnerships, some of them husbands and wives, continually remind each other of their goals and work together as a unit because it doesn't matter who gets the credit. Bureaucracy and policy manuals are rejected, as are job descriptions. Everybody does everything. Their only "rule" is to talk openly about any problems that may come up. Everyone rows together, just like in the picture on the motivational poster over the photocopier.

This is the place for motivational tapes, in the car, at home and in your Walkman. What you can believe, you can achieve. You can think you can or you can think you can't, either way you'll be right. There would be no mountains if there were no valleys. Attitude is the key. Your attitude determines your altitude. Today is the first day of the rest of your life. Something good is going to happen to you. Begin it now!

I love the Innocence Station. I never want to lose the belief that the universe will indeed take on the shape of my dreams. But no matter how positive my attitude, between here and there the game gets pretty rough.

INDEPENDENCE
The confidence that the business is going to make it corresponds

exactly with one's arrival at the **Independence Station**. This "baby" will live outside the womb! The proud corporate parents can actually take some money out of the company for themselves – a major symbol of independence, I might add. The other major symbol is the advent of referrals, which is proof positive that the tree has taken root. Yes, business is starting to roll, helped largely both by the entrepreneurs' ability to move quickly and creatively, and by the fact that they can play with the costs a little more easily than can their larger, more bureaucratic competitors. Great pride is taken in this. Little guy beats big guy at his own game. Soon gratitude turns into boasting about how unique their business is and indeed, they will be quick to point out, the difference between their product or service and that of their closest competitors is like night and day. Apples and oranges. *Anybody* can see that there simply is no comparison. "We are redefining this business," they will tell you. And who knows, maybe they will do exactly that.

The important point of the Independence Station is that corporate identity is measured by how far removed one is from the rest of the competitive field. Certainly this is understandable and, to some degree, even desirable. Independence, however, is becoming not only impossible, it's not even smart. The computer industry went through this, do you recall? At first, manufacturers made their own equipment in their own way. *Their* plugs. *Their* wiring. *Their* configuration. After trying to be successful independently, several of these firms realized that there was considerable advantage to collaborating on some industry standards, and collaborate they did. All except IBM who, at first, had the attitude that the world should come to them, not the other way around.

Back when I was consulting in and around IBM, the number-one customer complaint was that working with IBM was easy, as long as you did things their way. The truth was that IBM was big and powerful enough to get away with it for a while. While other products were advertised as "IBM compatible," IBM was becoming more "com*bat*-ible," trying desperately to hang on to its identity. But in today's global marketplace, Independence Breeds Misery. Once you get stuck in independence, it is difficult to get out, a lesson IBM learned very painfully. There are many books about the fall of Big Blue and we don't need to reiterate the whole story here. Today's IBM is very different. Their major promotional thrust is about how they can network with all other computer systems out there. Generally, they have become as warm and fuzzy as one can get while still wearing a pocket protector. Their reward has been a bottom line that is envied by everyone.

The relationship between Visa and MasterCard has been quite a different story, almost right from the start. They are fierce competitors and yet saw that success for either one of them could not be achieved through independent action; so they decided to collaborate on many fronts. In Canada, several of the major banks have announced unheard-of collaborative efforts. Rather than each bank maintaining its own incredibly expensive processing center, many banks will share one. Airlines that have no fiscal relationship are declaring themselves "partners," exchanging frequent-flyer miles, cooperating on schedules and so on. More and more we are recognizing that while each corporation needs to find its own identity, there is not much value in overdoing it. Even the big companies know they can't do it alone.

INSTITUTION

There are not many stories of companies moving quickly and smoothly to such heights of cooperation and collaboration. Corporations, like individuals, must sign up for the whole difficult journey or they don't get to go. Consequently, as an organization grows, it is inevitable that it makes a stop at the Institution Station. More business usually requires more people. From the moment that first person is put on payroll, institutional characteristics start to become evident. It begins with the first full-time secretary wanting to know if you would like her to work from 9:00 to 5:00 or 8:30 to 4:30. With the answer we celebrate the birth of the first institutional rule. Not a big deal, I know, but it is the beginning.

Success has a way of bringing on a tidal wave of institutional characteristics. For example, we soon see the rapid emergence of bureaucracy. Instead of everyone simply doing whatever job needs to be done, it is thought wise to divide up responsibility. This is tantamount to having departments, and, of course, there is the traditional philosophy that some*one,* as in singular, has to be in control or else the buck won't know where to stop. So now we have a designated president, which means that everyone else wants a title too. Fortunately, there is software on how to develop a personnel manual. It is a very short step from there to a full-blown policy-and-procedure binder.

There is nothing inherently wrong with any of this unfolding. I am almost convinced that it has to be this way or there would be nothing to frustrate people into the Irritation Station. We cannot forget that behind all of this lies our absolute intolerance of chaos and ambiguity and our fetish for control. The need for power, the hunger of the ego, the fear of losing identity, the loss of free choice, the need to measure anything that moves – all begin to blend into a dangerous but necessary corporate cocktail.

As the bureaucracy takes on a life of its own, its grip on those within it tightens. Like an attack of spiritual claustrophobia, we find it increasingly difficult to breathe, to create, to search for our "whys." Seldom do we feel deep connection with our institutions; instead, we begin to feel used by them. A sense of helpless dependency nibbles at our spirit. The old-timers sit around and lament about how work "used to be fun" and how "we all used to know what was going on because we were all involved in everything." What they are lamenting, of course, is the loss of innocence. The loss of innocence has been a favorite corporate complaint for a very long time. In the Old Testament book of Ecclesiastes, written around 977 B.C., we read this advice: "Do not say, 'Why is it that the former days were better than these?' for it is not from wisdom that you ask about this." People have been talking about the good old days since day two.

We become more and more restless, sometimes moving from one institution to another to see if, perhaps, there is more freedom, contentment and meaning to be found elsewhere. We leave home for our first apartment. We try another church or religion. We switch schools. We change jobs. Get new spouses. And each time we do, we look for our Selves, often to no avail. The restlessness is no longer assuaged by two weeks' vacation, nor is it peculiarly *our* restlessness. Apparently it is shared by many within the same institution, a fact we discover in cafeteria lines and during covert discussions in the parking lot. Restlessness picks up energy through such discussion, each example of perceived corporate foolishness becoming another log on the fire. All of this is for the benefit of the welcome that takes place at the gate to the **Irritation Station**.

IRRITATION

The feeling that we are losing our grip on our own life becomes more and more dominant. In our frantic desire to understand what is happening, and in the absence of any real insight or even simple information, we begin to make up circumstances. Of course there is not much point to starting a rumor unless it is destructive and juicy enough to be worth the retelling. An active and negative rumor mill is one of the primary signs that the organization has entered the Irritation Station. Rumors are the weapon of choice for today's corporate peasants, just like pitchforks and sickles were for the peasants of the French Revolution. They are cheap, easy to use and everybody has one. The rumor campaign has been successful if considerable confusion has been created throughout the organization. This victory can be confirmed by the scheduling of the "all-employee meeting" at which the president will, once and for all, "set the record straight." We've all been here before though, haven't we? Unfortunately, it is usually far too political a pronouncement and must, by law, include the statement,

"No further layoffs are contemplated at this time." We learned earlier how far this political stuff gets us.

These events rarely have a calming influence, which prompts the leadership group to attempt even tighter control over their restless subordinates. Bringing on even more institutional pressure is an interesting strategy, given that it was the institution's stifling tactics that probably brought on the irritation in the first place. Well, "Nip it in the bud," as they say. Once you've had your bud nipped, it becomes clear that there are certain things around the company that you don't talk about – unless you are determined to make an abrupt career choice.

As we all know, what is not expressed verbally will be expressed nonverbally. Nowhere is this more true than at the Irritation Station. Absenteeism is an expression of anger, for example. So are accidents. If you want to measure irritation, these two variables are a good starting point. Quality and service problems are also a popular way for employees to fight against the institution. A mining executive told me the story of how he went, in exasperation, to a group of miners to see if they had any ideas about how to solve a certain problem that was costing the company millions of dollars. That's easy, they said, just do thus and so. "How long have you known about this?" he asked in amazement. "A long time," they replied nonchalantly. "Why haven't you told us before?" my friend continued. "You never asked!" came the obvious reply. Irritated people don't usually participate very well in quality- and service-improvement programs. Ever wonder why there are locks on suggestion boxes? There's nothing in there except some gum wrappers and the occasional erotic suggestion that wouldn't likely win one of the cash prizes.

I remember working for a renowned children's hospital in which morale was as low as I have ever seen it in any kind of organization. You need to appreciate that every nurse, doctor and staff member in a children's hospital has the commitment of a saint to his or her work. These people are a special and wonderful breed. Though they often take on an inhuman amount of pressure, they too have a breaking point. These good folks had reached it. Not being willing to recognize the nature and severity of their anger, the president, in an odd attempt to boost morale, stood at the hospital entrance one Monday morning and handed out "We Care" buttons to the staff. You need no medical expertise to imagine into which of his orifices it was suggested he stuff the entire supply of buttons. He just didn't get it, and it wasn't long before he was gone. Taking an organization through the Irritation Station requires almost supernatural leadership skills. Actually, what it requires is spiritual leadership.

While at the Irritation Station, you will also notice a reduced level of creativity and initiative – even of the sort that carries relatively low risk. You can forget about high-risk initiatives, there is just too much fear throughout the organization. Come to think about it, for the more accomplished and successful employees, it may be apathy more than fear. Why should they bother to go out of their way to help an organization they feel has curtailed their power and freedom of choice? Ever noticed that it's often the good ones who are first to move out? It's not the marginal employees who take "the package"; they are too afraid they won't get another job. Truly talented employees love these windows of opportunity. They'll take the year's salary from you and have a job elsewhere by Wednesday. Or, even better, they will contract themselves back to you at twice the income. I know dozens of people who have done that, and from their perspective, it is an incredible deal. To this day I have never understood the financial logic from the employer's perspective.

We know all too well the many ways in which anger reveals itself in organizational life. I've mentioned some of the more blatant ones and you can add to these other manifestations such as interdepartmental tension or turf wars. Sales against Service. Manufacturing against Design Engineers. Head Office against Branch Office. Finance against Information

Systems. Union against Management. Everybody against Human Resources.

Of course, we can't go on without mentioning that universal favorite, communication. You have not likely ever attended a conference, or even a meeting, where there hasn't been a comment about communication problems. We keep having communication problems because we don't have the insight we need to resolve them. Right now, for instance, your organization has *exactly* the kind of communication it deserves, be it good or bad. Communication is simply the testimony of the degree of unity your organization is experiencing. When an organization has real unity – that is, unity in body, mind and spirit – it does not have a "communication problem." You will recall that the experience of unity is central to being spiritual. In other words, one major characteristic of a spiritually centered organization is that it enjoys and benefits from constant "common-unity-cation."

When an organization is experiencing irritation, it is virtually impossible to have unity. Do you know what irritated organizations that have no unity do? They try to cover up their disunity with instruments of communication. Everything from company newsletters to fireside video messages from the president. From forming an employee advisory council to hiring a public relations officer. From handing out company T-shirts to having a company song contest. From an employee attitude survey to casual Fridays. You name it and it has been tried because we all, angry or not, yearn for unity. Unfortunately, many of these efforts are like trying to paint over a rusty car you want to sell. You might get away with it if you can sell it within 24 hours. Anything longer than that and you have a rusty car again. When you don't have unity, nothing works. When you *do* have unity, everything works! Organizations at the Irritation Station don't have much unity.

I mentioned briefly that it takes spiritual leadership to bring an organization through Irritation. This kind of leadership is all too rare, unfortunately. As noted above, what management usually does is impose even tighter controls backed up by clearly defined rules and policies. Irritation among the employees threatens management's sense of control and consequently their egos. When managers can't power, manage and/or measure their way out of organizational anger, they panic. They are using the only tools they have, the same tools that got them to this exalted position, and now the tools appear useless. And, indeed, they are. The irritation or anger we are discussing is a spiritual, Second World problem that cannot be solved with First World strategies and techniques.

While I have tried to make it clear that this book primarily focuses on "Why?" and only slightly on "How?," it is inappropriate to discuss the Irritation dimension of an organization's spiritual journey without providing practical suggestions on how to lead people through it. The likelihood of an entire organization becoming forever stuck in Irritation is very high and is usually a terminal condition, just as it is on a personal level. Practical actions must, however, be laid on a foundation of understanding. Deep spiritual understanding. Particularly when we are trying to move out of the Irritation Station. When you get the "Why" right, the "How" comes easier. A shift in Spirit must always precede a shift in systems. Consequently, we are best to look for practical solutions from the relative safety of the **Insight Station.**

INSIGHT

Insights do not seem to come in huge tidal waves. They're more like little ripples. Each one is vital and the cumulative effect is immensely powerful. We reach for insights while still in the Irritation experience, so it's a little like trying to crawl out of a tar pit. It is very difficult to do. The anger keeps sticking to us and pulling us back. Sooner or later we grab an insight, assimilate it into our experience and then grab another. Each time we do this, we alter the state of our irritation until it is no more. Like the ocean wearing away a rock. As in our personal experience, corporate irritation is a divine source of energy that is to be used. If you can, be grateful for organizational irritation; it makes changing the situation much easier. Be glad you've been forced to recognize a morale problem; it is going to change your leadership influence for the better. Be glad that the company's departments are fighting overtly rather than covertly because this will lead you to a new and more effective organizational model. Be glad there is an obvious communication problem because it will spur you on to fashion real community in the company. When you get angry at the anger, you are shooting everybody else in the foot and yourself in the head. The troops can't follow you even if they want to because they can't walk and you are no good with a hole in your head. This is your first practical insight. You're welcome.

Having had the insight to accept rather than deny the anger, you can move on. Your best insights will come out of your specific situation and your approach to life. Your insightful view of the corporate inner journey will be *through* the lens of your personal inner journey. All insights are automatically customized to meet the yearnings of the viewer. No one can tell you what *your* insights ought to be, they can only tell you what insights have been precious to them. That is the situation between you and me at this moment. All I can do is tell you, in as practical and clear a manner as possible, what I have discovered about releasing your corporation's soul. For me, these have been important and freeing discoveries. They may disappoint you because they are not as prescriptive as you'd like. Or you may conclude that, obviously, I don't know *your* difficult situation. This, of course, is absolutely true. I have been through lots of forests though I have never been through *your* forest. But I do know what I have experienced with the clients who have honored me by taking me into their life as I have taken them into mine. They have helped me go deeper and I trust that I have helped them do the same. So, I will go as far as I can. It is your job to go the rest of the way. Again, the goal of accumulating insights is to move your organization out of Irritation and on to Integration and unity. If it doesn't make you nervous to put it this way, the real goal is to help you "in-spirit" or inspire your organization, to set it on its spiritual purpose.

There are three major insights that have been confirmed for me over and over in a great variety of organizational settings filled with equally varied challenges. You cannot lead your organization out of Irritation without:

- A significant degree of intimacy in communication, particularly on the part of the senior executive team.
- Organization-wide insight into the company's spiritual purpose.
- The liberation of the workforce.

Intimacy in Communication
First we will look at the level of openness and honesty in communication, particularly within the senior executive team. These are old words that have been damaged with poor usage for a long time. I have come to prefer the word *intimacy*. Intimacy does not refer to your deep dark psychosexual secrets, though that would add some much-needed spark to the meeting, but to your willingness to disclose how you really think and feel as it pertains to your corporate situation. As I listen to you talk and feel your relationship, am I absolutely confident that I am experiencing your very heart and soul? Or will I get the real story whispered out in the hall five minutes after the meeting? You can't imagine how many times someone has suggested to me, during a break in the meeting, that "no one is telling the truth." If you have an emotional and spiritual relationship with your team members, rather than one stalled on political and intellectual levels, I would consider your communication to be "intimate."

At the other end of the communication continuum I use the word *remote*. This is the political, game-playing, manipulative, non-disclosing and opportunistic behavior that many of us have witnessed for years.

If we give a value of 1 to very remote dialogue, and 10 to very intimate dialogue, we can place a mark where we feel personally comfortable most of the time. We'll slide up or down a little depending on the situation, but for most of us it doesn't vary that much. My observation is that male executives tend to hover around 3, with exceptions both up and down. When they meet as a group, the number drops to about 1.5. Must be a guy thing. Female executives, who are destined to become the saviors of many male-dominated teams, usually behave at a higher level, though not as intimately as you might think. So here is the problem. No executive team will lead an organization out of Irritation if their level of connection is somewhere on the remote side of 3. Just can't be done. Anger is a very intimate emotion and it must be engaged intimately.

At one of these "all-employee meetings," I have seen people tearfully express the workload stress they were experiencing since the company's downsizing. Anyone with even the lowest level of sensitivity could feel the anger in that room. The executive responding to all this said only that they "hoped to do a workload analysis sometime this year" and went on to the next question. No intimate engagement whatsoever. Not even eye contact. I'll bet money that his wife and children have experienced this same nonengagement a million times. Without a miracle, he won't be leading his organization out of anger and, even more sadly, he won't be able to lead his family out of it either.

With the serious and complex issues ripping through organizations today, we cannot afford remote, poker-faced, close-to-the-vest levels of connection. Start reaching out from your heart and soul, and continue to do so even though it may make some of your colleagues nervous. We are wrestling daily with level-10 issues and they require level-10 dialogue. Some of my clients actually announce "Level 10" meetings. That means you participate leading with your heart and soul or don't bother to come at all.

Intimacy also means that the corporate secrets have to be exposed. This can be scary territory. One common secret is that an inner circle of the executive team knows something that the others do not. Sometimes that is appropriate, but many times it is not; it prevents unity and breeds anger. The only way past this is to talk openly about how the whole group should handle sensitive information and why it is that the whole group isn't trusted.

Another issue could be that there has been long-standing tension between two team members that never gets discussed openly. When these two start to go at it, the others just look heavenward and roll their eyes. You can fill in the names here, can't you? No more! Have a "Level 10" talk with the whole group about how this power/ego thing is damaging the unity of the team and its ability to lead the organization.

Yet another difficult corporate secret to expose is what people in the organization think about the senior executive team, including team members themselves. The president and other executives need good team feedback about the way their behavior is strengthening or hindering team leadership and unity. But they rarely get it or give it to one another. We may be talking "Level 12" here, but I've seen it done many times and with very unifying results.

I am a strong advocate for team-performance reviews rather than individualized ones. What I like to see is the whole executive team sitting down for a day to reflect on the quality of their "team-ness" and to give each other feedback on their performance within the team. The president might go first, asking her colleagues how she is doing as leader of the team. How has she been successful in providing inspiration and purpose? Are there any ways in which she may be hindering the unity and influence of the team? Are there ways she could more fully provide spiritual leadership to this team and to the organization as a whole? Of course, there is no point to doing this if she is not going to get intimate answers. (The next chapter discusses what contributions senior leaders should be making to their team and how they might allocate their time.) Each member of the team would follow in turn. This is difficult the first time and you should probably employ a spiritually tuned-in facilitator who understands what you are trying to do. I also strongly advise that you **not** take this approach if there are major issues dividing the group. Resolve those first to the point where you have at least the semblance of unity. After that, this approach very quickly becomes a wonderfully unifying and freeing experience. Soon it will just happen naturally whenever the group feels it is needed. This goes far beyond the anonymously contributed 360-degree evaluation (where you get feedback from people above, around and below you in the organization) that is so much in vogue right now. There is no way in which anonymous feedback can contribute to team unity. It is not as "safe" as you might think.

Spiritual Purpose
The second insight that seems characteristic of organizations intent on their spiritual journey has to do with the struggle to identify spiritual purpose – the "Grand Why." Mission and vision statements have almost always given me a sense of sadness because they are written without insight and, consequently, have the spiritual depth of a dime. How many employees in your company have the corporate mission statement taped to their refrigerator at home because it excites their soul into action on Monday morning? One of the reasons that people are irritated and angry is that their lives aren't going anywhere. There is no Grand Why to their day. It's not a lot of fun to tread water year after year waiting for the great Retirement Day when you can finally get out of the pool only to spend your final years running on the spot. Purposeless, passionless people cannot build purposeful, passionate organizations or purposeful, passionate social communities. Henry Ford said, "No one is apathetic except those in pursuit of someone else's objectives." Odd quote coming from the inventor of the dehumanizing assembly line, but a truth nevertheless. For an organization to move beyond the Irritation Station, it requires the insight to see its ultimate spiritual purpose.

Here are a few of my favorite nonspiritual "missions." *"We want to be the preferred supplier in our chosen marketplace."* No kidding. *"Our mission is to provide the best possible service, within available resources, to every customer."* Boy, that's reaching for the stars, isn't it? The central line in another mission statement reads, " . . . *to return to the shareholder 15% return on equity."* I remember it well because this company had carved it on little pieces of granite that they gave to each staff member just to show them how flexible they were going to be. I asked them if that was really the purpose of their work, because if it was, they should go into porno films and make 800 percent ROE. And the team meetings are more interesting. You've seen them – to be the biggest, to be the best, the leading, the number one and so on. The lowest common denominator is that they are all self-seeking and fall short of answering "Why?"

Here is another insight for you. A statement of spiritual purpose will never contain bottom-line or positioning references. Save those figures and measurements for your goals and objectives, but don't put them in your mission or vision statement. How would you feel if, on the wall of your family doctor's office, you read this mission statement: " . . . *to reach a million dollars in patient billings."* Wouldn't that make you a little uneasy? And if, as the doctor's customer you don't like it, what makes you think your customers are going to react to your numbers-focused mission statement any differently?

I worked with a very successful drug company making a product that wonderfully cures a serious heart problem. At the annual conference, I listened as the new president told of his dream of hitting a hundred million dollars in sales by the year 2000. This was the new vision! As he sat down to the appropriate applause from his sales force, my heart felt sad. The issue for me was not about money and profit; I'd love to see them make *two* hundred million. It was spiritual purpose that was missing. As I took my turn on the stage, I asked how many lives would be saved, based on average consumption, if indeed they were to sell a hundred million dollars' worth of their wonderful product. It seemed as though they had never been asked that before and they huddled quickly to discuss it. I forget the real figure, but let's imagine that it was 150,000 people. Try this on as a mission, I suggested, *"By the year 2000, we will have saved an additional 150,000 human lives."* Now you tell me, which mission gives you a Grand Why? Which mission would make you eager to get to work on Monday morning? Which mission would make your grandchildren proud of you?

Here is another example that I think is rather noble. *"Our mission is to find meaning in our work and to help our members experience joy, satisfaction, happiness and celebration."* That didn't come from a golf club, it came from one local of the International Brotherhood of Electrical Workers. Doesn't exactly sound like a union mission statement, does it? To be honest, before I met these incredible people, I thought that leaders of strong unions like the IBEW would rather sit around and guess where Jimmy Hoffa is buried.

I cannot fully remember one of the most moving mission statements I have ever heard. It came at the tail end of a television documentary on a health clinic run by a few retired doctors in a poor rural region of the United States. It went something like this: *"Our mission is to bring hope and health to every person in our region without regard to income or race, and perhaps in the process, heal ourselves."* The impact may be diluted by my effort to recall the statement, but I remember not even paying attention to the television while this documentary was on until this old white-haired doctor began to recite, with tears in his voice, his mission statement. I just stood still in front of the television as if I were standing on holy ground listening to a burning bush. You knew beyond a shadow of a doubt that this man's purpose was Holy. Now *that's* the impact a mission statement should have!

The other characteristic of a truly spiritual purpose is that it literally lifts you into action. My favorite example comes from a strategic planning experience with the Solicitor General's Department of the government of Canada. They are one of the agencies responsible for law and order across the country. Their mission was so simple compared to the incredibly complex discussions that produced it. *"To make Canada the safest country in the world."* My reaction in hearing them proudly present their spiritual purpose was to ask how I could help. I wanted to help them fulfill this mission because I have kids. I see everywhere the posters of missing children and try to imagine what that must be like for a parent. Thousands of children across North America are battered, if not murdered, every year. International pedophile rings are being uncovered. Parents can barely go shopping anymore without worrying that someone will snatch their baby if they look away for a second. This is not the way life should be lived. If my Solicitor General friends were going to try to make Canada the safest country in the world by keeping these predators off the streets, I was determined to do everything I could to help them!

To be absolutely honest with you, there is a small cynical side of me that wonders if something as powerfully simple as "To make Canada the safest country in the world" could ever last in a government bureaucracy. Almost inevitably it will become a 56-page document with seven layers of sub-paragraphs in both official languages. I hope not.

Reading over some of these great mission statements reminded me of another insight. Many statements focus on a benefit for the *company* itself – "Make our shareholders rich!" "Make us your choice!" – and so on. You can't do that and still reflect a spiritual calling. Try having your mission or vision focus *on the people your company wants to serve.* Have the mission benefit the customer. If you look after the *giving*, the *receiving* will look after itself. That seems to be a spiritual law. When your customers want you to be as successful in fulfilling your mission as you want to be, you just can't lose.

Want to lift your organization out of anger? Help people find a spiritual purpose to their work. A grand transcendent Why that calls them to action with such power that they couldn't stay in their seats even if they wanted to.

Let me briefly tell you about my "Two Whys Theory" and then suggest a practical assignment for your management team. "Why?" is the most important question in life. Little tiny children show us that this is so. Right after learning to say "Mummy" and "Daddy," every child in every culture starts asking "Why?" It's as natural as breathing and eating. Who do you suppose taught the child to ask "why?" Parents didn't, that's for sure. There is the constant "why?" "why?" "why?" culminating with the ultimate parental insight, "Because that's just the way it is!" I doubt that any mother has leaned over the crib and cooed to her child "Can you say why? That's it – why."

I know who taught every child this most important of questions. God did. Frankly, I think it was God's sense of humor. God whispers to the baby in the womb, "As soon as you can after you're born, start asking, 'Why?' – it drives them crazy!" The serious point here is that children are born seeking insight and integration. Children are born spiritually aware. Unfortunately, the various institutions in the child's life soon let them know that it is not appropriate to ask "Why?" because the question is threatening to those in authority, especially when they don't have an answer.

As a corporate spiritual leader you must elevate and revere the question "Why?" Encourage everyone at every level to ask it. Instead of a Suggestion Program have a Why Program. Put up Why Boxes with no locks on them. "Why?" is the door to quality, to creative problem solving and to setting the organization's sights on what it is really meant to accomplish. This is what makes the *yearning* organization. "Yearning" starts with a "Why?" When we get the "*why*" right, the "*earning*" looks after itself. Corporate spiritual leaders know this, and they also know that the yearning never stops.

Here is the assignment. I have found that most mission statements fall two "whys" short of stating the spiritual purpose of the organization. At your next management meeting, read your mission or vision statement out loud and then ask yourselves, "Why?" "*Our mission is to be the leading firm in the Midwest.*" Why? Let the group wrestle with the answer to that question until they have a new, simple and succinct statement. In relation to that new statement, ask the group "Why?" one more time. Again, let them wrestle with it until they find a purpose that ignites their corporate soul. Now, if your current mission statement is all about money and profit, you are probably about five "whys" short of a spiritual purpose, so you'd better take the group away for the weekend. You'll need the time.

Liberation of the Workforce

There is a third major insight about what is required to move out of the **Irritation Station**. This has to do with the liberation of the workforce. Some readers will feel that I have painted organizations with a very negative brush. Even calling them "institutions" smacks of the evil psychiatric hospital hidden behind overgrown vines on top of the hill, whence no one has ever been seen to leave alive. It is not my intention to organization-bash because that only bruises the soul. At the same time, I'll do anything I can to stir the corporate soul into an awareness of itself and subsequently into changing our world. I can personally take you to companies that have found their soul. I can introduce you to spiritual corporate leaders or, even better, to corporate spiritual leaders, and will do so at the end of this book. (I prefer the term "corporate spiritual leader" because it has a stronger implication that the leader is affecting the soul of the organization in a significant way.)

I've come to the conclusion that organizations today are particularly in need of corporate spiritual leaders. There are organizations who have learned the awesome power of community. If I have sounded critical and harsh, it is because by far the majority of corporate institutions have imprisoned their people's minds, hearts and souls, and sometimes they don't even know it. There is an amazing abundance of resources available within our organizations, but these minds, hearts and souls are all still in boxes, mostly unused. I agree with those who estimate that most employees withhold about two-thirds of what they could contribute to their employer. There are gifts and talents. Skills and experiences. Information and ideas. A virtual warehouse containing the world that has yet to be created. So who has the key?

You do. I do.

Liberation requires free choice. Choice even at the risk of chaos. In the Biblical account of creation, God, after perfectly creating the world and all living things, gave Adam and Eve a choice. The very first thing human beings were given was choice. Choice was the starting block for life in an ideal world and it is still the starting block for life in a less than ideal world. Adam and Eve could be obedient and avoid the forbidden fruit, or they could go ahead and eat it. It was up to them. You know the story and we can only fantasize what might have happened had they made a different choice. Since then it seems people in authority have been hesitant and even afraid to give people choices. The fear is that people, free to make their own choices, just might send us further into chaos. The possibility that their choices might send us back to Eden does not seem to be given much credence.

When we recognize that people have choice, we also recognize that they have power. The only people who have any real power are those who are making choices. Everyone else is subservient and impotent. And they have to be real, significant and consequential choices. Making suggestions, giving advice and offering recommendations will not do. Those kinds of contributions are valuable but they do not carry the type of power and affirmation of our humanness that we are talking about. It is my opinion that in order to be fully human, every person needs a significant aspect of their life in which *they* get to make choices.

Think of life as one huge blank canvas. What I am saying is that we each, young or old, educated or illiterate, executive or staff, need to have our *own* piece of that canvas on which we can paint our *own* picture. Furthermore, a significant portion of that blank piece of canvas needs to be in the context of work. If people have a blank canvas to paint on at home and a paint-by-number set at work, guess where their passion is going to be.

The location and visibility of each person's portion of blank canvas will vary with the level of responsibility, experience, talent, training and so on. Maybe the chairperson of the board gets to paint the sky and the new mail clerk gets to paint a tiny flower in the bottom right-hand corner. Each is given the opportunity to express their soul and it is in the choosing of the expression that each finds Life. Both sky and flower contribute to making the painting a masterpiece.

When you give people choice, you give them power. When you give them power, you give them freedom. When you give them freedom, you give them back their individuality and their life. When they get their life back, they will choose to find unity and purpose. This is a natural human yearning and a requirement of the spiritually centered organization.

There are so many ways in which institutions take away choice unnecessarily. Like overbearing and overprotective parents who think they are helping their child by making choices for them, control-oriented corporate leaders generally have no idea of the damage their dependency-inducing management style is inflicting on the spirit of their people.

Here is a simple but good example. I arrived quite late at the airport, I forget which one now, anticipating an interesting conference at that city's major hospital the next morning. To my surprise and delight, the president of the hospital met me at the airport in order to drive me to the hotel. It's late, I'm tired and I am so grateful. Even so, I wondered what the real motivation was behind this kind act. As we got into the city, my host said, "Ian, I wanted an opportunity to describe to you our management style at the hospital." Here comes the real agenda, I thought to myself. "We have an extremely participative style of management," he continued, "and we believe in empowering our people." As an aside, I've got to tell you that just once in my life I'd like to run into someone who is straight enough to say, "I'm a dictator, I like being a dictator and I'm proud of being a dictator." I swear to you if Attila the Hun were alive today, he'd claim to be participative and empowering. Anyway, back to my participative and empowering host.

"Just this week," he said by way of example, "our housekeeping staff needed to order new uniforms. So I gave the catalog to their committee and told them to pick out any three uniforms they liked, any three at all. Then they were asked to submit their selections back to my executive committee and we chose one of the three and ordered it."

This was his example of participation and empowerment. When you read the story, the point is so obvious. Who kept the power? He had taken these people to the point of real and significant choice and then snatched the choice away from them just in case they thought they could actually and fully express themselves. There was no power in their recommendation and frankly it would have been kinder to have made the choice himself in the first place rather than go through with the pretense.

What possible harm could there have been in his saying to these good, hardworking and poorly recognized people, "I am very proud of the vital work you do in this hospital. Without you, we would have to close our doors, and in my books that makes you extremely important. Your uniforms are a symbol of that importance. Your uniforms are an expression of your pride and professionalism. They are part of your identity in this hospital. Here is the newest catalog of uniforms; you choose which one best suits you and go ahead and order the supplies you need. When you get them, we'll mark the occasion with a celebration in the cafeteria because I want all our staff to know how much confidence I place in you." What could possibly go wrong with such an approach? Would patients die? Would the hospital go broke? Would the president not like the color? What?

Another example: I was sitting in the office of an incredible woman who had gone from having nothing to owning a small but very successful chain of hotels. Someone from Human Resources interrupted to ask her to come and decide which of several flip charts she would like to order for their training room. There they were, all set up in the corridor for her to inspect and choose. Flip charts! Why was she making the choice about flip charts? Surely that piece of the blank canvas belonged to the training person.

I can hear some readers thinking that this kind of hands-on control is how she went from nothing to a multimillionaire. True enough. Remember, though, we are talking about what insights are required if one is going to lead an organization out of anger or Irritation to Integration, *not* about how you can make record profits. If that is all you want to do, you've been in the wrong book for some time. Making all the choices yourself may enable you to build a huge business empire, but it will be an angry empire. Does anyone remember Leona Helmsley? People who do not get to make real choices sooner or later become angry people because their life has been taken away from them. Spiritual leaders build successful people who build successful businesses.

These are very minor examples perhaps, but each piece of blank canvas was very important to somebody. The point is, if we cannot give people choices in matters like these, we will never liberate them to make even more consequential ones.

Some last comments on the fear of people running all over the place, making unwise choices and creating havoc and chaos in your business. I have to admit that there are a few people who distrust institutions so much they will find a way to create havoc no matter how much control you try to exert over them. These people are stuck in either Independence or Irritation and probably a little of both. One of the remnants of my Innocence experience is the theory that everyone can be loved out of their anger. For the most part, I still believe that. But, like you, I've met people who are so angry they almost cause me to abandon that belief. Every reader will have a story about the time they trusted someone to make a choice only to regret it. The answer to these rare occasions is not to get paranoid and start setting up controls over everybody you meet. That's how we got most of our corporate rules and policies: one person did something stupid, someone in the organization panicked and the next thing we knew we had a new rule to control everybody else from now to eternity. As Pat Pocock, one of the clinical leaders at St. Joseph's Hospital in London, Ontario, says: "Policies! They're just scar tissue over an error!" Organizations can heal without scars if they let in the fresh air of freedom.

In the literature on chaos theory, we learn that chaos is essential to the functioning of life. One purpose of chaos is to create a spiritual vacuum that draws your Self into it. When everything is in order, controlled by an external authority and governed by rules, there is no need for the Self. You walk into a room and find a large number of pieces of art piled up in the middle of the floor. Your job is to arrange the art around the room so that others can appreciate the beauty of these creations. The initial chaos of the pile of art is, in fact, what allows you to express your Self in the creation of the display. If all the pieces were nailed to the wall in an orderly fashion, we wouldn't need you at all, regardless of what talent and giftedness you might have. Spiritually-centered organizations are not afraid of a little chaos.

But how then do we bring free choices into harmony and alignment? Might the mail clerk, mentioned earlier, paint a skull and crossbones instead of a flower on his blank piece of canvas? Not if the mail clerk believes in the picture. You know by now that I believe everyone wants to be part of something meaningful, to make contributions of significance. Significance means they know where their contribution fits, how it relates to other contributions, and have a humble awareness that the painting simply would not be the same without them. It is this desire and yearning that draws people into alignment. Painting the picture becomes a transcendent and divine purpose for both mail clerk and board chairperson alike. Each is willing to sacrifice and do what it takes to fulfill their richly imagined future.

The other thing leaders shouldn't forget is that people need tools through which to exercise their contribution. It is not fair to simply fling blank canvas in front of people and order them to paint. They'll need equipment, some practice time and probably some art lessons. If you don't mind my swiping a truth from another metaphor, "Teach them how to paint, and they will paint for a lifetime."

INTEGRATION

It is the accumulation of *your* insights in the context of *your* corporation that will lead you out of irritation and on to **Integration**. This is the Station of alignment. The Station of passionate purpose. The Station where you just know that what you are doing as a corporation is right. Defeats and setbacks are handled with the same depth of understanding as victories and opportunities. Your organization will never have been so unified and at the same time so flexible. You've learned that most organizational inflexibility is caused by people who have power and don't want to give it up. Consequently, your management team has also learned that if they truly want more power than they've ever had before, they must first give up power to the people. The people, in turn, will gift management with their devotion, energy, creativity and, yes, even love. They do so because they have the choice to do so. Employees will speak daily of the corporate spiritual purpose as though they were talking about the purpose of their own lives. This is because they recognize that it is *through* the fulfillment of the corporate purpose that they are able to fulfill their life purpose.

Everywhere you look, there will be symbols and expressions of unity. From job titles and job descriptions to the composition of committees. From performance evaluation to compensation systems. From where people get to park to where they eat lunch. From how you deal with gender to ease of access for physically challenged people. From employees' access to the boss, to the boss's access to employees.

Unshakable trust will enable people to make choices and to take creative and wise risks, always in the performance of their Grand Why. In doing so, the organization will operate swiftly and sensitively with minimum controls. Every activity will be relevant to the spiritual vision and values that provide the foundation of the corporation. You will no longer sit around having repeated conversations about how you can't be all things to all people, because you won't be rethinking your values and purpose every time an apparent opportunity comes up. Every expenditure of time, energy, space and money will be made with your eyes fixed on the mountaintop. Surrounded by your values and with your goal sharply in focus, you will make decisions with faith and courage.

In the integrated company, there is a major interest by the corporation and its leadership in the health and strength of the families it affects. It does much more for its families than provide some form of employee assistance, activated when it is probably too late to help. It recognizes that only healthy and whole people can continue to build a healthy and whole company. A corporate spiritual leader whom I most admire is Mike Stephen, chairman of Aetna International, Inc. He makes it a point to tell every employee that under no circumstances are they to put the company ahead of their family. Another company I heard about in England turns off the power every night at 6:00. The message is that, "We, as your employer, cannot make you spend time with your family, but you will be unable to use work as a reason not to be home." Contrast that with the case of one manager, a single mother, who got an emergency call that her teenage daughter had just run away. The call came just as she was to go into a management meeting. So frightened by what the company might do if she wasn't there, she stayed for the meeting though her heart was wrenched, and then went home to try to sort out the situation. You can blame her for her lack of courage if you wish, and to a degree you have a point. But I am telling you, in many, many organizations across this continent, the unwritten but often enforced policy is: the success of this company comes before the success of your family. A spiritually integrated company is one where the employee's spouse and children love the company as much as they do.

Does all of this sound like a little much? Can there be a corporate heaven on earth? Can we return to a corporate Eden through our choices? Or are we so far removed from such ideals we cannot help but react with cynicism and disbelief? In more than 26 years of consulting to organizations around the world, I have seen enough evidence to believe that the truly spiritual, integrated organization is possible. We do not arrive at this Station all at once. We arrive piece by piece. Insight after insight. We cannot plan to arrive there by a certain date. More likely is the scenario where part of our corporate life is at the Irritation Station, part is stuck at the Institutional Station and, hopefully, a large part is celebrating peace and joy at the Integration Station.

Ever participate in one of those outdoor team-building exercises – the kind where you lower your boss over a cliff by a rope, thus building trust within the team? It seldom seems to cross anybody's mind that you also have this thing against being charged with murder, but that is another issue entirely. One of these executive games is a terrific metaphor for our corporate inner journey. All the participants are on one side of a marked-off space and they have to get to the other side by setting up various bridges with planks and overturned buckets. Part of the equipment they need is on the far side, which means they have to find a way to get someone over to the other side to bring back what is needed (insights). Back and forth they go, getting one person over at a time. Occasionally, one who has made it over will have to come back to help one of her teammates. At other times several will become stranded on one of the buckets and they can only cling to each other while others look for the insight on how to get them unstuck. Sometimes there is one member of the team who considers himself God's gift to engineering and, when the team does not respond obediently to his direction, shows signs of irritation. More often than not, this irritation delights the others who are more playful. Wouldn't it be terrific if we could learn to laugh instead of become angry? Finally, there is always, even from the most sophisticated executives, great cheering when the whole group makes it over to the other side and they experience the joy of integration.

See it or not, you and your company are being drawn toward this place. This is the intended purpose of your corporate life together. If you are willing to take the inner journey, to confront your shudderings and to experience the wonderful freedom of the other side, you will have reestablished a purposeful flow to that yearning spirit already within you. Your company will manifest the unifying spirit of God, and there is nothing more powerful in the marketplace.

Scientist and philosopher Gary Zukav writes about authentic power, as distinct from the external power most of us have witnessed. "External power," he says, "has produced our survival-of-the-fittest understanding of evolution, generated conflict between lovers, communities, and superpowers, and brought us to the edge of destruction." In his enlightening book *The Seat of the Soul,* Zukav shares his insight that:

When we align our thoughts,
emotions, and actions with the
highest part of ourselves, we are
filled with enthusiasm, purpose and meaning.
Life is rich and full.
We have no thoughts of bitterness.
We have no memory of fear.
We are joyously and intimately engaged with our world.
This is the evidence of authentic power.

EIGHT

The Beloved Leader

◆ ◆ ◆ ◆

How does one get to be-loved as a corporate leader today? For that matter, do you think many of our leaders care if they are loved by the people they lead? We have all heard the executive who claims that he doesn't care if the employees like him as long as they respect him. Frankly, I don't believe a word of it. My suspicion is that many people who talk like this do so because they are afraid that, in fact, their employees *won't* like them. Best defense is a good offense, they always say.

Imagine at your funeral, all your old employees are standing around reminiscing about the time you increased market share by seven points. Tears come to their eyes as they recall the quarter you finally achieved your goal of 23 percent ROE. Or how about that time you told the executive team that if they couldn't get costs under control, you'd find somebody who could. That was a magic moment. Well, as long as they respected you, that's all that counts. And at your funeral, they all pay their *last* respects, never to do it again.

Doesn't exactly feel right, does it? Chances are, you are not big on politically driven funerals, unless of course you've had a politically driven life. Most of us would like to be remembered for something a little deeper than our profit margins. We want our memory to be loved by those we led, just as our life and leadership were loved while we were alive.

I remember being in a plush corporate waiting room, carpet that came up to my ankles and woodwork that I dared not touch. Around the walls were ornately framed oil paintings of past chairmen. All male. All very austere. Not a single smile in the lot. A gallery of the dead chairmen's society. Shiny brass plates gave their names (in true corporate fashion, only an initial for their first name) followed by the dates during which they had ruled. I went from one to the next, saying a silent hello to "D." and then "H." On to two "J.'s" and a cigar-smoking "M." Though I didn't even have a name to call them, I asked each one if they had been loved. I wanted them to have been loved, even though their pictures looked anything but loving. I wanted there to be a grandchild somewhere who could tell me about how much she'd loved her grandfather for giving her the courage to be herself. I wanted to find the employee who'd loved his old boss for enabling him to make choices that were good for his family *and* his career. Maybe there was even a customer who'd loved him for his integrity and faithfulness through tough times. As I was called into my meeting and out of my fantasy, I knew in my heart that not all of them had been loved. And I thought, how sad. There they hung, in a place where nobody knows their name.

Some people, of course, feel that if we were actually to experience being beloved in the corporate world, it would be impossible to make the tough decisions. How do you lay off someone who loves you as their leader? How do you tell someone who loves you that they are not meeting performance expectations? Of course these decisions are difficult, if not heart-wrenching. But sometimes these things have to be done and, I suggest, they can be done in a growth-inducing and loving way. It is a risky metaphor in this case, but parenting is probably the best proof that it is humanly possible to love, guide and make hard decisions all at the same time. There may be parallels between corporate leaders and parents because parenting should be a form of leadership; however, I don't believe corporate leadership should be at all "parental."

There are hundreds of definitions of leadership and I have no inclination to go into them here. For starters, pick up any book by Dr. Warren Bennis and you'll have all the descriptions you need. While I have forgotten where I read it, my favorite definition is actually a comparison of management and leadership: *Managers operate on the physical or material resources of an organization, while leaders operate on the spiritual.* Because we are exploring the concept of corporate spirituality and the function of a corporate spiritual leader, this definition seems particularly relevant. We have to ask the simple and blunt question, "What do beloved spiritual leaders do?" We might even want to know what they look like. Surely they moan on Monday morning as their radio alarm wakes them. Surely they shower like the rest of us and check for hair loss in the steamy mirror. They put on pants or panty hose one leg at a time and hardly any of them wear orange robes. It is not likely that they have yet learned to beam themselves into work and they too occasionally bang their steering wheel in frustration at the traffic. So what's so different about spiritual leaders?

For me the difference can be found in:
1. the process through which they are able to influence their organization;
2. the nature and quality of their relationships; and
3. their sense of Self.

What I feel spiritual leaders should be doing with their time is described next, followed by some thoughts that blend points two and three.

If the purpose of real leadership is to take hold of the organization by its very soul and take it to a place where it has never been before, why do so many leaders spend most of their time mucking around in yesterday's problems and issues? Who is looking at tomorrow? Leadership is relevant only to the future. You cannot *lead* last month, you can only *manage* the consequences of last month's activities. Picture this: We are all on our corporate bus, most of us scrambling around at the back trying to fix last month's problems, looking out the rear window at what has already happened. The prospect of just getting caught up with yesterday seems like a far-fetched dream. We lift our heads up out of the mess long enough to get a glimpse of our president who is also looking out the rear window. She is trying to fix yesterday too. "Who is driving the bus?" we exclaim in alarm. Unfortunately, in many organizations, no one is. It's like the true story of the person driving a new mobile home who put the vehicle on cruise control and went to the back to make some coffee. No wonder we keep having accidents. No wonder we don't feel we are getting anywhere. No wonder we keep doing the same stuff over and over again.

Every now and then, prompted by the excitement of a new management fad, our most senior executives go to the front of the bus to try to get something new happening. Initially there is great promise until we realize that, even though they are in the driver's seat, they are spending most of their time looking in the rearview mirror, just in case someone is doing something outside of corporate policy.

Here is what I think spiritual leaders should be doing with their time. The formula to remember is **30/30/20/20**.

Brain Trust
Thirty percent of their time should be spent on what can be titled Brain Trust activities. Like thinking. When do you really have time just to think? Not *do* anything or *fix* something, just think. Ironically, the more senior in responsibility you become, the less time there is to think, to let your intuitive powers become an active part of your leadership skill-set. The expectation is that, because of experience, you should just *know* and not have to think or reflect. We don't stop to consider

that what you know, you learned out of yesterday's experience. Thinking, in this context, is what bridges the organization into tomorrow. Not many organizations expect people to set aside time devoted to thinking.

Reading is another of the brain trust activities. You won't find this in many job descriptions either. Many of us have wonderful libraries and, while we haven't read many of the books, we feel smarter just knowing they are there. Thank goodness I fly so much because that seems to be the only time I get any concentrated reading done. The other thing I've realized is that our reading can become very narrow, limited to our own profession or industry. Broaden the scope of your reading. Try out some of the books mentioned in the back of this one. Read the magazines your clients and customers read. In particular, read the biographies and autobiographies of great spiritual leaders. Start with books about Christ, Gandhi, King, Jr. and Lincoln. Don't hesitate to read books that stretch or even bother you. Get out of that intellectual comfort zone. Christians should be brave and read the writings of Joseph Smith, Mohammed and Baha'u'llah. Non-Christians might just try the Bible on for size.

It won't get me any reading credits, but Georgia and I went to see *Timothy Leary's Dead,* a film produced by Paul Davids and Todd Easton Mills. Frankly, this would not usually be our "first choice" for a movie, but you don't have to be an advocate of LSD to be shaken into new ways of thinking by that movie. We had the opportunity to sit and talk with Davids and Mills for a while and had a fascinating discussion that led us into all kinds of explorations. They didn't make that movie because they are flower children frozen in time. These guys are as white-collar as you can get. They made it because Leary shook up the establishment and made people think and his story deserves to be told.

Some other brain trust ideas. Try doing some research for yourself as a change from reading somebody else's research. It will change how you think. Spend time with your team members in chaotic and freewheeling "What if?" sessions designed to create new business ideas.

Based on a 50-hour work week, 30 percent works out to be 15 hours. Three hours *a day* developing your thinking and intuitive powers! Some readers will, right at this point, discard my 30/30/20/20 formula as totally unworkable. They want to get to the action phase as fast as they can. Their time is far too valuable to be spent thinking and reflecting. But spiritual leaders have very open, active, creative and constantly expanding minds. Recently I noticed a sign in front of a church that read, "Christ came to take away our sins, not our minds." Point made.

Communication

The second 30 percent of the spiritual leader's time is to be spent ensuring internal and external communication. This is an extremely important function. Central to our definition of "spiritual" is the notion of unity. Communication is the testimony of that unity. So when the spiritual leader goes about ensuring that messages are being heard, that people know what is going on, that they have the information they need to make wise choices and that they know how their efforts are contributing to the functioning of the whole, he is creating spirit and unity. When he visits the shipping department, he brings news from sales. When he visits administration, he brings news from production. He may bring news of struggle or news of triumph. Either way, the spiritual message is "We are one! We are one! We are one!"

It is much the same message externally. With confidence and in truth, the leader can tell the customer that the company is unified behind their needs. Again the cry is, "We are one with you!" Connecting the corporation to the community around it also falls into the portfolio of the spiritual leader. The story that needs to be told over and over again in schools and social-service clubs, as well as in the business community, is the story of why your corporation does what it does. Talk about its higher calling. Talk about the spirit and unity within your corporate family. Talk about why you are proud to be a part of it. These are not politically motivated speeches in which you tell the community how lucky it is to have you because you are the second largest employer and pay huge tax bills. These are speeches of humility, gratitude and hope that call for unity in the community. Your company is the first to congratulate the local high-school team for winning the championship. Should disaster hit, it is your employees who are first on the scene to help. We are our community's keeper and unity can overcome anything.

A few years ago, we all went through the MBWA phase as though it were an incredible breakthrough in management thinking. Management By Walking Around. Actually letting the troops see their leader. Thus, dutifully, the human resources director, as the warm and sensitive member of the executive committee, would try to get the president to walk through the building on the third Friday of every month. Out he would be led, awkwardly pressing some flesh, wondering how he could get back to the sanctuary of his office to make his 10:00 call without hurting anybody's feelings. For many it was, and maybe still is, a political rather than a spiritual exercise. Little engagement with the hearts of the people. "Keep up the good work," can get a little tiresome as an empty refrain, especially if one isn't sure what work is actually being done. It still amazes me that in some companies a visit by the senior executive arouses fear, the tribal drums beating out the warning, "He's coming, he's coming." When you see that reaction from the workforce, you know that beloved and spiritual leadership does not exist, at least not at the top.

So here are another three hours a day taken up with carrying the flag of unity. Along with unity comes faith, trust and hope. I have seen and heard my leader; I know we will get through this downturn in sales. I have seen and heard my leader; I know our purpose is good and that we are on the right track. I have seen and heard my leader; I know that she understands and cares about what I am going through. Think of the captain communicating with the passengers over the airplane's public-address system. He gives us his name and tells us there is another leader right beside him. We learn his name too. His confident and steady voice tells us about our progress, where we are in relation to our goal and when we can expect to arrive. Occasionally he points out things that we should see during the journey, things we would never have noticed without him. We even learn what it will be like when we get to our destination. If rough times are ahead, we usually hear about it before we actually experience it. He tells us how to be safe during turbulent times and lets us know when it's over. Sometimes he comes through the cabin to look at the people who trust him so. Then at the end of the journey, he thanks us for letting him lead and hopes that we'll give him that pleasure again sometime. Not a bad model to follow.

The most poignant description of this aspect of spiritual leadership that I have ever read comes from Max DePree in his book *Leadership Jazz*. DePree was the CEO of Herman Miller, the furniture maker that was named one of *Fortune* magazine's ten "best managed" and "most innovative" companies. He tells about his granddaughter Zoe, born so premature that there was only a 5 to 10 percent chance of her living even three days. Because Zoe's father was not part of the scene, Mr. DePree became a surrogate father. One day while visiting Zoe, a nurse told Mr. DePree to "rub her body, her legs and arms with the tip of your finger. While you're caressing her," she instructed, "you should tell her over and over how much you love her because she has to be able to connect your voice to your touch."

"At the core of becoming a leader," DePree concluded insightfully, "is the need always to connect one's voice and one's touch." Corporations, if they are to survive, desperately need to hear their leader's voice and feel their leader's touch.

Mentoring/Succession Planning
Six hours of a ten-hour workday have already been accounted

for. We move on to our first 20 percent allotment of time. Spiritual leaders, I suggest, should spend this percentage on internal consulting, coaching, mentoring and succession planning. We might call this allotment Developing People. This is where the facilitative role of the leader is so important. I have long advocated that good facilitation skills can successfully take you through almost every circumstance that involves human beings. Most people who have climbed the corporate ladder have rather directive tendencies, if not a fetish about control. These qualities got them to where they are, but they are not likely to get anyone else anywhere. At best they promote compliance, subservience and routine. Spiritual leaders help others do things for themselves, leaving the recipients of this guidance in a much stronger and wiser position than when they started. This is leader as teacher, perhaps one of the oldest forms of spiritual leadership known to us. Our models are Christ, Socrates, the Buddha, to name only a few. The CEO who can teach is a wonder to behold.

Some examples: One of your departments is struggling. Rather than taking it over, fixing it and expecting everyone to happily go along with the fix, spiritual leaders help marshal the knowledge, insights, ideas and talents of the people involved so they can see the situation clearly from above and form a corrective and collective response to that situation.

An employee committee has been formed to examine, improve and simplify the job-sharing option available to them. Most have not undertaken a responsibility like this before and all are enthusiastic about doing so. Your contribution is to coach them on how to access the information they need without violating corporate policies. You help them see the real meaning of this exercise, and how to document their recommendations in the most persuasive way. While you encourage and applaud them, you also let them stumble and learn from their own experiences just like you did. At the end they say, "We did it ourselves" and you couldn't agree more.

One of the vice-presidents shows signs of unusual depth in her leadership. One of the most intuitive people you have ever met in business, you see in her a special gift waiting to be bestowed on your organization. You decide to invest a considerable amount of time in her development. As her mentor, you arrange for assignments slightly beyond her competency level and then help her stretch to fulfill them. You see to it that her intuitive gifts are blended into the more traditional functions of analysis, measurement and decision-making, yet all the while you ensure that she remains her own unique self.

All the above are spiritual interventions into the lives of other human beings. The goal is *their* advancement, not yours. In *The Quest for the Corporate Soul,* Albert Koopman and Lee Johnson write: "Organizations are nothing more than people relationships. Unless you recognize them as individuals, as social beings, as spiritual entities, and as every other aspect of being human, your organization is no more than a cannon with people as ammunition."

With this 20 percent we have spent another 10 hours a week, two hours every business day, helping other people grow and become what they are able to become. Can there be a greater joy than this?

Operations

On to our last 20 percent where, finally, we get to monitoring operational details. To the measurements and spreadsheets and budgets. Even corporate spiritual leaders need to have a handle on what is happening on the fiscal side. Even the most spiritually attuned leaders, however, have trouble limiting themselves to the 20 percent level. This is where our training has been. All our professional lives we have been rewarded for our operational skills. It is concrete and controllable. This is the stuff that your CEO colleagues talk about most of the time. And it is undeniably important. My assumption on operational details is that there are managers in the organization who are well able to deal with the collection, analysis and application of operational data. This enables you to understand the situation well enough to be confident and responsible without getting into the common trap of micro-management. I really don't think one can be a spiritual leader and micro-manage at the same time.

So there it is – 30/30/20/20 – the business life of a corporate spiritual leader. The ratios will change depending on where you are in the organization. On the front line, for example, it may be 15 percent brain trust; 10 percent communication; 5 percent coaching and mentoring; and 70 percent operational details. The more senior your leadership level, the more I hope its makeup is spiritual.

An executive team and I were bouncing these kinds of ideas around one afternoon when a vice-president lamented, "If I did these things, when would I do my job?" These things *are* the job of leadership – spiritual leadership. The same kind of leadership that our entire country is desperate for. I do believe that many executives would love to live by the 30/30/20/20 formula. Usually they have no time even to think. The obstacle is that, like everyone else, senior leaders are rewarded for doing things, solving problems, keeping control and reviewing what has already happened. But give it a try. You may need the help of a secretary who used to play for the Green Bay Packers to do it, but I think you'll find it very worthwhile. Sadly, the general business culture is built to withstand spiritual influences, and only when it comes crashing to its knees does it open itself somewhat to spiritual change. Amazing how having a heart attack suddenly makes you interested in spiritual things. True personally. True corporately.

Just in case someone is asking, "When do I get lunch?" the answer is: "Whenever you want." Just decide which of the four categories represents the best way to use the lunch hour. Use it to coach and mentor, or use it for your own quiet time of reflection. Or to review quarterly results. Time is a nonrenewable resource and you already have all there is. You are given only one chance to use it, so use it to make a difference.

In an article entitled "The Power of a Minute," my friend and time management guru, Harold Taylor, points out that a 10-minute coffee break five days a week amounts to 43 1/3 hours during the year, or the equivalent of a one-week vacation. As a single 10-minute segment, of course, it seems very insignificant. Taylor goes on to point out: "Time is forgiving. Regardless of how you squandered time in the past, you get your full quota of 86,400 seconds every day of your future. Unlike money, it does not get you into debt. You don't have to pay off past bills and interest charges. You remain debt free with the opportunity of using wisely (or wasting) your full complement of time each day."

What you will discover as you try to take full advantage of the opportunity of time, is that you don't exactly "do" spiritual leadership, you live it. The doing looks after itself. It is Spirit that gives you life and connects you to all things. Because that is true, it is impossible to turn it on and off as though you were moving on to the next agenda item. And it certainly doesn't stop somewhere between office and home. If we do not have spiritual relationships with our mate and with our children, then this discussion of corporate spiritual leadership is very premature. What do you really see when you look out the kitchen window at your kids trying to put up the tent for an overnight backyard safari? Do you see spirit at work? What do you really see as you look around the conference-room table at your management committee trying to figure out where they are going to cut another three million dollars? Do you see spirit at work? Once you learn to see and experience the First World from a Second World perspective, it does not matter where you look or whether you are at home or work. It is all one thing.

Presenting ideas about how spiritual leaders might spend their time is relatively easy compared to describing how to *Be* spiritually in work and life. It is not a matter of time management or budgeting techniques. Nor is it a matter of training and managerial competencies, though it will not be long before someone will come along with an interactive CD-ROM program on *Spiritual Strategies for Success* complete with a graduation certificate. (If you are interested, just wait for the infomercial.) But that won't be it. Evidencing spirit comes from the inside out not from the outside in. We go now to the inside and a look at what flows through the veins of a leader who is tuned-in spiritually.

I'd like to suggest that there are nine internal and spiritual characteristics of those who have "It," that special and mystical quality telling us that we are in the presence of something very powerful. These characteristics define the nature and quality of our relationships as well as our experience of Self.

1. COMPASSION

For most of us, this word connotes the act of looking down at some poor, helpless, wretched soul much less fortunate than ourselves. Such condescension is hardly the desire of spiritual leaders. Nor do I mean sympathy. Nor even empathy. Sympathy says, "I'm sorry that happened to you." This can be a sensitive quality but it does not fit here. Empathy says, "I feel what you feel," which, while only partially true at best, can also be a comforting sentiment. It too is not quite on target.

I think of compassion as *wanting more for others than they want for themselves*. The spiritually compassionate leader looks at the struggling new employee and sees the magic and potential of that individual's life. She sees beyond the struggle and mistakes to the inner person who is yet to manifest. A spiritual ultrasound, if you will. You can see its shape while most others cannot. You see that it is a boy or a girl and you cannot help also seeing it as a child learning to walk, a teenager learning to drive, a young adult getting a diploma, an adult who, through loving and being loved, helps change the world. All that will be is there already whether it is known or not. The compassionate spiritual leader knows and rejoices.

When you see and desire for others the full unfolding of their lives, you are more than willing to go through the struggle of birth and growth with them. This is where the spiritual leader uses some of that coaching and mentoring time we talked about above. The leader becomes a birthing coach.

There is a story in the New Testament of Christ walking past two blind men sitting by the roadside. They sensed the presence of something powerful and called out to Christ for mercy. Christ asked them what it was that they wanted him to do, though the answer would appear to be self-evident. "Help us to see!" was the reply. St. Matthew finishes the story by telling us, "So Jesus had compassion and touched their eyes: and immediately their eyes received sight, and they followed him." A spiritual leader can see what is possible in the lives of other people, but until they themselves want to see it, they remain blind. Having the gift of compassion can weigh heavy sometimes. You see so many possibilities that are never realized. A young person throws away, or even takes away, her own life. Those who knew and loved her shake their heads sadly and sigh, "She had such potential!" It truly breaks your heart, especially if the person happens to be your son or daughter. Spiritual leaders, both home and work varieties, help others see themselves and the world differently. When that happens, as we saw in the story of the blind men, people find the purpose in their lives; they see their way and set out on their *own* path to spiritual wholeness and integration.

Compassion is not limited to a one-on-one application. A corporate spiritual leader can look with compassion on 50,000 employees spread over two continents. You see the unborn possibilities of this huge unlimited pool of talent. Your soul is so overwhelmed that you cannot even give voice to what you see. Put that against the fact that most of those people are scared to death that they are going to be gone with the next round of rationalization and you can begin to picture the challenge facing the spiritual leader. Sometimes leadership is a painful privilege. So often you see the pain of those desperate to be led and, because you have no answers, their pain becomes yours. "Have mercy, and help us keep our jobs!" they cry as you pass by. Through compassionate eyes you know that it is not their *job* that is their potential, it is what they are accomplishing *through* their job that they need to see. You strain your very soul to find a way to show them that this is so.

There is a company in Ontario, Canada, part of Northern Telecom, that makes very reliable and sophisticated switching devices. The combined leadership of the company and the union (a rather unusual and spiritual partnership in itself), decided that they were going to create an opportunity called Return To Learning through which employees could make themselves highly employable or even self-employable. Whether employees stayed with the company, were laid off or retired, they would be ready to continue to find meaning in their lives. The program makes every employee eligible for tuition fees of $2,000. The basic question employees are encouraged to answer is, "What most interests you in your life?" To help ensure wise choices, an employee submits her answer in a simple proposal format to a small company/union committee. Some of the interests are relevant to the company's business; therefore, a number of employees are able to take advanced engineering and technical programs. Many other interests, as you would expect, have been rather far-ranging. I heard of one employee who obtained a pilot's license. Another is studying Chinese. A woman who took flower arranging is now renowned in Ontario for her floral creations. She was an artist waiting to be born, and Northern Telecom was the midwife. How many companies *and* their unions do you know that would spend money on a flower-arranging course? Are Nortel employees dedicated to their company? You bet! It is a compassionate place.

2. CONFIDENCE

Confidence is *the courage to choose in the context of risk*. We have already looked at the connection between choice and power, stating the belief that only people who make real choices have real power. This thought is broadened when we add risk. Corporate spiritual leaders find themselves almost constantly in the context of risk. It seems to come naturally with the territory, something I will explain in a moment. First let's look at choice-making itself and then its connection to spirituality and spiritual leaders.

Choice is a major ingredient in a rich and full life. Choice is the bridge between our today and our tomorrow. When our lives stall and become stagnant and angry, it is because we are not making choices. When they are flowing like a river, we are making choices. Look up from this book right now and the first person you see will have choices in his life that he is not making. If you are alone, use a mirror. All of us are in this constant situation – we've got to make a choice, we've got to make a choice, we've got to make a choice. About this. About that. About the other thing. Most of the time we just do it, entertaining the consequences of the choice for not one moment. That second piece of pecan pie was sure good, wasn't it? Calories be damned! Life is for living! Should you buy the suit you saw on sale last weekend? Yes.

But then there are other times. The consequences loom larger. The choices are more difficult. Should you disrupt your career to go back to university for your doctorate? Should you leave your husband and two children after 17 years? Should you leave the priesthood? Should you enter it? Should you bite the bullet and fire the employee who has been causing such stress for so long? Should you take the package? Should you try marriage again? Should you invest your life savings in the franchise that seems to hold such promise? I am tempted to keep going until I hit yours. The last sample question comes close to one of mine right now. It's not a franchise, but I keep walking to the edge of a major marketing idea then vacillate on whether or not to risk jumping.

When we don't make the choices we know we have to make, we run the risk of suffering depression. Depending on the nature of the choice, the depression could be mild and temporary, or chronic. The point is, we all have a significant choice to make in our lives and we are not making it. I don't recall meeting anyone who has claimed that this isn't true for them. If that were the case, I think we'd have in front of us a truly stalled life. How could a life going anywhere not be continually confronted with choices? It is at this point that we can see why a spiritual person is constantly taking risks. Once we have this Second World way of seeing things, we continue to see more and more at a deeper and deeper level. The more we see, the more choices confront us. The nonspiritual person sees little and confronts little. The difference is like swimming in a wading pool or swimming in the ocean. The latter is filled with risk and demands a great deal of confident choice-making. In Life's ocean, we are always discovering, and the more we discover, the more we know the depth of the undiscovered.

When we don't know about the starving millions in Africa, we don't have to make a choice with regard to them. But we *do* know and we *do* have to make a choice. Having decided to help, we dig deeper into the situation and discover that the problem in the East is environmental and in the West it's political. We choose West and go deep into the political, uncovering a viper's nest of bribery and corruption. Deeper and deeper we could go, with each iteration confronting us with increasingly difficult choices. The more we look *through* anything, the more we are given the opportunity to choose. In much the same way, when we barely even recognize our own employees and don't know what is really going on in their lives, we can make "human resource" decisions rather easily, though superficially. If we truly know and love them, the choices are almost unbearably complex and difficult. We are no longer making choices about "human resources," we are making choices about Norm and Barbara, about dads and moms, about faithful friends.

In a very real way, the corporate leader without a spiritual perspective is fortunate. He has fewer choices. He can solve, almost by decree, the political and intellectual problems of the corporation. The more complex and difficult emotional and spiritual problems he doesn't see and so has no choice to make. Thus the phrase "Ignorance is bliss." Why do you think that soft organizational problems like poor morale, lack of commitment, low creativity – in short, people problems – are so often denied by senior executives? They can't see the problem because they are *spiritual* problems. When others who are able to see spiritual problems come along with a plan, they get a very poor hearing. The exciting conclusion? Corporate spiritual leaders have more problems, challenges and opportunities to deal with than other leaders. You might as well know that up front.

There's more. Not only do we each have a critical choice to make in our life that we are not making, we even know the right way to go. We know the right decision. Yes we do. There are two buttons in front of us: buy–sell. Join–quit. Commit–divorce. We know in our heart of hearts which one needs to be pushed. "I'm waiting for more information," you protest. Probably what we are waiting for is someone else to push the button. I learned a long time ago that if you wait until somebody else makes the choice for you, you can be a martyr if things don't work out. It wasn't your fault, *you* didn't push the button.

Deep down inside we have an awesome source of wisdom that tells us which way to go. It's the still small voice. It's the voice that we can listen to with confidence. It's the spirit speaking. Someone once said if we'd just keep quiet and stop analyzing so much we'd come up with a lot of answers. It is pretty hard to hear a small voice if we are doing all the talking. Corporate spiritual leaders see the choices that others do not. They listen to the still small voice within them and choose with confidence.

3. VISION

Vision is *seeing the prize as if you have already won it*. Corporate spiritual leaders have already been to their promised land. They have felt its soil, eaten its fruit and bathed in its rivers. It may have been a virtual visit but it was a visit nevertheless. Because these leaders see things differently, they see the prize before them so vividly, so digitally compressed, so vibrant in color, so holographic that they experience it as though it already exists. The mysterious truth is, it does already exist. As did Christ, today's corporate spiritual leaders go to prepare a place for those who follow. The streets may not be lined with gold, there will still be tears, and there will still be the contamination of the First World, but it will be a better place.

This depth of vision is not the stuff of goal setting or strategic planning. Here we do not care whether it is desirable, attainable, measurable and whatever else it is that goals are supposed to be. This is not the usual mission-statement fodder. All those perspectives were left back on the surface a long time ago. This is the mountaintop experience of Martin Luther King, Jr. This is Jacob's ladder to Heaven. This is the dream in which we see the spiritual "Why?" of our organization take on form and breathe on its own. Words come hard and are inadequate because we are describing something that transcends us. Moses at least had something to read when he came down from the mountain. We don't usually get that kind of break.

The corporate spiritual leader, in the English-speaking world particularly, fights an uphill battle to express what she sees from her mountaintop. Like the high-schooler who, when asked a question in an oral exam to which he actually knows the answer, fumbles in his eagerness for the words to express it. "I've got it, I've got it!" he exclaims convincingly. "Oh, I know it, I know it! Ummmm. Ummmm." And with the delay in finding the words, the examiner moves on, no credit given. Because the vision is transcendent, helping others to see it through First World language is a major feat for spiritual leaders. Often they are given no credit.

Recently I was speaking about such things to an international crowd and so language would have been an issue if I were talking about how to tie shoes. I was trying to talk about the role of spirit. Not the rah-rah team spirit that we are so familiar with, but that universal, connecting, energizing force that gives us and our organizations cause and power to live fully. This multi-language audience, who would not be completely open to this message at the best of times, was really making me earn my money. They had very little patience for this "Why?" stuff, this visionary, let's-go-deep, there-is-another-world, touchy-feely, airy-fairy ambiguity. What they wanted me to do was give concrete examples of other businesses that were spiritually centered, in true "Best Practice" style. If it turned out that these companies were actually making pots full of money, they would send a team off on a field trip to visit them and copy what they were doing.

Now, there is a part of even me that sees such a request as rather reasonable and, indeed, I could give them addresses to visit. You can visit them for yourself at the back of this book. But this "give me an example" response is a trap camouflaged by reasonableness. You've walked into it many times yourself. "That is not how it works," I explained in vain. "You guys want the blueprints and the cement so you can start building the cathedral, and you don't even know what religion you want to be." You don't become a Jew by doing Jewish rituals or a Mormon because you stop drinking coffee. Be-ing comes long before do-ing. Don't worry about the do-ing, it will look after itself once you understand and experience the be-ing. This is pure gibberish to people who live and die in the "How?"

At the break, a Chinese participant, feeling a little sorry for the abuse I was taking, came up to me and said, "I knew what you were talking about from the moment you opened your mouth. But that's because my people have understood it for thousands of years and we have a word for it: Tao-Dao, the center of all things." As he drew the symbol for me, he added, "They will never understand it because there is no language." Grateful though I was for his support and insight, I know that I simply cannot stop trying. My encouragement to all corporate spiritual leaders is: flounder away as you must with language, but above all keep your eyes and spirit focused on the vision of what is waiting to be seen. Your life and passionate confidence will be your ultimate language.

"There is nothing more tragic," said Helen Keller, "than someone who has sight, but no vision." Vision is what a leader sees through the windows of her soul.

4. PRIDE

This may seem an odd quality to attribute to spiritual leaders. We were all told that "pride comes before a fall," and so it seems that we end up either fearing pride to the point of being insecure or we overcompensate and become purely ego-driven. Do we really have only the two choices: self-flagellation or self-adulation? Neither extreme is very healthy or very spiritual.

The fundamentalist philosophy in which I was raised favored the self-flagellation, anti-pride side. We heard much more about our sinfulness and inadequacy than about the notion that we are actually created in the awesome image of God and share God's very spirit. "Worm theology," we called it. The "Me" generation came down on the other side. We were number one. We were to be satisfied before anything else. We were to pull our own strings and look out for ourselves. We were the source of our own power. Many current corporate managers came through this school, which is why few people are prepared to follow them. They put themselves ahead of the team and often see themselves as bigger than the team. However, as Romanian sculptor Constatin Brancusi said, "Nothing grows under big trees." People do not stay where there is insufficient nourishment, they go where they are fed.

Somewhere in between the two extremes of self-flagellation and self-adulation falls the sort of pride I consider to be a spiritual quality. Pride is *relishing the ultimate expression of influence, that of the ability to see others become leaders without becoming fearful of their success.* Spiritual pride is not about you, it's about others. The purpose of corporate spiritual leadership is to influence the world. As you show other people how to experience the world differently, to discover their own

THE BELOVED LEADER   177

compassion, confidence and vision, you also launch them into leadership. If you have done that well, the disciple will surpass the master. Pride is your way of celebrating that passing. Christ said to his followers, "You will do far greater things than I have done." That should be the joy of every true leader.

Unfortunately, this attitude is very rare and nowhere is it rarer than in family-owned businesses. A father comes to this country with only a nickel in his pocket and through sheer will creates a manufacturing empire that bears his name. All three sons and a daughter are in the business and one is even president. But you can count on this: ain't no one going to fly past dear old dad. The children, now university-trained and with children of their own, still cower when the old man comes into the boardroom. This isn't spiritual and it isn't leadership.

Wouldn't it be awful to know that your organization is just waiting for you to get out of the way so it can start growing again? Worse if you knew the rest of the executive team was waiting for you to die. So often I have heard something along the lines of, "The president is going to be retiring in the next year or so and until then we'll just sit tight." What a waste of precious time and what a comment on the president's leadership, or lack of it.

Let me tell you the story of a man who was a true leader. I had become good friends with a CEO who was due to retire in about 18 months. He was just not the tread-water type and yet he was anxious about starting "something new." In my book, 18 months is a lot of time for some pretty exciting living. "Remember when you first became president?" I asked him. "Do you remember how you came in with all that fresh energy and all those new ideas? How you changed the stale old ways and brought everyone a new kind of excitement and hope for better days?" "I sure do," he sighed as his mind flashed back over 15 years. "Go out the same way!" I said. "Point your people to an even higher mountaintop. Let them show you what they have learned from your leadership." Part of his concern was that perhaps he should leave new initiatives to a new leader. From my perspective, he could leave his successor a train stalled on the siding or a train going a hundred miles an hour. We agreed the latter would be better for the company *and* the successor, to say nothing of how people would remember him.

My hope is that you can, with pride, point to leaders who, with your help, have eclipsed what you yourself have done. If that's the case, as far as pride is concerned, you've got "It."

5. HUMILITY

It is dangerous to discuss pride as a spiritual quality without rushing immediately to its conjoint quality, humility. The mistake we made in the seventies and eighties was that we began to believe that our power and potential actually originated within us. *WE* were unlimited. *WE* had incredible gifts, strengths and talents. *WE* were the makers of our own success. *WE* were supreme within the universe. *WE* were kings and queens on the chessboard of life. I hope we have abandoned such foolish conceit. I am a positive person. I believe in our potential and responsibility to allow the creation that God began to come to its fulfillment. But folks, it's not me and it's not you. It's much, much bigger.

Humility means the recognition *that you do not have the gift of leadership, the gift has you.* You and I are channels, conduits, vehicles *through* which power, from well beyond us, flows. We are not the river and we cannot push the river. We can only ensure that it flows and nourishes, often by just getting out of its way. The greater the impact of our lives and leadership, the more I hope we gratefully recognize that it isn't us. The Gift has chosen us to lead the world to a new place, a new recognition of what already exists. How honored and humbled that should leave us.

My world revolves around professional speaking. Those of us who do this are always onstage. We are always at the front. We always get applause, if not a standing ovation. In this business it is extremely hard not to think that it's us – our irrepressible style, rapier wit, unquestionable knowledge and sexual charisma. As in every profession, some of us actually believe our own promotional material. Some professional speakers come as close to being a household name as one can get in that business and, frankly, they can sometimes be very full of themselves. I describe it as spiritual constipation. Nothing flows through them and after a while the self-adulation gets pretty tiring. They get top marks for "how," but the "why" seems to be missing. To be honest, my emotional reaction to these colleagues bounces between disdain, sadness and jealousy.

Others, of course, are exactly the opposite. They know they don't have the gift but that the gift has them. One of these, a true spiritual leader, died September 3, 1996. Magic in his oration, prolific in his writing, Og Mandino touched the lives of millions. In every one of his many books he showed people how to let the power flow *through* them. He touched millions and he made millions. Yet there are few of his stature who would be more humble and unassuming. I watched him accept applause at the 1996 National Speakers Convention with tears in his eyes, as though the honor were unexpected and undeserved. I've read some of his books but I didn't know him personally. The testimonials of people who were close to him made me realize that I had missed out on something wonderful. We can only hope that people will feel the same way when they hear about us. The gift had him. May the gift have you.

6. SELF-LOVE

This spiritual quality, like pride, is a challenge to describe in that it can very easily be distorted into something that is anything but spiritual. In our caution, then, let's look briefly at the concept of love itself.

In our efforts to find ways to have spiritually centered lives working in spiritually centered organizations guided by spiritually centered leadership, we have to go through many doors. All of these doors, and any other door through which we may go, must lead to love or we are going the wrong way. There is simply nothing higher than love. If it is the spirit that gives us our life force, it is love that lets the spirit live. Love unites us with God. Love unites us with each other. And love unites us with ourselves. Love defines our "personness."

I have been wrestling with and talking about corporate spirituality for a very long time. Years ago, when I first started to get bold about this topic, I was consulting with a major government agency, trying to get them in touch with their corporate spirituality, their Grand Why. To say this was new territory for these bureaucratic, do-it-by-the-book-oriented folks would be a gross understatement. After a particularly exhausting soul-searching session, one of the senior government leaders came up to me and said, "You know, Ian, there are only two spiritual concepts that you haven't mentioned yet – forgiveness and love." What was wonderful about the comment was that he thought I *should* be mentioning those concepts. Well, we've come a long way since then.

As an aside on the topic of forgiveness, I am very proud to point you to Union Central Life Insurance, a company which is headquartered in Cincinnati. They are an amazing group who have taken the corporate exercise of defining their values to a higher plane than any other organization I know. For example, they have actually enshrined forgiveness in their corporate values. They call it "Reconciliation in Relationships" and describe it this way: "We recognize that in any work environment there will be times of struggle, tension and misunderstanding. We also recognize that the ability to reconcile, forgive and let go is the ultimate mark of a mature community. It is from a position of harmony that we can most appreciate and benefit from the diversities among us. We encourage all Union Central associates to ensure that their relationships are a source of joy, energy and strength."

I called this last paragraph an "aside" but it's not really, is it? Do you see how love is reflected in the company's value of forgiveness? Forgiveness requires the forgiver to take on all the hurt and pain inflicted by another, without the option of revenge. If that is not evidence of love, of some power truly transcendent, mysterious and present, I don't know what is. All doors really do lead to love.

Let's go on with our job of connecting self-love to spiritual, be-loved leadership. Since love can only exist in a state of freedom and nonjudgment, self-love means *the quality through which we cease to judge ourselves, so that, in our freedom, we also cease to judge others.* We are talking here of that self-righteous judgment with which people often condemn each other. Once we quit judging ourselves and others, we are free to be in fellowship or connection with ourselves and others. We move from judgment to acceptance to unity. The key is that we must experience this wholeness "with-in" before we can experience it "with-out."

There are four concepts of love in the Greek language: *eros,* a sexual, physical love; *storge,* a strong family love and affection; *philia,* a warm personal friendship and deep affection between two or more people; and *agape,* a form of love that transcends all other forms, the significant among significants. All forms of love contribute to wholeness, but agape provides the richest ground from which to see the importance of self-love. It is the noblest form of love, seeing something immensely precious in its object. Agape brings all things into itself, bringing man to God, man to man, and man to himself. In *Love, Power and Justice,* theologian Paul Tillich concludes that through agape we are able to see others as God sees them. It is agape that transforms life and, indeed, love itself. "Agape is love cutting into love," writes Tillich, "just as revelation is reason cutting into reason and the Word of God is the Word cutting into all words." In her book, *A Theology of Love,* theologian Mildred Bangs Wynkoop writes that *agape*: "is a principle by which one orders life – or by which life is ordered." She goes on to say that through agape, "relations sustained with other persons are kept in balance by one's deliberate orientation to God and one's own self respect – in the right sense, self-love." Self-love, in other words, is what enables us to keep balance and perspective in our lives and in our leadership. When self-love is limited to love of self, the result is chaos and distortion in all our relationships. If it is focused on God and others, the result is harmony, creativity and meaning. Self-love is a sacred state and we cannot have ongoing influence as a corporate spiritual leader without it.

7. HOPE

Hope, strangely, is a much-maligned quality. It does not seem to be a very strong or confident variable in leadership. If you say to your committee, "We *hope* to have the contract signed by next Friday," many will immediately wonder what might go wrong between now and then. They will ask you why you are not more confident than that. *Hoping* it will be signed is a long way from *knowing* it will be signed. Knowing is strong, hoping is weak, maybe even naive.

Unfortunately, we live in an age in which people have lost confidence and faith in their corporations and their corporate leaders. The sacred contract between employer and employee, many feel, has been broken and nothing has replaced it. Recently, I saw a documentary on television entitled "Downsized Dreams." That's a sharp and clever title. More than that, its truth is heartbreaking. The grand old American dream in the land of opportunity is no longer relevant in our downsized and rationalized world. The spacious skies have clouded over. "You shouldn't have as much hope as you once did," is another way of putting this discouraging message.

People automatically default to the negative, it seems. If the president of a company announced an unexpected all-employees meeting in the cafeteria, hardly anyone, I guarantee, would excitedly say to her colleagues, "I'll bet it's good news, let's get there early and sit in the front row!" They would never hope for that because the last three all-employees meetings resulted in more layoffs. So we are left to decide whether or not hope is an arrow worth having in our spiritual quiver. You already know what I think.

Hope, as a quality of beloved corporate spiritual leader-ship, is *the insight to recognize and communicate those circumstances, large and small, that mark progress toward the realization of the vision.* Unfortunately, there are no nonstop flights to the dream. There are delays along the way, some scheduled, some not. For refueling. Because of turbulence. Maybe even mechanical breakdown. The reality is that we cannot always actually see the mountaintop because we are too busy trying not to get ourselves killed as we crawl along the edge of a cliff. People do get discouraged and disappoint-ed. People do want to quit. People do get tired and hope-less. Enter the corporate spiritual leader.

Between your organization's current reality and its richly imagined future is a virtual chasm filled with both negative or nonconfirming experiences and positive or confirming experi-ences. Think of yourself on a spaceship going through a zone filled with thousands of asteroids, some with minus signs on them and some with plus signs. You zig, you zag. You try to avoid the negative asteroids but you can't always. They bang into you, damage your craft and throw you off course, fright-ening everyone on board. Fortunately you are able to hit the positive asteroids as well and each time you do you get more fuel or a new life that energizes you to carry on toward your destination. Most people today, including most leaders, keep amazingly accurate records of all the negative hits. Any positive ones are regarded as accidental and inconsequential. And so we become self-discouraging and self-defeating. The enemy is us.

Frequently I have seen corporate leadership endorse a workshop during which the management group is finally able to talk openly about some of the debilitating things that are going on in the company. As you know, if you are not careful, this kind of thing can easily turn into an exacerbating bitch session in which people reminisce about all the negative aster-oids they've hit. It does not seem to be evident that the very workshop they are attending is a huge positive asteroid. In contrast, one hospital client used to have an annual "Review and Rejoice Rally," or "R & R," as we called it. The entire day was positive, with each department giving recognition and thanks to other departments and individuals who had helped them over the past year. We would list hundreds of wonderful accomplishments and almost overwhelm ourselves with good news. It was absolutely taboo for someone to mention anything negative. At the end of it all the group would give each other a standing ovation and a hug, enjoy a little wine and cheese and go off to make something grand out of the next 12 months.

Spiritual leaders are always pointing out the positive signs that the organization is moving steadily toward the mountaintop. You would think that such an encouraging message would be well received, wouldn't you? Not always so. There will always be people who, calling themselves "realistic," focus loudly on the negative. They make their lives hope-less. Even while you have read this brief section on hope, your mind may have wandered to what my friend and fellow speaker Warren Evans calls the "YABUTS." Hope is a very difficult seed to plant today. The YABUTS seem to destroy it before it can take root. Hope does not spring eternal anymore. Herein lies one of leadership's greatest challenges.

There *are* wonderful things happening in corporate life all over the world. Good changes. Spiritual changes. These too are real. Spiritual leaders are constantly recognizing these signs of hope and become hope-full to overflowing, rinsing the film of discouragement from those around them.

8. DETERMINED FAITH

Faith, St. Paul wrote, is "the confident assurance that something we want is going to happen. It is the certainty that what we hope for is waiting for us, even though we cannot see it up ahead." Faith expands hope beyond a confirmation of progress to a confirmation of purpose. Hope, in itself says, "We are getting there!" Faith says, "Act as if you *are* there!" The future that we are "faithing" is there already. It is we who are not there yet. It is not distant from us, we are distant from it. We are the ones who must move.

Some will think the phrase "determined faith" is redundant. I prefer to see it as reinforced. Since faith is confidently anticipating a world different from the one we have now, *acting* on our faith means we must disrupt our current state in order to re-create the desired one. The complication comes with the realization that the entire world is being re-created all the time. In the same way that our body's cells are constantly changing over, so is all of creation. Most of us over 40 wish that when our body produces new cells to replace the ones that have died, it would make better, thinner, more attractive ones than those we just got rid of. It seems to do that for younger people, you might have noticed. They become stronger and more flexible. Their bodies become the beautiful sculptures they were meant to be. Their skin is smooth and elastic. And what does your teenager do to deserve this beautiful re-creation? Other than eat and sleep, not much. You and I walked seven miles to school, uphill both ways, wore socks for gloves, worked our fingers to the bone, had our first job at the age of six – for what? Re-created body parts that turn gray, sag, dry up or fall off. Just not fair, is it?

The whole world is in a dynamic state of re-creation and sometimes it does not re-create fairly. The reality is that some of its re-creation is cruel. Determined faith means *not letting the unfairness of the world dissuade you from changing it*. We just cannot figure out why or how the world is what it is sometimes. In Brussels, the bones of children were found buried in somebody's backyard. In Toronto, an infant died because her father threw her around like a football. In the Carolinas, dreams built brick by brick were made rubble by the wind. Every day cruel people seem to prosper. The writer of the ancient Hebrew book Ecclesiastes was so despairing at the unfairness of the world, he felt "that the dead were better off than the living. And most fortunate of all are those who have never been born, and have never seen all the evil and crime throughout the earth." In another part of the book, he wrote, "I hate life because it is all so irrational; all is foolishness, chasing the wind." Watch any news broadcast and you have to fight not to get depressed. Only occasionally, if there has not been sufficient cruelty to report (they call that a slow news day), does the media stick in a "human interest" story about "man saves cat from tree." If these rare feel-good anecdotes are of "human interest," what are the other news items?

This *is* the First World we live in and it *is* despairing. But through it all, we live and work and have our being. Through it all, the beloved leader calls on people to join hands and begin to love and protect all that is precious in life. We must not be dissuaded from changing the world. The beloved leader starts with herself, then her leadership team, then her organization, and then the community it serves. Poet and novelist Kahlil Gibran said that "work is love in action" and it is through the action of determined faith and love that we will eventually see the holy purpose of our work and leadership.

9. JOY

When you were applying for the job you have now, did anyone ask you if you were a joyful person? We seem to allow people to move into leadership roles because of their intellect, their toughness, their control skills and so on. They may have all the experience credentials possible but we soon discover that they have the personality and soul of a pit bull. There is no joy in their lives. Can one lead without joy?

When I was a kid at church camp we sang a little song that began, "I've got the joy, joy, joy, joy down in my heart." Then somebody would yell out "Where?" and we'd repeat, "Down in my heart." What exactly is *the* joy? Anybody can be joyful because something good happened to him, but is there a systemic, fundamental quality called joy? *The* joy? Because if there is, it must be present when everything happens to us, positive or negative. And if it's down in your heart, it must be a spiritual quality and worth exploring.

Joy is a spiritual strength that *enables one to attach celebration to every victory* and *to every problem and obstacle.*

This ability and perspective is every bit a function of corporate spiritual leadership as anything else we have discussed. We need to celebrate victories because that means we are another step closer to our vision. We need to celebrate problems and obstacles because they give us the opportunity to have another victory. I cannot think of a better corporate application of this than the leadership philosophy of David Williams, president of National Grocers Ltd. I met him and his team when I spoke at their convention in Puerto Vallarta, Mexico. That was a joyful celebration, to say the least. Going to that expense is something many companies do *if* they have had a great financial year, and I mean great. Because I knew they had had a good year, I asked David if that was true for his organization. These conferences, he said, are needed *more* if it has been a difficult year than if it's been a good one. His intention is to hold them no matter what. There's one CEO who believes in the power of joy and celebration.

Like agape love, joy is a spiritual quality, not simply a temporary emotion. As with all the other spiritual qualities, one does not do joy, one is, or is not, a joyful person. For spiritual leaders, whether in the context of their personal lives or their corporate responsibilities, this quality shines through their activities and relationships. How contagious the joy is and what confidence it instills. You come to the joyful leader with your struggles and difficulties and the sunshine from within him seems to illuminate the darkness of the problem. Somehow it is not quite so big anymore.

Joy is an outward expression of inner excitement. Isn't this what our corporations need – something to be excited about? English essayist Sydney Smith, who lived from 1771 to 1845, said:

> *Thank God for tea!*
> *What would the world do without tea?*
> *How did it exist?*
> *I am glad I was not born before tea.*

What I want to know is, who on earth wrote that down? Here we are, at least 150 years later and we still know that tea brought Sydney Smith great joy. A hundred and fifty years from now, will anyone know that you and I were joyful about anything? For that matter, will anyone know tomorrow?

The joy anticipates a future state. *The* joy also loves the present and gives thanks to the past for both gifts and trials. *The* joy is the joy of the journey to the fulfilled vision made real through determined faith. The joyful corporate spiritual leader is able to see past obstacles and problems to that future state. This is why *the* joy is different from simply being glad something nice happened to you. When you are simply glad, it is usually about an event or good news that has already happened. *The* joy is about the future. The beloved corporate spiritual leader is joyful about things that have not even happened yet.

Finally, joy is best when it is spontaneous. Spontaneity is the pilot light of all joyful relationships. Back when the Mutant Ninja Turtles were saving the world on the silver screen, I was doing my part by spending a day with a large group of economists. The stereotype that just jumped into your mind fit exactly. Very bright and extremely conservative. They were working in small hushed groups trying to figure out some strategy or another, when one of them yelled "Kowabunga!" to signal a breakthrough. It furrowed a few of the more sophisticated brows, but I thought the joyful spontaneity was wonderfully refreshing.

Such is the fruit of spiritual leadership: Compassion, Confidence, Vision, Pride, Humility, Self-Love, Hope, Determined Faith, and Joy. When we think of "doing" spiritual leadership, this is heavy fruit indeed. We cannot do it. We fatigue at the very thought. Fortunately, our calling is simply to "be"; to be joyful channels *through* which God's Spirit calls the world to himself. This is the inspirational fire which, said architect and sculptor Walter Russell, "burns within the consciousness of great geniuses, fires which give to them an unconquerable vitality of spirit which breaks down all barriers as wheat bends before the wind."

Corporate spiritual leadership may not be dramatic. One does not have to be tall or beautiful or an extrovert. Know only that when you are in the presence of it, there is no doubt. As Russell put it, "There is some subtle light in the eye of the inspired one, or some even more subtle emanation which surrounds the inspired thinker, which tells you that you are in the presence of one who has bridged the gap which separates the mundane world from the world of spirit."

This miracle of Spirit lies within each of us. This is the significance that lies beyond success. This is the Life Triumphant. And to this I can only add, joy to the world, and may your heaven and nature sing.

NINE

Frontline Spirituality

✦ ✦ ✦ ✦

W e are not alone. There are many thousands of us out in the "real" world who know that there is another way to live and lead. Slowly we are giving each other permission to speak of these things as easily as we speak about profit and loss. Corporate executives, managers and employees of all descriptions are coming out of the spiritual closet to share the struggle of their shudderings, the joy of their insights and the peace that comes through finding meaning in their work. Philosopher Sam Keen is right when he says that we are at the forefront of an "emerging spiritual world view." What is driving this movement? Is it just another managerial fad? Is it happening because the new millennium is about to dawn? I don't really know and, frankly, the answers are unimportant to me. All I know is that something good is happening out there and I want to be right in the middle of it.

Leadership is a holy calling. It is with great joy that I introduce you in this chapter to leaders who understand this way of experiencing the world. The people you are about to meet are trying to live their own lives on a deeper level and lead their organizations from success to significance. They will be the first to tell you that they have not "arrived" at some utopian place, they are simply on the journey. I am more than honored that they were willing to join me in this exploration of spirituality in life, labor and leadership. I am truly blessed to know these men and women.

I asked these successful corporate leaders to comment, as intimately and candidly as they wished, on the relevance of the ideas in this book to their personal and professional experience. Like the rest of us, they are all still searching. They have each been through their own unique shudderings, some I know about and many I don't. Each has gained different insights and found his or her own truth. In various ways and to varying degrees, they have all experienced the joy of wholeness and integration in their life and work. Consequently, while I hope they found both benefit and pleasure in reading my book, do not assume that our insights into the deeper life will match. Indeed, we will all learn more if they *are* different.

Some of my discoveries may not at all connect to their experiences, and they have been enthusiastically invited to say so and to share their own insights. Where our truths coincide, we rejoice in our mutual discoveries. When people openly share their truth with each other, there is no need for judgment or defensiveness.

Before we jump into their lives and hear a little of their story, let me provide introductions.

Michael Stephen

You feel Mike Stephen's "spiritual centeredness" the moment you meet him. I can't really describe how that is – it's just there. He is a truly wise man, and the times I've spent working with him and his executive teams are treasured chapters of my life. Mike is the chairman of Aetna International, a company that employs more than 12,000 people and brings in almost 2.5 billion dollars in annual revenue. He is leading a bold expansion into complex marketplaces like China, Indonesia and Argentina.

This is not his most important accomplishment, however. He has taught thousands of employees so much about centered living, especially about putting family and people first.

Dr. Marti Smye

I don't know if I am in awe of Marti Smye or if I'm just envious of her many accomplishments. An amazing entrepreneur with a very successful track record, she consults with organizations worldwide, has written a couple of books, is an engaging speaker *and* has a life! She genuinely cares about people and, as she'll tell you, her life isn't just about reaching goals. It is in the journey toward those goals that her spiritual awareness is evident.

Greg Cochrane

The first time I met Greg Cochrane was at a late-afternoon planning meeting. He stood out because, just before 6:00, he excused himself mid-discussion to head home and have dinner with his wife and kids. This man has his life together and his priorities clear. He brings that same level of engagement to his employees and clients. As a result, his company, the Mariposa Communications Group Inc., is highly successful by every measure. Greg is real, he is open, and I've got a lot of time for him.

Phil Hassen

I sit here looking at the picture of my friends from St. Joseph's Health Centre in London, Ontario, and wonder how to tell you what they mean to me. Phil, Peggy, Jane, Karen and Sandra – we've been through so much together. Laughed. Cried. Danced. Argued. Planned. If you ever want to see what "team-Spirit" really means, this is the group to visit. St. Joe's is a client of mine, but we flew past that level of relationship a long time ago. They came to my wedding. I was expressing my surprise and gratitude that they'd found the time and traveled that distance to attend a "consultant's" wedding. Phil explained, "Ian, it's an important day for you, and that makes it an important day for us." I love them for that.

Jon C. Madonna

I kept meeting Jon Madonna at various places around the world – Burgenstock, Prague, Orlando, London. He was chairman of KPMG International at the time and I was privileged to be part of the company's innovative partner-development program, which originated out of Brussels. Although our encounters were brief, I wanted to get to know this man. Jon has an unmistakable aura of leadership that fills a room and, to be frank, this guy is as "bottom-line" as you can get. Yet it was Jon who first initiated discussion about spiritual meaning into one of the world's most successful financial consulting firms. My invitation to him to be part of this book caught him in the middle of making some huge choices in his life and I am thrilled and honored that he was willing to share some of that personal process with us.

Larry Pike

Larry Pike and I hit it off almost instantly. He was attending a conference at which I was speaking and we had the opportunity to connect – a connection that has endured for several years. Larry felt I could help his organization, Union Central Life Insurance Company, particularly the senior executive team. It was clear that Larry knew there was something else he could bring to this incredible organization and, without hesitation, I wanted to help him find it. As mentioned earlier, there are few better examples of a values-based company than Union Central and that is largely due to the fact that Larry lives his life that way, too. As with Jon Madonna, this book caught Larry in the middle of some big choices that are now part of his spiritual journey.

Beverly Topping

Beverly Topping is one of those people whose natural presence can only be described as loving. We met at a conference in Arizona where my wife, Georgia, and I felt a connection with Bev right away. Bev had been widowed only months before we met, while Georgia's first husband had died just a little more than five years earlier. So the two of them found a special bond. I didn't really know about the shudderings of Bev's life when I asked her to contribute to this book. The fact that she has shared her story so intimately makes me feel blessed just to know her. She is a remarkable, remarkable woman who can teach us about what is really important in life, labor and leadership.

◆ ◆ ◆ ◆

Breathing Life into Organizations

Michael Stephen, Chairman, Aetna International, Inc.

Mike, his wife Bea and (from left) granddaughters Madeleine and Michelle

Dr. Paul Rubyni, a partner in the former firm of Ernst and Whinney of Montreal, was one of my early mentors. He introduced me to the notion of organizational "spirit." For Paul, an organization was not an inanimate object but, rather, a feeling being with a life of its own. In his view, organizations must be nurtured to reach full potential; otherwise, they will waste away. "Mike," he said, "if morale is bad in the organization, it's the fault of the CEO." The CEO's critical responsibility, he claimed, was to create an environment in which individuals can legitimately aspire to become the best they can be. Failed organizations reflect failed individuals at the top. If they want to achieve organizational success, leaders must celebrate the nobility of the humanity that makes up their companies. Paul passed away several years ago, but his message stays with me. For 20 years, I've tried to be the kind of leader he envisioned.

What Ian Percy has brought to my understanding of the responsibility of leadership is the recognition that you don't earn the right to lead because you occupy a prestigious office and have an impressive title. You earn the right to lead by modeling leadership in a way that is indeed spiritual, persuasive and inspirational. Ian brings home the truth that there is no organizational transformation until there is serious personal transformation.

Successful organizations are led by strong interdependent management teams who challenge employees to take ownership and responsibility for results, who make employees feel important and recognized, who allow the spirit space to grow. But the basis of this success, and the basis of this growth, is trust. Leaders earn trust by taking the risk of personal transformation.

What Ian invites each leader to learn is that success in life and success in business come from fully understanding our spirituality and its defining role in our relationships with our peers, employees and God. Organizations are not made great "by" leaders. They're made great "through" leaders who allow the spirit breath and scope. No easy task.

I first met Ian in Toronto, through an associate. I had been appointed president and CEO for Aetna International's Canadian operations and was looking for a professional to help my group become a high-performing executive team. We wanted someone who could persuade us to think and act "outside the box."

Enter Ian, with his wickedly irreverent and captivating style. With humor and finality, he ridiculed our pet biases about management and its responsibilities. With merciless wit, he parodied our pet platitudes (charitably identified as "management principles") and poked fun at a number of entrenched beliefs. He exposed for us the inconsistencies and shortfalls that commonly dog management decisions. In short, he laid before us the spectacle of organizations trying to function without passion, without hope, without soul.

Going Deep reminded me once again how much I miss talking with Ian on a regular basis. The book's wit, irreverence and laserlike focus are exceptional in today's hurly-burly business world. Its frank exploration of the author's relationship with God is not the usual fare in business conversation. In *Going Deep*, Ian holds out a serious challenge to today's leaders while playfully pointing out the pitfalls, the dangers of taking oneself too seriously. The book spoke to me in a very personal way. I need to effectively improve and intensify my relationship with God if any organization is to benefit from my leadership.

Ian is particularly caustic about leaders who are oblivious to the anger and frustration of those employees who stay on beyond organizational downsizing and re-engineering. Uncommunicative and detached management teams with their myriad corporate games come in for a strong dose of Percy scorn. Leaders can, for a time, disregard the notion of human spirituality and its place at work. They can pound away at the organization and make it more powerful. The bottom line may improve in the short term, but the workforce becomes angry, irritated, explosive. Whether or not such organizations will survive the challenges that face our society as we move into the next millennium is highly debatable. In my view, it's unlikely.

Without leadership, there is no "followership." There is no "followership" without honesty and inspiration. These must radiate and pulsate from management to assure lasting organizational success. Just as our children reflect the care and love that they experience in their relationships with us, so too do organizations reflect the quality of its senior leadership. Our children get confused and messed up when, as models, we are inconsistent or deviate from the principles we once espoused. Similarly, an organization – as a living being – deteriorates when official communication is inconsistent and out of character with what's touted as its "values and beliefs."

Ian's reminder to leaders of their spiritual responsibility led me to recall those people, like Dr. Paul Rubyni, who helped me understand what leadership is about. A group of young people I worked with right after university taught me an essential truth about leadership. For two years, I worked as a teacher with a group of students who were slow learners. They were teenagers with a reading level of Grade 2. These kids were labeled "mentally retarded" and that's how they came to identify themselves. So they lived the part; they didn't want to disappoint us. Working with them, I learned the importance of believing in someone's potential. I can't think of a better training ground for a business leader.

Recently, I was invited back to my home province to receive an honorary doctorate from the University of New Brunswick. At first, I thought they'd confused me with another Mike Stephen. I hadn't even graduated from UNB. But, no, they said they'd followed my career, and wanted to honor me as a New Brunswick native. I was thrilled. I took my wife, my children, my grandchildren. But the greatest honor came, not on the stage, getting hooded, but out in the lobby. First, a prosperous-looking man came up to me and said, "Mr. Stephen – Dr. Stephen, I want to congratulate you and thank you. Do you remember me?" He told his name. He had been my hardest student, way back then, a rowdy, unmanageable kid – he really got my goat. And I was determined he'd read; I knew he could. And here he was. "I want to thank you for what you did for me. I thought I'd never learn anything, but you hung on. I've got a great job, a great life. You were some teacher."

Then another fellow came up to me. He was a Supreme Court judge. He introduced himself and asked me if I remembered a certain person, whom he named. The name was vaguely familiar. "When you were at St. Joe's College together, he was really depressed for some time. He wanted to quit, didn't know what he was doing with his life. You were his ear. You listened to him through it and convinced him to stay on. He's now an Appeal Court judge. Couldn't be here tonight, but wanted me to say thank you for him." Those two encounters brought home to me what leadership is all about. Helping people believe in themselves.

The people who first helped me believe in myself and believe in the power of relationships were my high-school teachers in Saint John, and my father. Those teachers were some of the most focused, dedicated people I've ever met. You knew they cared about the students. I never had a teacher to match them, even when I had the privilege of going to Harvard's School of Advanced Management. Then there was my father. He came to Canada from Lebanon in his early teens. He married Eva George, his childhood sweetheart, and together they raised 12 children. All the time I was growing up, I never heard a negative word from him. I've never known anyone as optimistic as he was. I never heard him tear anyone down. He was always so appreciative of this country and of the opportunity he had to work and raise a family. He showed us what joy there can be in work and in life.

Staying true to that sense of joy is something I had to learn the hard way, for myself. Early in my career, I worked in sales. I was very successful. After five or six years, I was asked to go into management. In those days, management was not about sharing power – that's something more and more leaders are learning now, but not back then. I was "successful" as a manager, but I reached a point when I didn't feel a sense of accomplishment. For a while, I was a very angry guy, embittered. I resigned. The bosses asked "Why? You're so successful." But I could only say "By whose measurement?" Not my own, that's for sure. I didn't feel I could use all I had in that environment. I told them right out, "When you don't believe, you don't belong. I don't believe in this system."

My wife was great about all this. Although she didn't want to, she agreed to leave Montreal and go back to Saint John. We spent a year there. I did well in real estate, then got my bearings and resumed my career. I guess you'd call that experience a "shuddering." I had to come face-to-face with my own integrity and discover the kind of work I needed to do to preserve it. I needed to go through that painful experience to find out what I could do best, as a leader.

The key thing I've recognized is that, in North America, we're so task-oriented. The "rugged individual" doing heroic things is still an ideal. But the rest of the world doesn't function like that. As we work increasingly with companies in Asia, we see the power of paying attention to relationship building. Aetna staff who do a lot of business in the East are getting more and more captivated by that approach. The bottom line does fine, *and* so do the people – when they feel valued, recognized, depended on.

My worst fear as a leader would be to have people say of me, at the end of my career, "He didn't pay enough attention; he didn't care; he was phony; he didn't walk the talk." The business world in North America is trying to shake off a fixation on growth and material gain, power plays, self-interest. These things, in many ways, became a substitute for spirituality. Maybe today is a new beginning. People like Ian Percy are trying to remind us of the dangers of neglecting the soul or spirit of organizations and the people who spend their lives there. Maybe the pain and alienation of thousands of workers today will become a blessing in disguise. The corporate world may come to recognize the centrality of spirit in personal and organizational success. Let us hope.

Lasting "vision and values" are rooted, Ian claims, in an understanding of the loving relationship between God and creation. Those who lead need to consider that relationship and must themselves treat people with love, reverence, and respect. That's the way they'll breathe life into organizations. A tall order, for leaders, and a personal, spiritual challenge. But it comes with the title.

Mike Stephen is chairman of Aetna International, Inc. (AII). AII and its subsidiaries have annual revenues of approximately US$2.3 billion and employ more than 12,000 people outside of the United States. Under Mike's leadership, Aetna entered the newly emerging markets of Argentina, Peru and Indonesia and expanded its insurance lines in

New Zealand and Chile. Three years ago, representative offices were established in Shanghai and Beijing in preparation for entering the insurance business in China. In addition to his incredible business success, Mike meditates daily, enjoys jogging, hiking with his grandchildren, swimming and politics.

◆ ◆ ◆ ◆

Spiritual Leadership: Helping People Discover that They Are Good . . . and Scared

Dr. Marti Smye, PRESIDENT,
PEOPLE TECH CONSULTING, INC.
(A division of Right Management Consultants)

I'll never forget an exercise one of my professors had us do in a graduate psychology class. It was a simple and, like a lot of simple things, *powerful* sentence-completion exercise. Finish this sentence:

Marti and her dog Bailey

"People are . . ." "People are," I said, from real conviction, "good." I paused, then added, a bit surprised at myself, ". . . and scared." The prof, seeing me rather pleased with my own insight and wit, said, "Now finish this sentence: 'I am . . .' " I started off firmly: "I am good," (then slowly, with a bit of a shiver) ". . . and scared."

Ian's suggestion that I'm one of those leaders who've been on a spiritual journey is an honor. I guess I am on a journey. But the recognition is humbling; I sure feel like I've a long way to go. My journey, and my work, are about facing up to being good and being scared myself and helping others face that, as leaders.

I never had a problem knowing I was good; my family reinforced that. They were hardworking farm people; they gave me such a sense that I could do what I dreamed of, that I could do more than I ever thought possible. I will never forget one of the two greatest compliments I've ever received. It was from my brother; he's a bank president now, not one of the most emotional – or maybe not one of the most expressive – people around. But he said to me, one time I was home from university, "When you come home, you light up the house; you're a 100-watt bulb in a 60-watt world." My upbringing made me believe I had a light that could shine. My work now is about helping other people discover that they too are 100-watt bulbs.

But knowing you are good and knowing you are a light that can shine brighter involves facing the fact that, underneath, you are – we all are – scared. Often, it's fear of letting that light shine that gets in our way; it's a lack of hope for the self.

My path through childhood and on into my career certainly seemed well lit; it sure looked as though I was living out my 100-watt potential. In Grade 8, for example, I knew I would be the valedictorian for my high-school graduating class. My mom was, so I would be too. And I was. In university, I blazed through my courses, except French, and my research, and finished my Ph.D. in Applied Psychology a whole year ahead of the usual time. I was, in all things, incredibly goal-oriented.

But it took one of those "shudderings" Ian talks about to let me see that my real 100-watt potential was not just about achieving. It was also about breaking through to intimacy and helping others do that too. And intimacy, a focus on process, on the human struggle for growth, is what I was scared of. I discovered this about myself when I was working with a group as a consultant/facilitator. I was really driving them. One very astute, very kind man said to me, "Marti, we really love working with you, but relax; we get the feeling that you're mainly focused on seeing how we'll turn out at the end of the week –

what you'll make out of us." There it was; I was found out. I wasn't seeing the human process, I was so fixed on the goal, on the product, my own achievement.

That experience made me reflect – something unusual, maybe, for such an extrovert. I realized that, while my child-hood was happy and very oriented to achievement, there was little sense of what I'm calling "process." My one enduring memory of that dimension of being, though, is in my relation-ship with my pony, Sue. Times with her were incredible times of connection, of peace. I remember walking along beside her, leading her though a field. It was one of those blue-sky Midwest summer days. Quiet, a sense of huge peaceful space. I remember picking up a milkweed pod and bursting it, letting the silky seeds fly in silent grace on the summer breeze. How can I express the sense of utter oneness that surrounds that memory? That was intimacy, with another being, with the world.

When I discovered that, as a consultant, I was not yet strong on process, I shifted gears. I saw I had a strength in bring-ing people together and getting them focused on a mission. I formed People Tech and developed a group of 50 associates, specialists in Industrial Psychology, Organizational Consulting, Human Resource Strategy, Process Engineering, and Communi-ations. We form contracts of two to three years in length to assist organizations to get focused on their goals and relation-ships. In building the company, I wasn't sure, after my recent "shuddering" realization, that I could develop among them a sense of connection. I now know I can.

This team feels like a gift someone gives me every day; they really care about their work. Whenever someone leaves, they say, "I'll never have the relationships I've had here." They were the ones who gave me the second big compliment of my life – when they urged me to write a book about what our work is all about. I did, and called it *You Don't Change a Company by Memo*.

People Tech has worked with clients in consumer packag-ing, food and beverages, financial services, health care. (Funny thing, in health care, you'd think it wouldn't be hard to find meaning in your work, but it is; they're so fearful and exhaust-ed.) When we are negotiating contracts, we do have a lot of dis-cussions inside the company about whether or not we should take on certain clients, whether the client's work is really valu-able work. We wonder about the ethics of their business. But what we realize – and it's part of my own personal realization – is that it's not the product so much as the workplace, the work-ing relationships, that are important. How they find meaning in the way they work with one another, how they affect others, the fit of their work with their families. Our mission at People Tech is very much the mission I formed for myself, as a child, "To help people do more than they ever dreamed of, more than they ever thought possible." And we mean that in business terms, and also in personal terms.

Some of my work now as a practitioner involves what I call "CEO Reflections." I go on retreats with leaders who are going through major organizational change, and help them tell the truth about that process – what it means to them as a com-pany, as a team, as individuals, and as spouses and family members. I often have the spouses at our sessions together. Telling the truth is central to building the kind of healthy orga-nizations they want. In the past, in my view, we've tried to put the whole puzzle together in an industrial-age way. In the information age, work is about meaning and people bringing their hearts and souls to the sharing of information and creat-ing ideas. We can't do that unless we really connect and tell the truth. That conviction is what's behind the book Lesley Wright and I wrote titled *Corporate Abuse: How "Lean and Mean" Robs People and Profits*.

People are ready for this new focus. The clients I work with are way beyond that 1980s focus on the dream of success as a three-car garage. They're more interested in what they have a chance to experience at work, a sense of community, of what's been called "flow." People want to belong to something beyond themselves. I hear a lot of talk about "legacy" – not just leaving something to children, but leaving something through their work, that makes a difference in the world.

Where my work feels most meaningful these days is summed up in an experience I had coaching one executive. He sought the coaching. And he fought it. I had him up to my cottage one time for a coaching session. In the course of a long conversation, he did break through to an admission that his real self was just not as consistent and true as his projected image. No sooner did he make the realization than he drew back from it, drew back from his own "shuddering." He was one tough cookie. He did not want to participate any further. He was boiling with anger. But I did *my* job of telling the truth, of what I was seeing and hearing. He listened hard. He had a lot of courage. Then the tears came. He put it simply, "I've had a lot of things backward in my life, with my work, my family." What a turning point. He couldn't wait to continue the conversation, and the real hard work together, the next morning. Now we meet for coaching once a year; that experience of coming to some truth together never goes away, for the client, or for me – I'm wholly in it. The client is not my product anymore; their experience feels like my own. Every time they face a truth, I face my own.

What our clients are going through is very much the spiritual turning that Ian has found words for. There is definitely a revolution happening in the work world, in people's lives. My work, like Ian's work, isn't simply teaching people *about* this movement; it's about helping them free themselves to seek the meaning they yearn for, to be all they want to be, as people and as professionals. To be 100-watt beings!

I love this work. I love my life. It's about helping people see hope. I'm a short person, but, boy, having opportunities like this, I feel tall!

Dr. Marti Smye is president of People Tech Consulting, Inc., an international leadership consulting firm specializing in large-scale organizational change. Marti jogs, golfs, sails and treasures time to unwind at her cottage. Recently, she took part in Harley-Davidson's Corporate Ride for Presidents.

◆ ◆ ◆ ◆

The Leader's Spiritual Challenge: Engage

*Greg Cochrane,*CHAIRMAN & CEO,
MARIPOSA COMMUNICATIONS GROUP INC.

*Greg and his sons (from left)
David and Jim*

There's a scene in the 1980s movie *Top Gun* where Maverick (Tom Cruise) is in mock combat with his flight director. The mock combat isn't going so well because Maverick is in real combat with the self-imposed demons who have occupied his mind and soul since the tragic death of his copilot. Maverick blames that death, in no small part, on himself. At a pivotal point in the dogfight, Maverick goes blank; he won't take the shot. His new copilot yells out "Take the shot, take the shot!" The flight captain himself growls tensely, "Goddamn it, engage, Maverick, engage!" To me, this point in the movie is one of Maverick's decision points in life. As Ian would say, it's a "shuddering." He has a simple choice: to engage, to connect, to experience his potential, or to fall short.

In my view, each of us is faced on a daily basis with the decision to engage or not. The question becomes: "When do you stand up for what it is you truly want and believe in?" I believe Ian has helped us better understand what is important in life. He's helped us see how to live for what is important through his description of the Six Stations of the Inner Journey. I don't know about you, but I live in all these stations each and every day.

I know there are some things I'm not going to change, like paying taxes or having to get a driver's license. I also know what is truly important to me and what irritates me. Knowing these things pushes me into doing what I need to do to engage the status quo and seek to change it for the better.

Ian says to accept your irritations. After that comes the challenge of learning how to energize and pick the battles we want to fight. We need to head right into the shudderings that help us change as leaders of business, as members of communities, as friends. To fearlessly create a little havoc for the better. The call, in my view, is to get involved, get passionate, get engaged.

As head of a communications company that executes major corporate events like new-product launches, employee-recognition programs, mission-and-vision exercises, I find myself wanting, more than ever, to help corporate leaders hear that call. It's a wake-up call. Wake up and listen.

Here's what happens all too often during a corporate mission-or-vision roll-out because passion and commitment are missing "at the top":

1. The president and executive team spend months working on a mission and plan of action formulated by a consulting company or a facilitator.

2. By the time the mission/vision is ready to be communicated,
   a) the employees already know it's coming and aren't too excited;
   b) the environment, competition or market has changed;
   c) at least one or more of the executive team has moved on.

3. The task of communication *always* gets passed to Human Resources or Public Relations because the CEO has moved on to other things (for example, watching the numbers).

4. The launch of the program is just that – an event, not a process.

5. In about half of the mission roll-outs my company has done, the CEO has left the company within six months of the communication plan.

So, while Ian asks "Why?" I ask "*When?*" When will leaders get truly committed enough to be passionate about their business and their people and go the journey with them?

Go the journey. Here's where I take issue with Ian's 30/30/20/20 guideline for the use of a leader's time. In my view, leaders had better be on the front line. Sure they need the vision, the road maps, but they'd better also be great with the customer, the technology, the deal – whatever the business they're in. The leaders I admire spend most of their time communicating with their customers, their fellow employees, their communities. For them, the time division seems more like this (though I doubt if any do a conscious count):

- 60 percent communication;
- 30 percent day-to-day process;
- 10 percent strategy and planning.

One of the leaders I have in mind plans months in advance for his trips to branches and centers across his retail network. In his words, if you don't know what the front-line problems are, you don't know what the company's problems are. He notes the birthdays and anniversaries of the many people he works with directly in his organization, and sends them notes or calls them to mark those occasions. He stays connected. He is the heart and soul of an internal reward-and-recognition program to ensure that those who deal directly with the customer are the ones who are rewarded first, not the managers of those people. He also gives tirelessly to nonprofit organizations because he doesn't think corporate Canada does enough. I don't think he needs to spend 30 percent of his time thinking about the "what if." He knows the "why" of it all and he acts on the "when."

In my work, I try to encourage the senior leaders who are my customers to be single-minded in their communications. I try to get them, in their speeches, to focus on the people in the company. Not to bore them with content everyone knows, not to focus on strategy, but to energize them with personal attention. I try to get these leaders to quit focusing solely on end results, to look at a mission, for example, as a process, a continuation. A relationship.

And what I urge my customers to do is really part of what I'm trying to do. The struggle for focus is part of my journey too. I go into my organization of 100 people each day and try to think about who needs help on an emotional plane today. At any given time, there are four or five pregnancies, two divorces, at least one person facing a major health scare. So I try to connect as much as possible on a daily basis through E-mail, calls, chats, attending celebrations. In our managers' group, we make the people the first item on the agenda. The question isn't about the service, the numbers, the customers; it's "How are we as people?"

Keeping the people-relationships at the center is no easy job. I don't blame leaders, or anyone, for saying, "It's hard enough to get through life as it is and you want me to put something into it? You want me to take the time to encourage, to advise, to listen, to connect?" I know the effort involved is taking my relationships to a higher ground.

Most relationships can be pretty superficial. We say, "Hi, how are you?" as if we're ticking something off on a to-do list. We haven't heard. The struggle is to stay awake, to say what we mean and mean what we say, to be there with all our senses. The real breakdowns in business, like in any relationship, come from not listening, from forgetting to connect on a deeper level.

To do this at work, I need to have some really close relationships in my personal life. You can't have that with many. It takes commitment and time. For me, it's a matter of keeping my family at the center, and keeping the connection close and strong with my wife. I get up really early for work so I can get home at a decent hour to have a family life, to be there for the kids. I also go home ready to step out of the leadership role, to sort out with my wife, Linda, which of us is going to take the lead in different situations. The main thing for us is to keep checking in with each other, not to take anything for granted when things are going well, when everything seems to be happening right. That way, we keep the communication meaningful, not just about tasks or events, but about how we're doing together, as a family, as a couple. If we do that, when the kids leave home, we'll have more in our lives than a barren to-do list.

It's a matter of staying engaged, of knowing I'm on a journey, just like everyone else I work or live with. It's a journey of knowing and experiencing, of being fully focused on what you know is the right thing. Right now, the right thing for me is engaging on the deeper level Ian's book invites us to explore.

Greg Cochrane is chairman of the Mariposa Communications Group Inc., a Toronto-based sales and marketing communications company. Mariposa's nearly 100 passionate people provide strategic, creative and production expertise in sales force, franchise, employee and consumer communications. Greg's own energy and passion spill over into his involvement with several volunteer organizations, as well as his love for golf and family time at the cottage.

◆ ◆ ◆ ◆

Conversations and Reflections on Letting the Spirit Lead

Phil Hassen, PRESIDENT;
Sandra Letton, VICE-PRESIDENT;
Jane Parkinson, LEADER – TOTAL QUALITY MANAGEMENT;
Karen Shuttleworth, EDUCATOR; *Peggy Roffey,* TEAM LEADER –
EDUCATIONAL SERVICES,
ST. JOSEPH'S HEALTH CENTRE

Peggy's reflections:
It's Springbank Park. Our 1989 yearly Run for Research has wound down; people have sprinted or hobbled off home. The cleanup crew is left. One person, youngish but balding, is stuffing coffee cups and bedraggled stream-ers into a garbage bag. "Who's that?" *one of the staff volun-teers asks.* "Don't know," *says another.* "Thanks for the help," *he says to the unknown fellow.* "I'm John from the labs, what department you from?" *They shake hands. The new guy has a shy grin.* "Admin. I'm Phil. Phil Hassen." "The new CEO? Well, geez."

(from left) Peggy Roffey, Karen Shuttleworth, Sandra Letton, Jane Parkinson, and Phil Hassen

The first eight years of Phil Hassen's leadership at St. Joesph's Health Centre, London, were ones of turbulent change in the health-care system in Canada. At St. Joe's, those years were marked by vision, courage, emotional highs and emotional lows, hope and loss, hard decisions, new directions and, above all, compassion – in Ian's sense of the word.

Phil saw earlier than many that the health-care system had to change. It had to streamline its complex, often wasteful processes and reorganize itself around the patient. So Phil introduced Total Quality Management in 1990. The approach was adopted as St. Joe's primary "strategy for excellence." It precipitated radical organizational restructuring. Structures, relationships, processes were realigned to create a more flexible, less hierarchical organization. Teams were called on to find ways to improve quality and maintain quantity of service while driving down costs and protecting a good quality of work-life. This was leadership vision in action.

All this rapid change brought on a good deal of personal soul-searching for everyone in the organization. The stability and comfort of the recent past was fast receding, the present was in a state of wrenching, and sometimes exhilarating, flux, the future was uncertain. There were layoffs and losses, a lot of personal grief – and personal growth. In the midst of all this change, St. Joe's really became a place where just coming to work could, if you chose, turn into a spiritual journey as difficult and potentially rewarding as Ian describes it.

THOUGHTS ON SPIRITUAL LEADERSHIP DURING RADICAL CHANGE:

Phil: What's all this change been about? Not just surviving or coping, but really trying to create something new in health care. We're about health and wholeness, for the people who come here for help, for the people who work here. It's wholeness for the community as a system. In a way, we had to create chaos. We had to move into the "irritation" Ian talks about, so something new could come about. You don't ever create chaos just for the sake of chaos, but because you know in your bones that something is out of alignment. We'd been bumping along with our wheels out of kilter, focused on illness. The way the system was built, it wasn't going to get us to health.

But being at the center of chaos, leading people into it, is not a lot of fun. The attacks from angry and frightened people hurt; it's so personal. And you feel for them. But as a leader, you have to trust your intuition and your conviction that where you're going is right, it's good. With TQM and with restructuring, there was a large element of intuition, backed up with all the information we could get. In both cases, I had the overwhelming sense that these initiatives were good, the timing was right. When we started restructuring, we had no proof that we could come through it to the other side. It took such an enormous amount of belief, not just intellectual conviction, but a deep belief that this was the way to go.

I wouldn't have set us off on this path if I hadn't believed that our staff have so much more potential in them. In our new structure, with fewer people in every role, with greater reliance on teams, what everyone thinks and does every day is important. What everyone brings to the work really counts; it can make a difference. We've reduced from 120 managers to 36 team leader–managers! With so much less management, we are seeing more leadership arise, in all sorts of places. People, I think, are discovering there's no more relying on someone else to do the thinking and choosing for you. You have to take responsibility for the work that is yours. You truly have to collaborate and connect with others.

Sandra: In the midst of all this change, a lot of great things have happened. We've seen clinical teams agree on "best practices." We've seen teams persevere and persevere through multiple attempts to improve techniques of care. A lot of excellence is happening right in the middle of huge budget reductions. That says so much to me about the human spirit and the sense of mission.

Phil: But I still ask, how can we help more people take hold of that vision, really take hold of it? While my challenge has been to create chaos, it's also to bring people into harmony, to help them know they are part of the spirit that moves this organization. I can't do that with rhetoric. I know I've got to model the change I'm trying to bring about. And that challenges me personally, at a fundamental level. This makes the negativity that comes out sometimes so hard to take. How can we – how can I – help people find new meaning in all that's happening? Have hope for the organization and for themselves? What is my role as a leader in helping staff discover their spirituality?

Karen: When you talk about the painfulness of those attacks from angry staff, and when you ask the questions you ask, I think I see some of what's involved in spiritual leadership. It has something to do with what a person believes about emotions. Our open forums, where staff can come and be as angry or challenging, as open about their suffering as they want to be, are living proof that, as senior leaders, you know the healthy side of anger or "irritation." It must have been awful for you to say "I don't know" or to hear and feel the terrible mistrust that came at you. But you seemed to know that anger can become creative. You know it has to be spoken; otherwise it goes underground and becomes destructive. All this anger is about hurt and loss, and that needs to be acknowledged, right alongside a new vision for St. Joe's. People are so passionate because they care, about their work here as well as their livelihood.

Sandra: The emotion involved in all of this has been incredible. The response that is hardest to take is the distrust. During restructuring, I felt relationships change, from being really open to being closed. There were, it seems, more "undiscussables." During restructuring, I kept feeling we should be able to do more to build trust, to show our trustworthiness. You never knew when a conversation would send people "looking for their lawyer." I guess you have to accept that you can never do enough; you can only build trust, maybe, by being clear yourself, being reliable, and building relationships one at a time.

Karen: As a staff person, I feel moved and rejuvenated when I feel that someone has heard me and understands me, my issues, what I care about. Being understood or even sensing that a leader is trying to understand helps me clarify my own contribution to the work; I do it with more heart.

Peggy's reflections:
Ian Percy is on the scene. Tough times are beginning at St. Joe's. It's our first foray into downsizing and redesign, shifting around services and staff for better efficiency. People are losing their positions, having to exercise seniority rights and "bump" others out of their jobs – the first time we've ever done this at St. Joe's. Hearts are heavy at the change and discombobulation. But it's Valentine's Day and we go ahead with two full-day sessions with Ian called "Join the Dance." Come into the conference hall and write on the wall, on heart-shaped cards, what's in your heart – what breaks your heart, what mends your heart. Have heart-to-heart talks with your table group. Laugh at skits depicting the "old way" and the "quality way." Serve a family-style luncheon, everyone pitching in to fetch a dish, share it around. Hear Ian's reflections on spiritual growth and change. Seventy to eighty people each day. And best of all, the whole crowd gets up to learn to linedance. Kitchen staff and social workers, nurses and secretaries, vice-presidents and maintenance staff, even the president – all shuffling and tripping and bumping and hey – getting it right! – side by side, to "Achy Breaky Heart." Learning to learn together. Who's leading it? The spirit leads.

Jane: With Total Quality Management, we disrupted the status quo. We gave people a model, a language and a way that spoke to many people's deepest sense of why they want to be in health care. It said what they longed for: to find ways to make things better, to put the patient and anyone else who depends on your work right at the center of the work. It's been an effort of vision.

But we failed to remove the old, incongruent structure. So, in many ways, the organization stayed hierarchical, segmented, bureaucratic. It worked against the new vision. The irritation of that incongruence was good. Restructuring helped us deconstruct the roles and the structures that were blocking collaboration. In the process, the Senior Leadership Team really learned that no one person could do it all. I think the change to our basic structure has brought in something more sustaining for our quality principles. It's also taken us beyond our comfort zone.

Leaders need to take people beyond their comfort zone, but it takes a spiritual leader to help them explore that zone, and discover more about themselves when they're there. I think spirituality has something to do with accepting our limitations and imperfections along with feeling a sense of joy in striving for something better.

Sandra: We *have* taken people beyond their comfort zone. We've created real pain, or, in spiritual terms, real suffering.

Phil: That's so true of our management group. Reduced to 36 system-wide leaders, they really had to reconceive their roles. They had to get out of their silos and detach from the old territorial loyalties. They were expected to grow into a team that shared responsibility for the whole organization. I remember their anger in 1995, when we restructured leadership. I know they were stressed-out and confused, and wondering if they could handle so much more scope in their work. I recall them challenging the Senior Team: "If we have all this new responsibility, if there are no more line-reporting relationships with the V.P.'s, then why do we need V.P.'s at all?" Then there was the director group – a whole layer of hierarchy folded into the one team, becoming "equals" with people who once reported to them. Those people really struggled with the loss of identity; some could find new meaning at St. Joe's, others couldn't and so they left. But at least they left *because* they had to find meaning and an identity that fit. I think that was a sign of great health, fundamentally.

It was a challenge for the Senior Leadership Team to watch the 36 managers struggle. It was downright uncomfortable to see them floundering, impatient with their own sense of shaken competence and confidence. And we sure weren't consistently patient with their struggle either.

But it's exhilarating for me to see their growth. We are all becoming, every day, more of a team, a self-organizing body that is flexible and can face some of the most incredible challenges. We're more resilient, more connected. As one leader who joined this team two years after it formed said, "You people really like to talk to one another; you actually seem to enjoy one another!" I think that's great, someone coming in and noticing something like that.

Sandra: People really seem to understand that they need one another to do this work. They've shaken the old patriarchal structure in every joist and joint. I guess if sharing power isn't spiritual, what is?

Jane: Sharing power seems central to spiritual leadership because it's such a sign of respect. I also think spiritual leadership is a matter of taking people to a different level. And that takes self-mastery and insight. With internal clarity, you can give meaning to people's struggles. You can help them not get stuck at the "event" level, but to see further, broader, to see the pattern, the whole. You help them, I believe, by hearing the meaning they are making out of their experience.

Karen: In my work, I hear people struggle with a sense of incompetence and I hear them frustrated with the effort to learn a new role and work in new relationships. Stretched by fear and insecurity and with so much newness, our familiar shape gets unrecognizable. We lose our definition. When I sense in people's anger or frustration a lack of hope in themselves, then I know that the job of leaders is to patiently show them the meaning in their suffering and to help them get up the courage to learn.

Jane: The effort to regain competence may be the hardest work any of us does. And it's never finished. Leaders keep confronting their own need to grow. It's so important to know that, to handle it and to tell it. Because that's exactly what staff are facing. Leaders can't take people further than they themselves have gone. They can't lead people to the discovery of all that is in them unless they have taken that journey themselves and faced their own inner blocks. They can't lead unless they've discovered the meaning in this work, the "why" in all this change. They can't lead people unless they connect with them. That goes way beyond the intellectual. It's not a matter of being smart, as a leader; it's a matter of having a calling, to give that much of who you really are.

Peggy's reflections:
Phil is speaking with the Team Leader–Managers' group. He speaks quietly but passionately in the hushed room. We are in the midst of a citywide effort to rationalize services and create a seamless system. Any talk of the various hospitals "winning" or "losing" in the process is completely unacceptable, Phil is saying. This is about something larger than "my personal interests or needs," or any one organization's separate agenda. It's about making a system, not about power. It's a process based on principles, and the key principle is sharing power. It's about decentralizing and having lots of conversations so the right connections are made. The group is still and attentive and Phil paces a bit as he speaks. His hands go into his pockets, his head bows briefly as he searches for words. Then the hands are out, helping to shape the words as they come. "This isn't about you and me; it's about making something good happen." Minds and hearts are raised a notch above personal anxiety as people feel themselves in the presence of truly passionate and principled disinterest. In the presence of spiritual leadership.

Phil: Ian says compassion is helping people realize their wonderful potential, calling out the best in them. Believing in one another enough so we each begin to believe in ourselves. On this journey to believe in ourselves, St. Joe's has been through what Ian calls "shudderings" – both the terrifying and the blissful. But I guess we can only speak of shudderings from our own experience.

There are two levels where I find myself deeply moved. On the first level, I am deeply burdened, saddened. I have to find a new piece of me to deal with it all, and that hurts. This "shuddering" alters the foundation in me. I know something is not working anymore. The awfulness of the situation on the outside is matched by how awful and how terrible I feel on the inside.

The second level is hard to describe. Here my "shuddering" is wonderful and comes from knowing I have done something really good, something that made a difference. It occurs when someone understands deeply the vision I'm striving for. When they see the whole picture and see that it is good. That affirms the foundation of all that I am or believe my life to be about. And it's not the acknowledgment they make. It's that moment of sharing the knowledge, the vision. It's when someone else gets a glimpse of the intention that moves me. For a moment, then, there's a culmination of an intention that is good, a purpose that is meaningful.

In those moments, there is, in me, a great stillness, a kind of chill of sudden intense clarity and awareness. It's a moment's experience, beyond the intellectual, beyond the physiological. It's a sense of culmination, of transcendence, a consolidation of thinking and being. I feel then that I'm part of something bigger, something that is good. In those moments, I feel genuine, without pretense, as whole as I can be. There is such a sense of the wonderment of the world.

Peggy's reflections:

One of the darkest hours during our restructuring. Joan, one of our truly beloved leaders, only 34 years old, is in intensive care; a cerebral aneurysm blew. The chapel is packed; we are having a prayer service, trying to send our collective spirit to her, in hopes of healing. She does rally for three days, then more damage occurs and we lose her. But during the prayer service, the love is palpable. A couple of people have been asked to do readings. Our president approaches the lectern. Silence. Not a word will come, only a sob. Never has he been more eloquent than when he cannot speak.

The Health Centre is in the midst of a visit by a group of surveyors – experts who measure our care against national standards. A cluster of team leaders is in the main hallway outside the coffee shop. Jean, a feisty person, if there ever was one, is telling us the story of the surveyors' morning visit to the Hemophilia team. Her usual bluster and irony are gone. She is absolutely glowing, thrilled. Sandra and Phil walk up. "You've got to hear this," one of us says. Jean starts all over: "It was incredible. Five patients showed up for the presentation to the surveyors. They literally took over. They each stood up and said what this service has meant to their lives. What the care-givers have meant to their lives. They described in detail every process involved in the service, how we'd improved the steps over the years, how they'd been involved in changing the way things were done. 'We owe our lives to St. Joe's, and we remember that every day we live,' they said. The surveyors gave them a standing ovation at the end of it. 'You've covered everything,' they said, 'What more could we ask?' "

So, there in the hallway, outside the coffee shop, one month away from the next effort to take 10 percent out of our budget, that group of leaders laughed and cried and delighted in the staff's good work, the patients' loyalty and confidence. Who's leading here? The spirit leads.

Phil, Sandra, Peggy, Karen and Jane are just part of one of the most innovative and compassionate management teams in health care today. St. Joseph's Health Centre is a 950-bed teaching hospital in London, Ontario. Their remarkable story is told in **Rx for Hospitals: New Hope for Medicare in the Nineties**, *published by Stoddart Publishing, Toronto, Ontario.*

◆ ◆ ◆

The Reward is in the Journey

Jon Maddona and his wife Lynn finishing a particularly good round

Jon C. Madonna, VICE CHAIR, TRAVELERS GROUP

I suppose I'm more familiar with the football notion of "going deep" – a long pass to a wide receiver. So it's intriguing to think how my years in leadership have taken me deep into other territories. How they've been a journey, personal and corporate, that's by no means done.

It's interesting to think that Ian puts me in the category of "*beloved leader.*" I believe that leadership skill is developed at a young age. Everybody has leadership skills, more than they usually give themselves credit for. It's just a matter of stepping out and using them. To bring that natural ability forward, though, it helps to have a strong support system, people around you to help you know who you are. As I grew up, my family gave me that support in abundance. From childhood on I seemed able to influence a group in terms of its objectives or goals, and did so in a self-assured, confident way. For me, decisiveness has always come when the goal is clear, and that's when I go for something with passion and commitment. Without a doubt, clarity, decisiveness and passion are central to leadership in any capacity. So is listening well and refusing to go in for pretenses.

When I was younger, I also had the sense that school isn't the "be-all." Like the army, it was just something you had to get through, one of many necessary steps. But it wasn't the center of my life. I saw people achieving there, but it didn't matter to me. I always knew that wasn't the real game, at least not my real game.

What I wanted was to achieve success in life, to be able to accomplish something. Be good at business. Take good care of myself and my family economically. Do the best at what I was doing. That's what I still want. My recent job change, from chair of KPMG to vice chair of Travelers, is part of a search to achieve, on my terms, ways that satisfy my sense of what is worth doing.

I've been in a lot of leadership positions and I know the kind of influence and contact with people that really satisfies me. My former position at KPMG brought with it a very large audience, and therefore more influence. It was a position where a leader with broad vision could affect very many people. In that role, you had to know how to leverage the situation to get the desired impact. I learned you can move a lot of people if you can sell the people close to you on your ideas and goals. You have to paint the picture, preach the message. I love sports, so I think about the satisfaction of all of this in sports terms. It's the satisfaction a coach gets in helping his team meet the competition and win. There is tremendous joy in doing something great together. The coach sees it all from the top, sees the whole thing.

In that kind of role, though, while you touch a lot of people, you don't get really close. You don't *personally* do a lot. You can't get into each person's head. To do that you need time with people and that's what I missed in that job. That's part of what drove me to look for a change. I wanted to provide vision *and* support, to *personally* create a place for people to succeed. I wanted to create an environment where things and people grow, where they connect to that environment, not just observe it from a distance.

Ian's description of the "Institutional" stage of this journey of leadership relates well to my recent experience. So does his description of "Irritation." My former company has been in business for many, many years. Very successful years. As so often happens, a very large bureaucracy established itself and a lot of things became very set. For example, as chair, I had a calendar that was scheduled a year in advance. Then there's the decision-making process. It's an admirably democratic process, but it is also very slow, as you'd expect with 1,500 partners. About two years before my term as chair was up, I was beginning to feel that it was all too slow and too set for me.

The company had been going through significant transformation, but many felt the change should end. The desire was strong in the organization to slow down, to protect the status quo. But I felt a need to continue to make even more dramatic changes, faster. When the end to my term as chair drew near, I began to ask myself if I could be satisfied for much longer with the slowness of the process and the relative lack of freedom I was feeling in that position. As my tension grew, I also began to think what it would be like to do for another four years what I had already done for six. I would be 57 at the end of another term as chair, not an ideal age to start something entirely new. Let's face it, for most, the older you get, the more reluctant you are to change. So, if I was going to make a new start, this was the time. And that's exactly what I was feeling a desire to do. To be in a new field, to make a meaningful contribution, to be really challenged again by something new, to work closer with a smaller team. I knew I wanted to run something and I was open to anything. Mainly I longed for freedom and connection.

Interestingly, that longing first expressed itself as a desire to move out of New York and back to the West Coast, where I grew up. The strength of that longing, coupled with the decision not to seek a second term as chair at KPMG, led me to announce my intention to leave the company. I didn't know where I'd go, but it had to be somewhere where I could escape the restrictions I was feeling. I was happy and eager to face the unknown and find a new place to prove myself.

The Travelers Group turned out to be that place. I'm working closely with a small team. The company is more informal, and has a smaller feel although it is really huge. There just aren't the same restrictions here. As vice chair, of course, I'm not the most senior person, as I had been for so long, and I'm still adjusting to that. But that too is an exhilarating part of the new challenge. The current CEO has a fabulous track record. He treats people like adults and gives them free rein. He gives you a challenge then gets out of the way. So it's a pleasure to be a follower. It really is true that, to be a good leader, you need to be a good follower.

The change in jobs that I've just made seems to have had a lot to do with the kind of leader I see myself being. It helps to think of that in terms of the attributes of a corporate spiritual leader that Ian describes in his last chapter. I need, though, to start with one attribute Ian doesn't name – *Integrity*. Integrity is reflected in a lot of the other attributes he talks about, like confidence, pride, compassion. If you are going to have an effect on people, integrity is vital. The people I deal with know I'll be straight; they know how I see them fitting into the big picture and how we fit together. They know that I don't do something just to be, as Ian puts it, "political."

What Ian calls compassion makes real sense to me. I am very demanding as a leader, as I am demanding of myself. I don't go in for a lot of harsh self-judgment or spend a lot of time thinking about being worthy, for example. Fundamentally, I accept myself and then expect the best. And that's my approach to other people. I usually see more potential in individuals and groups than they tend to see in themselves. Consequently, I set the goals high and invite people to stretch toward them.

I see with understanding and compassion the trials people go through when they try to change. As a consultant, for example, I believe in taking great care of clients. Part of that care is to help them be more effective than they think they can be. It's not really a matter of making them be something *different*, but getting them to play to their strengths, to break out and grow bigger. If I'm able to help others do that, it's because that is where I've been myself. Each successive role doesn't change who I am, it just invites me to act and perform at a very different level. At each point I see the world differently.

Gratefully, I've seen others grow under my leadership. Though I was dissatisfied with the speed of change in my former organization, I did see it grow, change and get better. It became more market-focused, more skilled and diversified in all its services, and more relevant to clients. Getting the whole group to that point wasn't easy for any of us, but we accomplished a lot in a relatively short period.

Now, as a leader committed to seizing a new reality and making the dramatic changes it requires, I know the people involved feel their lives are on the line. My job as a leader is never to lose sight of the fact that I'm there to help them succeed. A leader needs to have vision, confidence and faith. For himself and for the team. I don't let people's fears consume me because I keep my eye on the goal. I don't look at the gorge under the high wire, I look at our feet on the wire, walking to the other side.

Some people would say that this is the behavior of a risk-taker. But I don't really take risks, and view myself as quite conservative. My plans or ideas for change may sound crazy and far-out, but before I put them forward I've thought them through as thoroughly as possible. The challenge is to help others visualize that future and see the path toward it.

There *is* a new reality. Unfortunately, many people tend not to want to put the facts together because the answer means something has to be different. They start by denying the facts, arguing that what is inevitable just isn't going to happen. They simply don't want to see a new reality and they get stuck in their present, or even worse, in their past. Fortunately, the future of a particular situation is usually something a new pair of eyes can see much more easily than those who have been in it for some time. The job of a new leader is to lay it out, get the facts clear, encourage confidence and calmness, and communicate the potential of the new reality.

If I have what Ian calls faith, it's because I believe the future will be better. And if I have hope, it's because I really believe we'll get there. I never lose heart. When I see people get discouraged, I just believe *for* them that they can be part of the vision. I know they want to be on a winning team. People treat you as you treat yourself. If you act like a loser, you'll be treated like a loser. We all need to believe in ourselves as winners. I try to help others see winning opportunities, but if their performance isn't up to it, I deal with them honestly. It's in their best interest in the long run. I suppose some could view that as ruthless, but I won't sacrifice the end goal; too many other lives depend on it.

Can you separate the person from the leader? Ian is saying that you're a good leader *because* of the person you are. Often, and this was especially true in my last role, I feel that not many people really know the *person* I am. I regret that, but if people get some good out of the way I lead, and are positively affected by the attributes I bring to leadership, then maybe they do know something about me after all.

While I am getting my bearings in a new environment and with a new team, something I always find a bit hard, I'm also feeling a lot of excitement again. What amuses me is that I'm still in New York. I didn't have to move to the West Coast for rekindling. I didn't need to make a geographical change because I'd made a psychological, or in Ian's language, a spiritual change. This new job gives me a "West Coast" of the spirit.

Part of my excitement comes from the fact that there is a radical change happening in the way business is done within financial services, and everywhere. Most of that change is coming from technology. Those who recognize this, get a good understanding of the reality of it and communicate that reality will come out ahead. I know some people are afraid of these changes, but technology doesn't have to hurt people. It can create incredible opportunities.

This is a time of tremendous opportunity for the United States and the world. We are in a position to achieve great success economically. If you work to get an education and really pursue meaningful work, success will come. Some are finding it hard to get an education right now, and that too is a challenge this country must step up to. Essentially, it is a challenge of leadership. Our times call not for the kind of leadership based on scientific formula, but for leadership that demonstrates a power of spirit. Something that comes from the gut, the heart. It is intuitive leadership, as Ian suggests, that tells you how and when to seize the opportunity.

In the final analysis, I really like what Ian says about humility. I buy his idea that the gift of leadership flows *through* us. A position can only give you the *opportunity* to do something great. It is up to you, as a leader, to take advantage of the opportunities provided to you. And, if you do, it is because lots of people see something worthwhile in the project. It's opportunity that gives the power.

When all is said and done, a leader needs humility to keep perspective. I was recently on a combined tour-conference in Jerusalem. Something really stirred me there. I found myself "going deep" in a new way. Being there, I was reminded of all the events of history, and what a journey the whole human race has been on! Being given a chance to influence that journey in whatever small way is a real privilege. Having just made a new start myself, I feel that privilege and that responsibility keenly. The opportunity to make your own journey part of that journey is, in my view, the real reward of leadership.

Jon is vice chair of the Travelers Group, one of America's largest diversified financial services companies, with approximately $151 billion in assets. Previous to that, he was chairman of KPMG International, leading that firm to a market-focused strategy and record revenues. Jon and his wife, Lynn, live in New York City and Desert Mountain, Arizona. Jon gives generously of his time to many civic, professional and educational organizations and plays golf every chance he gets.

❖ ❖ ❖

Handing on the Vision

Larry Pike, CHAIRMAN, PRESIDENT AND CEO,
UNION CENTRAL LIFE INSURANCE COMPANY

*Larry, his wife Sandy and
(from left) daughter Christy,
grand-daughters Karin, Meredith,
Renata and Ashley*

My travels down the road of corporate spirituality began about 16 years ago, in my position as senior manager at Home Life, with a staff of five. The six of us were off-site for a day of planning and annual objective-setting. At some point in the day, the discussion took an interesting turn. From our talk of business objectives, we moved into a reflection on the growth and development plans of staff members. How would we build into a busy work-life ways and opportunities for them to become the best they could be, as professionals and as people? An important consideration.

As the day came to a close, one of the group asked me, quite pointedly, what *my* vision was for my own growth as a manager, and what I wanted to accomplish in the days to come. The question gave me pause. What *did* I want to accomplish? I told the group that I didn't have a good answer at the moment and promised to think about the question and get back to them in two weeks.

Over the following weeks, I found myself thinking back over the past years of my career, looking for examples of management styles that had had an impact on *my* life. Unfortunately, my memory seemed to be full of examples of "what not to do" as a manager. What was I trying to do that was different from the management I'd experienced? The realization dawned that an important ingredient had been missing: how you treat people as human beings. I realized that what I'd been trying to do, and what I yearned to do more consciously now, was base my leadership on a Christian ethic of caring and mutual respect. That yearning and that vision are what have guided my choices and efforts for the past 16 years.

This process of clarification and reflection took me longer than the two weeks I'd originally promised my team; it takes time to think and sort out weighty matters. But at one of our staff meetings, I did put into words my dream of the kind of company I wanted to work for as a senior manager.

My desire was to have a team that, besides setting clear objectives and sorting out options, also sets aside time for introspection and for testing our actions against internal feelings and beliefs. My desire was to have us find ways to enrich the whole so we'd have a working environment we enjoyed. My yearning was for a place where people *wanted* to come to work, where they could use their talents and expertise for a good purpose, for personal development and for true reward. It was a tall order, it seemed. I thought at the time, "Help!" and prayed that God would give me the opportunity to manage in a way that would make this vision come true.

A few years after this breakthrough started me off on my own spiritual journey as a leader, I was faced with what, in Ian's terms, was a bit of a "shuddering." It also turned out to be one of the opportunities I had prayed for, but didn't recognize at first. Home Life went through a major restructuring. I was given a new position, but it wasn't the job I'd wanted. My new role was to lead the data processing, comptroller, accounting, planning and auditing functions. I had worked with these people but hadn't managed or led them. Times were difficult at first, but a friend said, "Hang in there, Larry, you'll be a better manager for it."

This position did turn out to be the testing ground for a management approach that matured into a commitment to spiritual leadership. From there, my career took another turn in 1987 when the opportunity arose to join Union Central as executive vice president in the Individual Group.

When I started with Union Central, the company had had a bad year. After I'd been with them just over a year, the CEO retired and I was named the successor. The greatest opportunity to accomplish what I'd dreamed of as a senior leader was here, and I could use on a broader scale what I'd learned with my previous group.

It was clear to me from the start that a real culture change was needed in the organization. There was a lot of turf protection, and, as in my previous organization, not much interchange between the various strategic business units. With all the fragmentation, the company had lost momentum, so I started to work on these issues with a Senior Team of about nine leaders.

These professionals were all highly skilled, but they really worked in "silos," with little coordination or collaboration. The challenge was to help them break down barriers and grow as managers. My job was to teach them to manage and work together. These people were put in responsible positions that made them stretch. My approach, I suppose, was marked, most of all, by patience. I never do get excited about little things and I'm not one to go around blaming people.

We entered a real learning mode, figuring out how to do budgets, plan and make decisions in full recognition of the impact the various areas had on one another. Gradually, this group that had been such a collection of isolated functions became a team capable of cross-the-board thinking about the company as a whole. To my great delight there was also very little "politics" or game-playing or putting people down. Where I never compromised was in how people treated one another. People knew that unfair and disrespectful treatment of another person meant you were "out of here."

Gradually, the structure I'd originally found started opening up, and the people within it were opening up as well. Our efforts as leaders took us a good ways, but there came the recognition that the team and I were hungry for something else – something we couldn't even name. That's when we called in Ian to help make clear the vision of spiritual leadership we were striving for.

Part of making this vision become real was to establish a new operations team, a mid-level group of managers responsible for all operations, actions and plans in the company for an 18–month time line. The Senior Team would be responsible for longer-range planning and overall direction-setting.

At first, the Senior Team really resisted establishing this new structure; they had a lot of personal and corporate anxiety about handing on the day-to-day responsibility to this mid-level group. Ian worked with us on this and he didn't let us get away with anything that would compromise the journey. The new structure required a lot of trust, faith, compassion and confidence. Giving people the opportunity to stretch and grow by handing power and opportunity over to them was a spiritual act. We needed to do it to establish the kind of caring, respectful culture that was the heart of the vision.

Again, as a senior leader, my role was to teach and to help the operations team learn their new roles and lead with a clear sense of values. As these new values began to take effect, we charged a group of employees to articulate the values that made this company unique. Their task required input from across the employee base. Senior management acted as coaches in this process and did not have final approval. It was an employee effort guided by the mid-level team, who were themselves, in turn, learning the coaching role. They, and the employee group, were also learning through this effort, to be keepers of the vision.

The company's culture was changing for the better and people were growing. Of the nine senior leaders who started the journey, eight are still on board. One retired, another came in, found he just couldn't fit with where we were going and left. During the change process, I never gave in to the impulse to dictate and stuck with the hard way, which is to patiently, but unwaveringly, help people go through the growth process. The hard part, in my view, is first to determine what is right. Once you've done that, the hard way – the patient way – is easier in the long run.

Another reason why I've been able to persevere toward my vision is that I've also never shied away from conflict. I'm very straightforward. For me, there is no difficulty in talking about performance issues and working with people on improving. That comfort, I think, comes from my early experience as well. As a young person, I never gave in to peer pressure or felt any fear of standing out from the group and saying, "That's not right." That attitude can get you into trouble, but it always seems to me that, when all's said and done, you have two people to answer to – yourself and the Lord.

But when you take a company on a journey of change, you don't avoid the discomfort of change yourself. In June 1996, I began to feel unsettled. I had a vague but persistent sense of discomfort. I didn't pay attention to this at first and wrote it off to a busy schedule and outside demands. By October, though, I realized that a major struggle was taking place within me and that somehow I was losing the battle. I had to force myself to stay at peak performance and to meet the demands of my responsibilities. I wasn't having much fun, and, to my dismay, not getting much satisfaction out of striving for my vision.

By mid-December I was really on the ropes. But then one of those events occurred that I call a *co*-incidence. God and me. During a two-hour meeting I had to attend for appearance' sake, I received the answer to my struggle. Right there in the meeting, I started writing at a furious pace. The writing clarified for me why I had this inner tension and conflict.

I had let go of a lot; shared power *was* working. But my history had always been to take hands-on risk, to be active, to make change, to seek and enjoy challenge. I now had to accept that, on the operations level, I was a little worn-out, weary. My "points were burned" – for those of you who remember when automobiles had points. The realization came that the inner me was still seeking to adjust to the different role; I *still* had not, internally, truly let go.

In a little more than three years, I plan to retire. In one and a half years, I expect to recommend to the board of directors the individual who will replace me as the new president and CEO. To prepare for these events, I need to become even more of a teacher, a coach, and a champion of the vision. The challenge now is to make sure that my attitude, outlook and values are agreed upon and accepted – by myself as much as by the rest of the corporation. I need to help us all incorporate that understanding and those insights into action. This is integral to my "succession planning" and it will weigh on me during the next year and a half.

Right now, the insurance industry is going through some difficult times. Yet I believe that we can do a lot of good. At our meetings, we make a point of sharing stories about the individuals who have been served well by the work we do. And we don't just talk about the shareholders but about the people whose family businesses were saved by the proper insurance coverage. We talk about the children who were left well-protected after losing their father and then their mother.

Our customer service has strengthened since we've broken down old barriers. Now we blend products, do one-company marketing, share resources across divisions for the sake of the whole company's viability, recruit people from one another's areas, house the different product groups together and have one annual conference so everyone knows where the company as a whole is going. We know that the customers aren't interested in the details of who does what; they're interested in getting their problems solved. Working the way we do now, we can answer that expectation. The vision is coming true.

The final few years I have to lead the corporate journey will be years during which my work will be accompanied by two things:

- the belief that the old "bottom line" will take care of itself and flourish if you do what's fair by people and treat them with real care and respect; and
- the prayer that God may bless our efforts to treat people at all times as human beings.

Larry Pike is chairman, president and CEO of the Union Central Life Insurance Company, headquartered in Cincinnati. Founded in 1867, Union Central ranks among the top 30 mutual insurers in the country. Licensed in all 50 states, the company's subsidiaries include The Manhattan Life Insurance Company. It provides a broad range of financial products and services for the individual, group and pension markets. Under Larry's leadership, Union Central has grown and strengthened by adhering to the values of quality, integrity and financial soundness. Active in industry affairs, Larry currently serves on the boards of several key associations. He is also involved in local civic and philanthropic organizations, as well as in his church. Larry and his wife, Sandy, married for 43 years, have two daughters and five grandchildren.

◆ ◆ ◆ ◆

Finding Meaning in Life

Beverly Topping, PRESIDENT AND CEO,
TODAY'S PARENT GROUP, INC.

Spirituality. I think the puzzle of spirituality is a chicken-and-egg kind of puzzle: can you know it if you don't have it? Can you learn it? It is not so much a question of whether *corporations* can develop spiritually, but a question of what helps *individuals* develop their inborn spirituality.

*Beverly and her sons (from left)
Michael and Chris hiking on
Baffin Island*

I believe that each person can, with nurturing, make their personal presence a gift to the group. I also believe that most of us learn by example. We learn from leaders and lovers and friends who are examples for us of all that is worthwhile in the business of living. And, yes, our response to the spiritual dimensions of living can be deepened by what Ian calls "shudderings."

If I am a leader who helps others discover their own spirituality and develop their gifts, it's because I was given the gift of believing in myself, from day one. It's also because I strive to see my own shudderings as opportunities. They're events that were meant to be, even the most wrenching ones. Happenings that deepen my sense of life's meaning.

I spent the first three years of my life on a prairie farm, following my dad around. Mom worked as a nurse, so I was immersed in a male world and grew up unafraid of it. I loved being in the grain elevators with the huge trucks. I loved being with my dad, who had a great sense of humor, and a real easy-going style. He could talk to anybody.

Later, when my father entered the military, he still took me everywhere, to racetracks, to army-navy boxing matches. I was a terrible tomboy. I'll never forget a sudden consciousness I had once, of myself as a girl and a tomboy all in one. I was washing my hands at a pump, when I felt my trousers falling down; swiftly, without thinking, I hitched them up. It was the same gesture the farmhands used! In the midst of that, in spite of it all, I had a very clear sense of my own femininity; it was just part of who I was. Being in the male world, I think, is part of what helped me become a leader. I always moved forward assuming I, as a person and as a woman, *could* – a kind of "bulldozer with a heart."

That clear sense of self helped me through the wild teenage years. I ran with kids who drank, but I never did – really! I had so much energy I just knew that alcohol would put me over the top. And I had no problems with peer pressure. I had a great social life, but I'd been given a strong sense of values, so I could stand my ground. I always had boyfriends, too, but I wasn't ever, am not today, a woman who needs to be on the arm of a man to feel real.

Mainly, I think I came at leadership through motherhood. It was a great advantage being a mother *before* becoming a leader. I married early, at 21. John proposed to me only two months after we met. He had that inner knowledge, very quickly, that we belonged together, and he was right. I became a mother when I was 23; I was young, but I was ready. John and I were equally committed to helping our two boys be their own separate beings. We were prepared to let them go through the necessary, painful, awkward stages of growing up. We stayed close enough to guide them, but never so close that we smothered them.

If they wanted to go bootless in winter, for example, to save face in front of their 10-year-old friends, we backed off in respect of that child's scale of values that puts a cold much lower than belonging and saving face. But when they wanted to go as 15-year-olds for a kids-only cottage weekend, we said no, knowing that the dynamics of teenagers in groups can get dangerous. We explained that to them. When Mike was 17, we actually did give in and let him go once – I'm not sure why. But he came home after only one night and said it wasn't for him. They grew up with a strong sense of values, and they're lovely men now. I love being with them.

When I decided to become an entrepreneur, and bought the magazine *Great Expectations,* a magazine on pregnancy, I didn't do that as a bold leadership step. It was probably more because I simply didn't know the consequences. One thing I did know was that, for me, and my career, it was time to make a change.

Great Expectations provided a wonderful opportunity to talk to people, and to provide services to them at one of those points of great change in their life. Pregnancy, like puberty and menopause, is a central event, physically, emotionally, psychologically. But I wasn't some crunchy-granola mom who wanted to have 10 kids herself and persuade everyone else to do the same. This was both a great marketing opportunity and something I could relate to.

It was also an opportunity to take my learning in the school of motherhood into the world of leadership. The business started with seven women, 14 years ago. Six of the original seven are still together, and the company has grown to 85 staff, with another 50 to 60 freelance writers and photographers. Just as John and I worked to help our sons gain a strong sense of themselves and of their values, I also try to ensure people in our business have the opportunity to surpass their own expectations of themselves. I love to see young women start in the production department and a few years later become associate publishers. Everyone in our company gets exposed to all of the business issues. They come to see and understand the work as a whole. So everyone works for the success of the whole enterprise. They're encouraged to learn, to accomplish, to move on to something else.

One thing I never want to lose as a leader is the opportunity to be hands-on. If the staff are stretched, they call and tell me, "Beverly, we need you to focus on such and such for two weeks." So, for example, I'll help out with sales, going out and looking for sponsors for our TV show "Spilled Milk." Or I'll go to hospitals and try to convince them to take our bedside patient-education programs. I love it when I can stay close to the front line like that. I always say to my colleagues, "Good, I feel like I've contributed to the bottom line and earned my salary!"

As a leader, I keep the near and far perspective in balance. I get ideas and realize I'm often three months ahead of where the company is ready to move. My partner in charge of operations is great. With tremendous humor and respect, he'll say, "Beverly, I don't see it yet, but give me six weeks." I have patience with that, patience with the way people process things. It's all part of being there while someone goes through the stages that are necessary *to them*. It's what a leader does, and what a parent does.

The belief that going through things and coming out better for it is probably the one piece of wisdom, as a leader, that I want to pass on to the people I work with and the people I relate to. And to pass it on mainly by example.

Five years ago, I was diagnosed with breast cancer. I did not go the route of chemotherapy and radiation. Instead, I practiced traditional Chinese medicine, as I had been doing for some years already. I had a conviction that I wasn't going to die, that it wasn't my turn yet. So I worked with my Chinese doctor on getting my immune system back in balance. I intended to come out of that experience a smarter person. With

Chinese medicine, you get an approach to health that has as much to do with getting your bodily fluids in balance as with getting your mind-body-spirit in balance. To avoid getting obsessed with work, to remember to sit on a beach with your kids and your partner, to take a two-hour lunch once a month and laugh till your sides ache.

Women I know, and even women I don't know but who are part of a network of connections, call me now when they learn they have breast cancer. What do we do? Talk. Listen. I counsel, and help them believe they can get through this. My friends tease me by calling me the "grandmother of breast cancer." All of this happens for a reason; you can turn anything to the good. I decided I was meant to have scars on my body because they were a language that helped me say to others some things that would help them.

That conviction was really put to the test when my husband, John, died suddenly just 18 months ago, from a ruptured aneurysm. He'd been on a brief holiday, fishing in the Queen Charlotte Islands. He died the day after he came home. One of the most lovely things anyone said to me at that time came from a friend who told me a little anecdote. He said he'd seen a couple in their late forties walking hand in hand the very weekend that John died. He remembered thinking how wonderful it was, to have a love that seemed to be both mature and eternally fresh. He said that, when he looked closer, he recognized the pair. It was John and me.

It was wonderful to have that image given back to me. It reminded me that my marriage had been a gift. This man and I had loved each other steadfastly and well for 30 years. He died loving me.

John had lived wonderfully. He was an entrepreneur as well, and we always arranged our schedules together so one of us would be home for the kids at the crucial parts of the day. I remember he used to have breakfast meetings at the house so he could be there to get the boys off to school! He did his part to nurture my success and my growth as a leader. He never smothered me. He always made me laugh. He had clear, strong values. He was and remains one of those exemplars that are necessary to another person's spiritual growth.

When I returned to work after John's death, I could feel the sadness in the air like an enormous burden. People felt so terrible. I guess it was an act of leadership, but it was also just a true gut feeling, when I asked them, straight out, please not to let the air fill with the awful negative energy of grief. It wouldn't help me and it wouldn't help them. I needed them to focus on their work, feel the delight and excitement in it that would fill the place with positive energy. That's the way they could most help me, and I knew they wanted to. If they wanted to come to me, one-on-one, for a hug, or a cry, I welcomed that. But I needed them to celebrate John with me, through their work. I could see that just being direct like that helped everyone. I could feel the energy change and the spirit reanimate.

The loss of John is a wound that will gape a long time. The part of me that melded with him into a couple is exposed and open – the whole right side of me that was his place beside me. I know this will heal into scars. And I know the scars are the language of meaning. They speak of the tremendous importance one person can hold for another.

My own experience has taught me that the meaning that has filled, and continues to fill, my personal life actually fuels my work-life, and vice versa. Recognizing that the personal and professional parts of our lives have to nourish each other is perhaps the key to what my colleagues so generously call my "inspired" leadership. I want work to be fun and creative. I get an intuition that a certain business move would be exciting, good for the company, and I go for it – like a "whirlwind of energy," as my operations partner always says. I trust my instincts, and I like risk.

I want the people who work for me to feel that same keen enjoyment in their work. This desire is behind some of the unconventional, freewheeling approaches we take in this company. When I hire someone, for example, I'm more interested in discovering the person they are than in scanning their résumé for the list of standard credentials. Or, if people tell me they'd be more creative, productive and happy working out of their home office, so be it – whatever brings out the best in them.

When I go looking for developmental opportunities for the group, or consultant help, more often than not it's in the direction of personal growth and inspiration, not Harvard-style business courses. Recently, I sent about six of the staff to a course on innovative leadership. Why? I wanted to double the size of the business. But I knew that that wouldn't happen if people weren't really happy in their work. To be successful, a business needs 100 percent of its people to be giving 100 percent of their best creativity. They've got to be doing what they really want to be doing with their lives. If their work-life is causing problems in their personal life, they can't give that 100 percent. I wanted them to take this course to help them in their own beings.

The results were startling. One woman came back from the course perfectly clear she had to end a bad marriage. Another came back and immediately proposed to his lover and got married. Another decided to commit to the company for five years, then take a sabbatical to do relief work in the Third World.

What energy these redirections brought into their work! *Tapping that energy and bringing out the best in people is the leader's most important mission.* If, as a leader and a person, I can help bring meaning into other people's lives, help them see life and work and relationships in their true importance, then this whole journey *is* a spiritual one, as Ian claims, and worth it.

Beverly Topping is president, CEO and founder of Today's Parent Group, Canada's largest parenting communication and marketing company. In the business community, Beverly is an executive board member of Canada Trust Financial and Cara Operations Limited. Beverly loves the outdoors, skiing, kayaking, hiking and feels particularly creative when she is cooking.

Last Words

What if all of us who have held this book were together sharing our stories, our spiritual journey? Each one would be different and yet all part of one divine and human Story.

For Mike, it's about basing leadership on a loving relationship between God and creation. For Marti, it's about helping people see hope. For Greg, it's about truly and fully engaging in what you know is right. Phil and his team call us to the wonder of letting the Spirit lead – through the valley as well as to the mountaintop. For Jon, it's about freedom and the yearning for real connection. Larry prayerfully faces the challenge of handing on a corporate spirit that now burns so brightly. And for Beverly, it's about helping people find spiritual meaning in their lives.

All of us know there is a wonderful and holy mystery out there. All real change is first spiritual change. It is becoming increasingly imperative that our families, our schools, our religious organizations, our governments and our businesses discover the awesome transformative power available to those willing to go deep and experience the joy of the soul set free.

As we learn to live the integrated life, the aligned life, may we be irresistible to one another and to those who, in faith and expectation, look to us for leadership.

Other Highly Recommended Explorations

Scott Adams. *The Dilbert Principle*. New York: HarperCollins, 1996.

James Autry – anything by him, but especially – *Love and Profit*. New York: Avon Books, 1991.

Richard Barrett. *Spiritual Unfoldment – A Guide to Liberating Your Soul*. Alexandria, VA: Unfoldment Publications, 1995.

Geoffrey Bellman. *The Consultants Calling*. San Francisco: Jossey-Bass Inc., 1990.

Nathaniel Branden. *Taking Responsibility*. New York: Simon & Schuster, 1996.

Glenn Clark. *The Man Who Tapped the Secrets of the Universe*. Waynesboro, VA: University of Science and Philosophy, 1946.

John Dalla Costa. *Working Wisdom*. Toronto: Stoddart Publishing, 1995.

Max De Pree – anything by him, but especially – *Leadership is an Art*. New York: Dell Publishing, 1989.

Wayne W. Dyer – anything by him, but especially – *Your Sacred Self*. New York: HarperCollins, 1995.

Matthew Fox – anything by him, but especially – *The Reinvention of Work*. New York: HarperCollins, 1994.

Gay Hendricks and Kate Ludeman. *The Corporate Mystic*. New York: Bantam Books, 1996.

Arianna Huffington. *The Fourth Instinct*. New York: Simon & Schuster, 1994.

Sam Keen – anything by him, but especially – *Hymns to an Unknown God*. New York: Bantam Books, 1994.

Albert Koopman and Lee Johnson. *The Quest for the Corporate Soul.* Vancouver: Infra Management Ltd., 1995.

Ernest Kurtz and Katherine Ketcham. *The Spirituality of Imperfection.* New York: Bantam Books, 1992.

Victoria Lee. *Soulful Sex.* Berkeley: Conari Press, 1996.

Copthorne Macdonald. *Toward Wisdom.* Toronto: Hounslow Press, 1993.

Jack Miles. *God, A Biography.* New York: Vintage Books, 1995.

Thomas Moore – anything by him, but especially – *Soul Mates.* New York: HarperCollins, 1994.

Paul Pearsall. *Making Miracles.* New York: Avon Books, 1991.

Nido Qubein. *Stairway to Success.* Mechanicsburg, PA: Executive Books, 1996.

Robert Roskind. *In the Spirit of Business.* Berkeley: Celestial Arts Publishing, 1992.

Lance Secretan. *Reclaiming Higher Ground: Creating Organizations that Inspire the Soul.* Toronto: Macmillan Canada, 1996.

David Whyte. *The Heart Aroused.* New York: Doubleday Currency, 1994.

Gary Zukav – anything by him but especially – *The Seat of the Soul.* New York: Simon & Schuster, 1960.